SAMS
Teach Yourself

Microsoft®
Office XP

in 24 Hours

Greg Perry

SECOND EDITION

SAMS 201 West 103rd St., Indianapolis, Indiana, 46290 USA

Sams Teach Yourself Microsoft® Office XP in 24 Hours
Copyright © 2001 by Sams Publishing

International Standard Book Number: 0-672-32508-X

Library of Congress Catalog Card Number: 00-109551

Printed in the United States of America

First Printing: October 2002

05   04   03   4

Trademarks

Warning and Disclaimer

ACQUISITIONS EDITOR
Betsy Brown

DEVELOPMENT EDITOR
Linda Bird

MANAGING EDITOR
Charlotte Clapp

PROJECT EDITOR
Elizabeth Finney

COPY EDITOR
Rhonda Tinch-Mize

INDEXER
Sandra Henselmeier

PROOFREADER
Tony Reitz

TECHNICAL EDITOR
Georgena Harrison

TEAM COORDINATOR
Amy Patton

INTERIOR DESIGNER
Gary Adair

COVER DESIGNER
Aren Howell

PAGE LAYOUT
Lizbeth Patterson

Contents at a Glance

Contents

About the Author

GREG PERRY is a speaker and a writer on both the programming and the application sides of computing. He is known for his skills at bringing advanced computer topics to the novice's level. Perry has been a programmer and a trainer since the early 1980s. He received his first degree in computer science and a master's degree in corporate finance. Perry has sold more than 2 million computer books worldwide, including such titles as *Sams Teach Yourself Windows Me in 24 Hours*, *Absolute Beginner's Guide to Programming*, and *Sams Teach Yourself Visual Basic 6 in 21 Days*. He also writes about rental property management, creates and manages Web sites, and loves to travel.

Dedication

*The Seven Sees, Steven, Julie, Allison, Jacob, Sarah, David, and Timothy,
are not just wonderful neighbors, they are blessings to everybody who knows
them. I dedicate this book to each of my friends in the See family.*

Acknowledgments

I want to send special thanks to Betsy Brown whom I've only had the pleasure of meeting in person once, and she doesn't realize it but she impressed me in that brief encounter as a wonderful lady who is also great at what she does with books. Thanks, Betsy, for putting up with me on this project.

Rhonda Tinch-Mize made sure that the missing pieces and bad writing were handled. That's not a simple task when one considers the authorship of this book! In addition, Elizabeth Finney kept patient while my e-mails got stranded between here and there. Elizabeth, thank you so much for following up those times when I needed it.

Linda Bird somehow took my words and developed them into meaningful words and that was quite a feat. I have learned a lot about Linda since we began this project, and I know how special she is to this book, but even more so to her family. Georgena Harrison, this project's Technical Editor, had to wade through all the problems I put into this book's first draft. The repairs are all hers and any problems that may be left are all mine. In addition, the other staff and editors on this project, namely Tony Reitz, Sandy Henselmeier, and Liz Patterson made this book better than it otherwise could be.

My lovely and gracious bride stands by my side night and day. Thank you once again. You, precious Jayne, are everything that matters to me on earth. The best parents in the world, Glen and Bettye Perry, continue to encourage and support me in every way. I am who I am because of both of them.

—*Greg Perry*

Tell Us What You Think!

As the reader of this book, *you* are our most important critic and commentator. We value your opinion and want to know what we're doing right, what we could do better, what areas you'd like to see us publish in, and any other words of wisdom you're willing to pass our way.

You can e-mail or write me directly to let me know what you did or didn't like about this book—as well as what we can do to make our books stronger.

Please note that I cannot help you with technical problems related to the topic of this book, and that due to the high volume of mail I receive, I might not be able to reply to every message.

When you write, please be sure to include this book's title and author as well as your name and phone or fax number. I will carefully review your comments and share them with the author and editors who worked on the book.

E-mail: consumer@samspublishing.com

Mail: Mark Taber
            Associate Publisher
            Sams Publishing
            201 West 103rd Street
            Indianapolis, IN 46290 USA

Introduction

Microsoft Corporation's Office products have an installed base of more than 22 million licensed users. More than 90% of the Fortune 500 companies use Microsoft Office. Microsoft designed Office XP to be more user friendly as well as more integrated among applications and the Internet. You won't regret your decision to learn and use Office XP. With the Office XP skills that you master in these 24 lessons, you will know the most popular application software on earth.

You probably are anxious to get started with your 24-hour Office XP tutorial. Take just a few preliminary moments to acquaint yourself with the design of this book, as described in the next few sections.

Who Should Read This Book?

This book is for both beginning and advanced Office XP users. Readers rarely believe that lofty claim for good reason, but the design of this book and the nature of Office XP make it possible for this book to address such a wide audience. Here's why: Office XP is a major improvement over the previous Office products.

Readers unfamiliar with Windows–based environments will find plenty of introductory help here that brings them quickly up to speed. This book teaches you how to start and exit Office XP as well as how to manage many of the Internet-based Office XP elements that you need to use Office XP in today's online world. If you are new to the Internet, this book helps you get started and shows you how to make the most of the Internet and Office XP. This book talks to beginners without talking down to them.

This book also addresses those who presently use a Microsoft Office product. With your fundamental Office understanding, you will appreciate the new features and added power of Office XP. Keep in mind that Office XP is similar to previous Office versions but includes plenty of new features, improvements, and Web-based add-ons to keep Office gurus intrigued for a long time. This book teaches the Office XP Professional Edition, the edition that includes all the Office XP products and the one that sells the best.

What This Book Does for You

Although this book is not a complicated reference book, you learn almost every aspect of Office XP from a typical user's point of view. Office XP includes many advanced technical details that most users never need, and this book does not waste your time with those. You want to get up to speed with Office XP in 24 hours, and this book helps you fulfill that goal.

Those of you who are tired of the plethora of quick-fix computer titles cluttering today's shelves will find a welcome reprieve here. This book presents both the background and descriptions that a new Office XP user needs. In addition to the background, this book is practical and provides more than 100 step-by-step walkthroughs that you can work through to gain practical hands-on experience. These tasks guide you through all the common Office XP actions you need to make Office XP work for you.

Can This Book Really Teach Office XP in 24 Hours?

Yes. You can master each chapter in one hour. (By the way, chapters are referred to as *hours* in the rest of this book.) The material is balanced with mountains of tips, shortcuts, and methods that make your hours productive and hone your Office XP skills.

Conventions Used in This Book

Each hour ends with a question-and-answer session that addresses some of the most frequently asked questions about that hour's topic.

This book uses several common conventions to help teach the Office XP topics. Here is a summary of those typographical conventions:

- Commands, computer output, and words you type appear in a special monospaced computer font.
- To type a shortcut key, such as Alt+F, press and hold the first key, and then press the second key before releasing both keys.
- If a task requires you to select from a menu, the book separates menu commands with a comma. For example, File, Save As is used to select the Save As option from the File menu. All menus in this book are shown in full even though Office XP users can elect to display only the personalized menu options they use most.

In addition to typographical conventions, the following special elements are included to set off different types of information to make them easily recognizable:

Special notes augment the material you read in each hour. These notes clarify concepts and procedures.

You find numerous tips that offer shortcuts and solutions to common problems.

The cautions are about pitfalls. Reading them saves you time and trouble.

Coffee Break Sidebars

Take some time out of your 24-hour tutorial to sit back and enjoy a more in-depth look at a particular feature. The coffee break sidebars are useful for exploring unusual Office XP features and uses and show you additional ways to utilize the hour's material.

A glossary in the back of the book provides any definitions you need in one handy location.

Start Your 24-Hour Clocks

You are about to begin. Let's synchronize our 24-hour clocks and turn the page to enter the world of Office XP.

PART I

Working with Office XP

Hour

HOUR 1

Getting Acquainted with Office XP

Microsoft Office helps you work more efficiently and effectively. Office offers integrated software tools that are powerful, yet easy to learn and use. Offices large and small can use Office–based applications for many of their day-to-day computer needs, as can families and home-based businesses who want simple but robust writing and analysis tools for their computers.

If you have used previous versions of Office, Office XP takes you to the next step by adding more products, voice dictation, extra content in new window task panes, and extra Web-based tools not included with previous Office versions. Office automates many of your computing chores and provides products that work in unison by sharing data between them. This hour shows you how Office tackles many of the standard software requirements of today's offices.

The highlights of this hour include the following:

- What Office contains
- When to use an Office product
- How Office supports different environments

What's in Office XP?

Office contains Microsoft's most popular applications, such as Word and Excel, in a single package. The programs work well together now that Microsoft has combined them in the Office collection of programs. Microsoft offers multiple versions of Office, such as the Office Professional Edition and the Office Standard Edition. Program collections such as Office are often called a *suite of programs*. You can still purchase many of the Office programs individually, building a suite of products, but the Office package offers the best deal.

The following is a quick overview of the primary Office programs included in all versions of the Office suite:

- Word 2002 is a word processor with which you can create notes, memos, letters, school papers, business documents, books, newsletters, and even Web pages.

- Excel 2002 is an electronic worksheet program with which you can create graphs and worksheets for financial and other numeric data. After you enter your financial data, you can analyze it for forecasts, generate numerous what-if scenarios, and publish worksheets on the Web.

- PowerPoint 2002 is a presentation graphics program with which you can create presentations for seminars, schools, churches, Web pages, and business meetings. Not only can PowerPoint create the presentation overheads, but it can also create the speaker's presentation notes.

- Access 2002 is a database program with which you can organize data collections. No matter what kind or how much data you must organize, Access can analyze, sort, summarize, and report on that data. Your Web pages can reflect your latest data when you incorporate an Access database into your site.

- Outlook 2002 is a *personal information manager (PIM)* that organizes your contact addresses, phone numbers, and other information in an address-book format. Use Outlook to track your appointments, schedule meetings, generate to-do lists, keep notes, manage all your Internet e-mail, and keep a journal of your activities.

All the Office products share common features and common menu choices. Figure 1.1 shows the Word screen, for example, and Figure 1.2 shows the Excel screen. Both screens display the open File menu. As you can see, the two program interfaces look virtually identical even though the programs accomplish entirely different tasks. The data in each program differs in format due to the nature of the programs, but the interfaces are uniform.

FIGURE 1.1

The Word interface behaves like that of Excel.

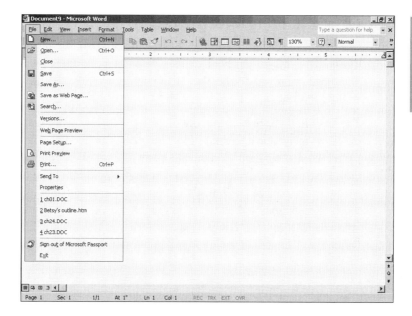

FIGURE 1.2

The Excel interface behaves similar to that of Word.

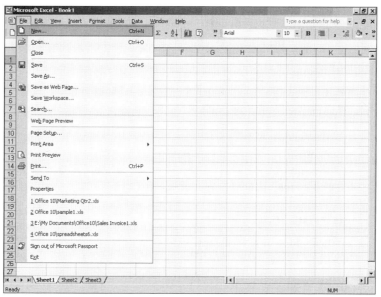

In addition to common interfaces, data that you create in one program can be inserted into another program within the Office suite. If you create a financial table with Excel, for instance, you can put the table in a Word document that you send to your Board of Directors and embed the table in a PowerPoint presentation to stockholders. After you learn one program in the Office suite, you will be comfortable using all the others because of the common interface.

Office Is Fully Integrated

One of the most helpful features of Office is its capability to adjust menus and toolbars to work the way you do. For example, Word does not display all menu commands on the File menu when you display the File menu. Instead, Word displays only those commands you use most often.

The less often you use a menu option, the more likely Word will remove that option from the initial menu that appears. All the commands are there, however, so when you click the arrows at the bottom of a menu, the menu expands to show all its commands. The Office products, thus, attempt to keep your screen as free from clutter as possible. As you use these personalized menus, Office analyzes the menu options and buttons you use most; those options and buttons you use infrequently will begin to go away so that only your common choices remain. You can always access these hidden menu options, but Office puts them out of the way until you need them.

> This book always displays all menu options although your Office installation might show the personalized menus that reflect the options you use most. You can show the full set of menu commands by selecting Tools, Customize, Options and checking the option labeled Always Show Full Menus.

The Office products are general purpose, meaning that you can customize applications to suit your needs. You can use Excel as your household budgeting program, for example, and as your company's interactive balance-sheet system.

You can integrate Office into your network system. This way, Office provides useful features whether you are networked to an intranet, to the Internet, or to both. You can share Office information with others across the network. Office fits well within the online world by integrating Internet access throughout the Office suite of products.

Introducing Word

When you need to write any text-based document, look no further than Word. Word is a word processor that supports many features, including the following:

- Automatic corrections for common mistakes as you type (see Hour 3, "Welcome to Word 2002") using special automatic-correcting tools that watch the way you work and adapt to your needs
- Wizards and templates that create and format documents for you (see Hour 4, "Formatting with Word 2002")
- Advanced page layout and formatting capabilities (see Hour 4)
- Numbering, bulleting, and shading tools (see Hour 4)

- Multiple document views so that you can see a rough draft of your document or the look of a final printed page as you write (see Hour 4)

- Integrated grammar, spelling, and hyphenation tools (see Hour 5, "Managing Documents and Customizing Word 2002")

- Newsletter-style multiple columns, headers, footers, and endnotes in your publications (see Hour 6, "Advanced Word 2002")

- Drawing, border, and shading tools that enable you to emphasize headers, draw lines and shapes around your text, and work with imported art files (see Hour 22, "Sharing Information Between Programs")

- Web-page development for Internet users so that they can turn their documents into Web pages (see Hour 24, "Creating Web Pages with Office XP")

Figure 1.3 shows a Word editing session. The user is editing a business letter to send to a client. Notice that the letter is well formatted thanks to Word's advanced page layout capabilities.

FIGURE 1.3

Word helps you create, edit, and format letters.

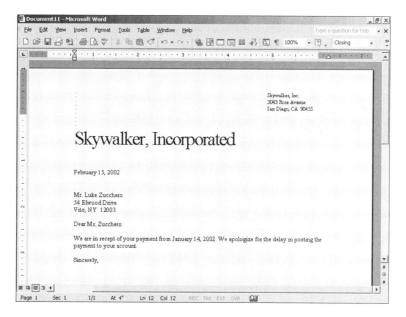

Introducing Excel

Although Excel can be used to organize and sort non-numeric information, the primary goal for Excel is to help you organize and manage financial information such as income statements, balance sheets, and forecasts. Excel is an electronic worksheet program that supports many features, including the following:

- Automatic cell formatting (see Hour 7, "Excel 2002 Workbooks")

- Automatic worksheet computations that enable you to generate worksheets that automatically recalculate when you make a change to a portion of the worksheet (see Hour 7)

- Built-in functions, such as financial formulas, that automate common tasks (see Hour 8, "Restructuring and Editing Excel 2002 Worksheets")

- Automatic row and column completion of value ranges with AutoFill (see Hour 9, "Using Excel 2002")

- Turn your worksheets into professionally produced reports (see Hour 10, "Formatting Worksheets to Look Great")

- Powerful charts and graphs that can analyze your numbers and turn them into simple trends (see Hour 11, "Charting with Excel 2002")

Figure 1.4 shows an Excel editing session. The user is getting ready to enter invoice information for a sale. As you can see, Excel can start with a predesigned form. If you have worked with other worksheet programs, you might be surprised at how fancy Excel can get. The wizards make creating advanced worksheets easy.

FIGURE 1.4

Excel helps you create, edit, and format numeric worksheets.

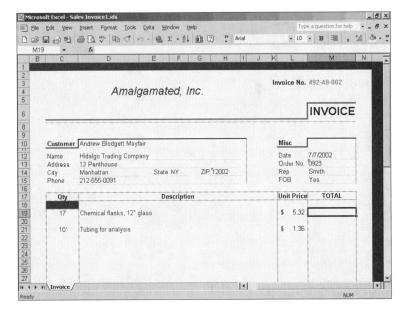

Introducing PowerPoint

Before PowerPoint's original version, users had no way to generate presentations without making a tedious effort to design each color slide using some kind of graphics drawing program. Although presentation products similar to PowerPoint now exist, PowerPoint is recognized as a leader. PowerPoint supports many features, including the following:

- The capability to turn Word document outlines into presentation notes (see Hour 22, "Sharing Information Between Programs")
- Using the AutoContent Wizard to generate presentations automatically (see Hour 12, "PowerPoint 2002 Presentations")
- Sample design templates that provide you with a fill-in-the-blank presentation (see Hour 12)
- Excel displays your presentation on your screen just as a slide projector displays slides (see Hour 13, "Editing and Arranging Your Presentations")
- Complete color and font control of your presentation slides (see Hour 14, "PowerPoint 2002 Advanced Features")
- A collection of clip art files, icons, sounds, and animations that you can embed to make presentations come alive (see Hour 14)
- Numerous transitions and fades between presentation slides to keep your audience's attention (see Hour 15, "Animating Your Presentations")
- The capability to save presentations as Web pages that you can then present on the Internet (see Hour 24, "Creating Web Pages with Office 2002")

Figure 1.5 shows a PowerPoint editing session. The user is getting ready for a presentation and has only a few minutes to prepare seven color slides for the meeting. With PowerPoint, a few minutes are more than enough time!

FIGURE 1.5

PowerPoint helps you create, edit, and format presentations.

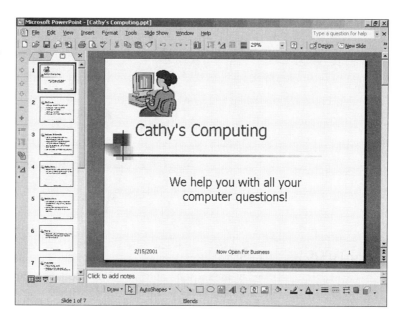

Introducing Outlook

Outlook is a simple-to-use tool that manages your business and personal meetings, e-mail, to-do lists, contacts, and appointments. Outlook provides many features, including the following:

- The capability to track your contact information, including multiple phone numbers and computerized e-mail addresses (see Hour 16, "Communicating with Outlook 2002")
- Management of your e-mail, phone calls, and to-do lists (see Hour 16)
- The capability to track your computer activities in a journal (see Hour 17, "Planning and Scheduling with Outlook 2002")
- The capability to schedule appointments (see Hour 17)
- The capability to plan which people and resources you need for meetings (see Hour 17)
- The capability to sound an alarm before an important event (see Hour 17)

Figure 1.6 shows an Outlook calendar screen. The user is getting ready to schedule a meeting on a particular day. As with all the Office programs, you can modify screen elements in Outlook so that they appear in the format most helpful to your needs.

FIGURE 1.6

*Outlook tracks
appointments and
events.*

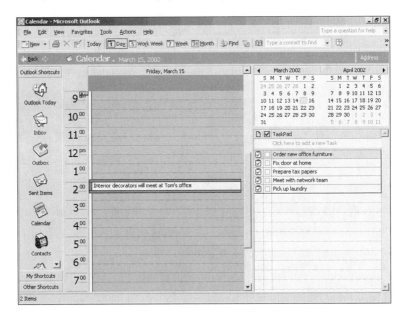

Introducing Access

Access provides one of the most comprehensive relational database systems available today. If you want to organize large collections of data, such as customer and inventory records, Access makes your job simple. Access goes far beyond other databases in power and ease of use by supporting features that include the following:

- Simple table-creation wizards and data-entry tools that enable you to set up and enter database information easily (see Hour 18, "Access 2002 Basics")
- Complete relational database support to reduce data redundancies (see Hour 18)
- Form-designing tools to ease data entry chores (see Hour 19, "Entering and Displaying Access 2002 Data")
- Information retrieval query tools that enable you to quickly get to the data you need (see Hour 20, "Retrieving Your Data")
- The capability to filter data rows and columns so that you see only data you want to see (see Hour 20)
- Report-generation that enables you to track and publish your data (see Hour 21, "Reporting with Access 2002")
- Sorting of data by any value (see Hour 21)
- The capability to produce custom labels for any printer (see Hour 21)
- Automatic summary provisions such as totals, averages, and statistical variances (see Hour 21)
- The capability to save databases in Web pages so that Internet users can view your database's information (see Hour 24)

Figure 1.7 shows an Access editing session. The user is editing employee records. Notice that Access accepts and tracks all kinds of data, including numbers and text.

FIGURE 1.7

Access manages your database data.

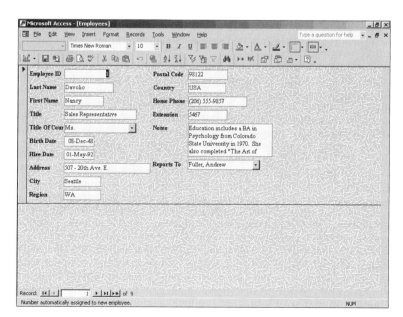

The Microsoft Office Shortcut Bar

Generally, you'll start one of the Office applications by clicking your Windows Start toolbar button and doing one of the following:

- Select New Office Document and select one of the icons that appear in the New Office Document dialog box (shown in Figure 1.8). Windows automatically starts the correct Office program that works with the document you want to create.

FIGURE 1.8

Select the type of Office document you want to create.

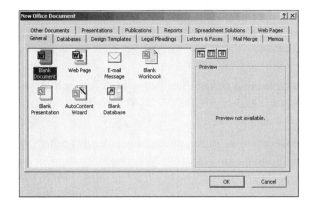

- Select Open Office Document and choose a file you've created already with one of the Office programs.
- From any Windows Explorer-like window that displays a file listing, select any file created by an Office program to start that program and load the file for editing.
- Use the Windows Start menu's Programs option to start a specific Office program.

You can forsake the Start menu altogether and select from the Microsoft Office Shortcut Bar to start one of the Office programs. Figure 1.9 shows a typical Microsoft Office Shortcut Bar, which automatically appears to the right of your screen when you select Microsoft Office Shortcut Bar from the Windows Start menu's Microsoft Office Tools menu option. (If a dialog box appears when you first start the Microsoft Office Shortcut Bar, select either Yes if you want the bar to appear every time you start Windows and No if you want the Microsoft Office Shortcut Bar to appear only in this session.)

FIGURE 1.9

Start Office programs quickly with the Microsoft Office Shortcut Bar.

Depending on your installed options, the Microsoft Office Shortcut Bar shown in Figure 1.9 might look different from yours. You or whoever installed Office on your computer might have changed the shortcut bar's display options by right-clicking on the bar and selecting one of the shortcut menu choices. If you want your Microsoft Office Shortcut Bar to appear across the top of your screen, simply drag the bar with your mouse to the top of your screen.

The Microsoft Office Shortcut Bar offers pushbutton access to any Office product. You can open or create an Office document by clicking the appropriate button. The Microsoft Office Shortcut Bar stays *active* and appears on your screen even if you work non-Office programs. Therefore, you can always access Office programs and documents from wherever you are.

If you use certain Office programs more often than others, you might want to select the Shortcut Bar's Customize option and add those specific program icons to the Office Shortcut Bar. If the Microsoft Office Shortcut Bar contains buttons you rarely use, such as the New Journal Entry button, use Customize to remove any of the existing buttons.

To get rid of the Microsoft Office Shortcut Bar, perform these steps:

1. Click the Office Shortcut Bar's colored Control icon to display the drop-down menu.
2. Click Exit.

You can change the size of the icons on your Microsoft Office Shortcut Bar by selecting from the shortcut menu's Customize option and selecting Large Buttons.

Euro Support

Europe is quickly moving toward a single economy. This will surely impact the entire world as the single economy becomes one of the largest economies on earth. Office provides support for the single Euro currency. Each individual country's former currency symbols still reside in Office as well.

Enabling Office for a specific language is easier than ever before. To activate a specific language, select Start, Programs, Office Tools and select the Microsoft Office Language Settings option. Select the language you want to enable from the Enabled Languages tab and click OK to apply that language to the Office environment.

Summary

This hour introduced the Office programs by showing you a little of what each program can accomplish. Before learning Office specifics, you need to get the big picture. This hour provided that big picture and introduced the Office tools that you will use.

All Office programs share a common interface. After you learn one Office program, the others are easy to master. Some users find that they can use Office for all their computer needs.

The next hour begins a tour of Office's features so that you can begin to see what Office can really do.

Q&A

Q I've used Word and Excel. Do I need the other Office products?

A Only you can answer that question because only you know whether you need a program to keep track of your appointments and contacts (Outlook) or your database (Access). Only you know whether you will be called to present a topic in a meeting or at a conference (PowerPoint).

If you need word processing and worksheet computing only, you might not need the other Office products. In that case, you need to install only those programs that you want to use. If you have truly mastered Word and Excel, however, you will be glad that Microsoft kept the same uniform interface throughout all the Office products. This enables you to use what you already know.

Q Why don't I see the Microsoft Office Shortcut Bar every time I start Windows?

A Just rerun the Microsoft Office Shortcut Bar from the Windows Start menu and select Yes when asked if you want to start the Office Shortcut Bar when Windows starts. If the dialog box does not appear, you can right-click the Microsoft Office Shortcut Bar, select Customize, and then select Show Title Screen at Startup. The next time you start the Microsoft Office Shortcut Bar, you will be able to state that you want the bar to appear every time Windows starts.

Q **Suppose that I want to keep track of names and addresses. Which Office product would I use?**

A This is actually a trick question. Word, Excel, Access, and Outlook all track names and addresses! Word keeps track of names and addresses for mail merging (sending the same letter to many people); Excel includes a simple database feature that can track items such as names and addresses; Access's primary purpose is to track virtually any data in an organized list; and Outlook records all your name and address records. Generally, use Outlook for your names and addresses (all the other Office products can read Outlook's data) and save the other Office products for their primary purposes.

Q **Is it true that the Office programs are simple after I learn one well?**

A The Office programs share common interfaces, such as uniform menus and dialog boxes. After you learn how to use one Office program, you already understand the basic interface of the others. Therefore, you can concentrate on the specifics of each product instead of having to learn a new interface in each program.

HOUR 2

Preparing for Introducing Office XP's Powerful Features

This hour previews Office XP by showing you some of its more impressive features. If you are new to the Office environment, this hour whets your appetite for Office. Once you get the overview, you'll be ready to study the specific Office programs and learn how they work.

Office attempts to move beyond the normal Windows-based help system. If you have used Windows programs in the past, you have probably read online documentation, clicked hypertext links to other related topics, and searched for keywords with which you need help. Office includes all these standard online help tools, but takes that help to a new level of functionality. Office provides some rather unusual help with the Office Assistant and Office XP's support for plain-language help queries. In a way, Office looks over your shoulder and offers advice about a better way of doing things.

In addition to improving the Windows online help system, Office helps disabled users by providing several accessibility options. These options magnify the screen's views and offer keyboard shortcuts that the user can define and control.

The highlights of this hour include the following:

- What the Office Assistant is
- How to ask Office XP questions
- What Office does when disaster strikes your computer
- How to recover from a disaster while using an Office product
- How you can utilize Office's install-on-demand feature
- How to use voice commands for controlling the Office programs
- How to customize your Office work environment to suit your accessibility needs.

The Office Assistant

When you start any Office program, one of the first features you will notice is the *Office Assistant*, an online cartoon character that hangs around as you work. Figure 2.1 shows the default Office Assistant (named Clippit), who appears when you start an Office product.

Clippit is here to help you

FIGURE 2.1

Clippit, the helpful assistant, remains faithful as you use Office.

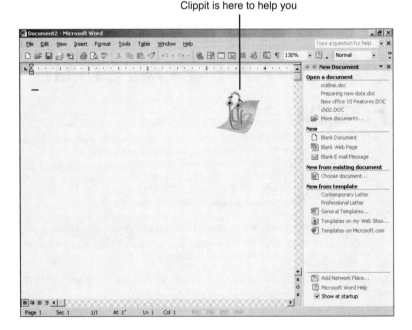

 You might see a different character. The next section, "Customizing Office Assistant," explains how to change the Office Assistant's animated character.

Keep your eyes on the Office Assistant as you work because you will be amused at the contortions it goes through as it provides advice. If you have your speakers turned on, the Office Assistant makes noises to draw your attention.

Move the Office Assistant to a different screen location by dragging the character. If the Office Assistant is about to cover an area in which you are typing, it automatically moves out of the way.

Suppose that you want help italicizing Word text. You can search through the online help system (via the Help menu), or you can click the Office Assistant and type a question, such as How do I italicize text?, and press Enter. The Office Assistant analyzes your question and displays a list of related topics (as shown in Figure 2.2). Click the topic that best fits your needs, and the Office Assistant locates that help topic and displays the Help dialog box.

Office Assistant's
help topics

FIGURE 2.2

The Office Assistant offers a lot of advice.

If you do something and the Office Assistant sees a better method, a yellow light bulb that you can click for shortcut information displays. If you begin to create a numbered list using menus, for example, the Office Assistant might display the light bulb to let you know that you can create a numbered list by clicking a button on the toolbar.

Customizing the Office Assistant

If you work on a slow computer, you might want to disable the Office Assistant to keep things moving a little faster. When you right-click the Office Assistant, a pop-up menu appears with these options:

- *Hide*—Gets rid of the Office Assistant. Display the Office Assistant again by clicking the toolbar's Office Assistant button.

- *Options*—Displays Figure 2.3's Office Assistant dialog box, from which you can control the behavior of the Office Assistant (such as the Office Assistant's response to pressing the F1 key).

- *Choose Assistant*—Enables you to change to a different animated Office Assistant character. As you work with Office, check out all the Office Assistants (they are fun to see). You will learn how to change the Office Assistant character in the steps that follow.

- *Animate!*—Causes the Office Assistant to dance around its window; the Office Assistant likes to show off. Select Animate a few times to see the Office Assistant's contortions. As the Office Assistant offers advice, it also moves through these animations. If you attempt to exit a program without saving your work, for example, the Office Assistant gets your attention. (You will even hear Rocky, the canine assistant, barking if you use Rocky as your Office Assistant.)

FIGURE 2.3

Control the way that the Office Assistant behaves.

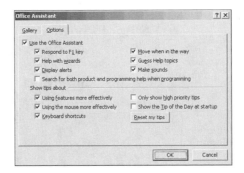

Office includes several Office Assistants to help you do your job. They differ in animation, but not in their advice. Suppose you get tired of Clippit and decide that you want to see a different Office Assistant. Try this:

1. Right-click the Office Assistant.

2. Select Choose Assistant. The Office Assistant displays an Office Assistant Gallery screen.

3. Click Back and Next to cycle through the Office Assistants. Each Office Assistant goes through a song and dance to convince you that it is the best.

4. When you come to an Office Assistant you like, click the OK button to begin using that Office Assistant.

By default, the Office Assistant does not appear until you activate him. If you don't see an Office Assistant when you start an Office program, select Help, Show Office Assistant and the Office Assistant will appear. In reality, you might grow tired of this fun guy rather quickly. The Office Assistant is cute at first and then becomes a nuisance in many people's opinions. Those people turn him off. Do what you want; Office XP is designed to provide what you need and hide what you don't want to see or use.

If the Office Assistant appears when you press F1 but you want to use the normal content-based help system, right-click over Assistant to display the pop-up menu. Select Options and uncheck the option labeled Respond to the F1 Key to disconnect the Assistant from the F1 keypress. Office uses a Web-like, HTML-based help so that you can navigate the online help the same way you might navigate Web pages. As Figure 2.4 shows, when you display non–Office Assistant help, Office displays two panes with the help text in the right pane and a condensed Office program screen in the left pane. (You can drag the center bar left and right to adjust the width of the panes.) With the help shown in a second pane, you can keep working in the left pane while referring to helpful instructions in the right pane.

2

Help stays here...   Help topics   Ask a question

FIGURE 2.4

Office products provide a two-pane help view.

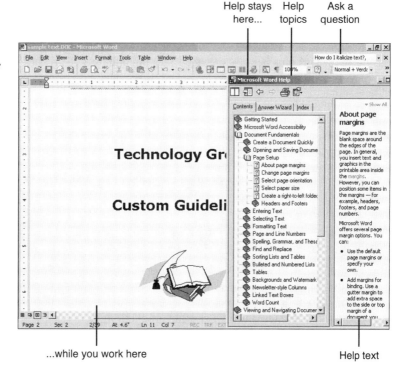

...while you work here   Help text

Type Your Question

Figure 2.4 shows a text box where you can type a question. When you want help and the Office Assistant is not showing, you can click this Ask a Question text box and the Office program will show a list of topics that attempt to answer your question.

The beauty of the Office XP products is that they all have a consistent interface. The Office Assistant and the online help system work the same way in all the Office programs. In addition, the Ask a Question text box appears to the right of all Office XP applications. Therefore, when you learn how to use the helpful tools in one program such as PowerPoint, you leverage that knowledge in the other applications also.

The Office XP Self-Repair Feature

Although it happens rarely, your Office installation can get damaged. Perhaps another program's installation overwrites one of the Office system files. If you start Access and Access does not behave in a normal manner, indicating that a system problem might have crept into your system, one of the first places to begin fixing the problem is in Office XP's Detect and Repair feature.

When you select Help, Detect and Repair from any Office application, the Detect and Repair dialog box in Figure 2.5 appears. The dialog box is designed to do these things:

1. Warn you that the Detect and Repair feature requires your original Office XP CD-ROM files because damaged files might have to be replaced.

2. Let you specify whether you want your settings kept or if you want the Detect and Repair system to restore all installation defaults.

FIGURE 2.5

Let Office repair itself.

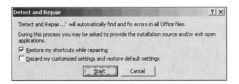

If you have used Office XP for a while and set several options throughout the Office programs, such as customizing the menus and automatic correcting features, be sure that you keep the option titled Restore My Shortcuts While Repairing checked. Otherwise, Office will restore all options for all the applications back to their original installed values, and you will have to re-enter all your options, preferences, and dictionary entries that you had entered while using the product.

Airbags for Office

In what is referred to as "airbags for Office," several crash recovery features are built into the Office products. If a system crash or power outage occurs before you've had a chance to save all your Office data to your disks, when you re-start the Office product, you will be given a chance to recover whatever file or files you were working with before the disaster.

Most of the time, the Office XP products are all smart enough to recover most, if not all, of your work. At worst, you typically have to save the recovered data under a name that differs from its original name before the problem began. Even early test releases of Office XP recovered files very well, which was fortunate considering how often the early Beta test versions of Office XP crashed!

Installing On Demand

When you or your system administrator installed Office, the installation routine offered several installation choices. You might not want to install a full version of Office XP Professional, for example, because of the massive disk space the full installation requires (more than 500 megabytes of space). You can install only the features that you predict you'll use most often.

If you later decide to use a feature that you had not installed, Office displays the dialog box shown in Figure 2.6, which reminds you that the feature is not installed and gives you a chance to install the feature or move onto something else.

FIGURE 2.6

Install a feature only if you need it.

More than likely, the install on demand feature requires that you locate and insert one of the original Office XP CD-ROMs, usually the first CD in your Office XP set. Office requests this CD if needed, loads the feature you were trying to use, and puts you at that feature the moment the install completes.

Parla Italian or *Habla* Spanish?

The Office XP programs will not only help you enter and format your data, but also Office translates between several languages. Simply select a word or phrase, right-click the selection, and choose Translate from the pop-up menu that appears. The Translate Task Pane appears on the right side of your screen, like the one shown in Figure 2.7.

Select the translation dictionary from the drop-down list box titled Dictionary if Office did not guess correctly at the language you wanted to translate to and from. (Actually, Office remembers your most recent choice of languages once you use this feature.)

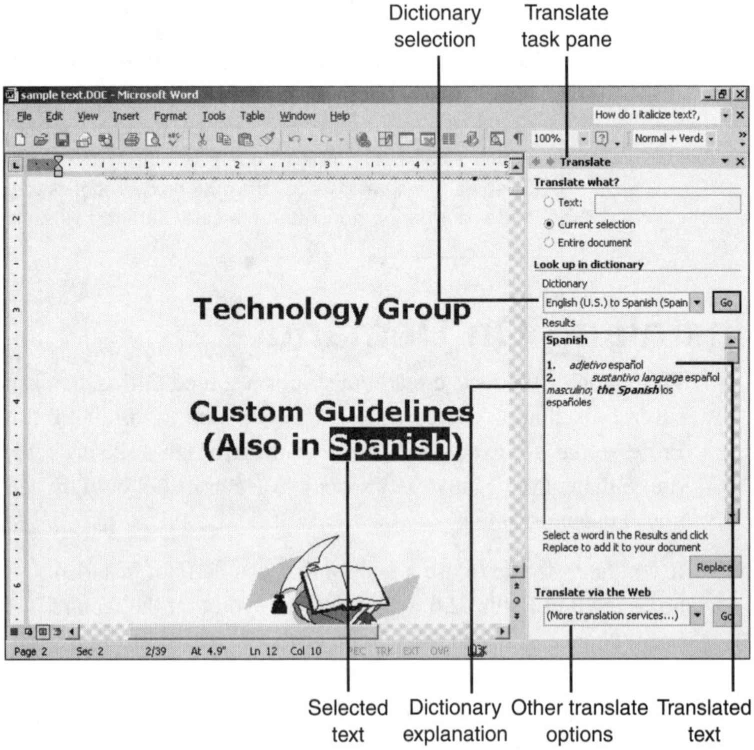

FIGURE 2.7
Install a feature only if you need it.

Dictionary selection

Translate task pane

Selected text   Dictionary explanation   Other translate options   Translated text

If the dictionary does not have all the languages you require, click the Go button at the bottom of the Task Pane to search the Internet for the languages you need. Microsoft's Web sites will contain several more translation dictionaries than your Office XP CDs come loaded with.

As you can see from Figure 2.7, the Translate Task Pane offers to translate not only selected text, but your entire document if you want. After you've used the Translate Task Pane in your editing session, you can once again display the Translate Task Pane by selecting View, Task Pane and clicking the Task Pane's navigation arrows at the top of the Task Pane until the Translate Task Pane comes into view. Simply type a single word or phrase in the text box titled Text, select your translation dictionary, and click Go to translate only the word or phrase that you typed.

The Task Pane is a feature new in Office XP. Hour 3's lesson, "Welcome to Word 2002," explains more about the Task Pane.

Even Simpler: Just Say It

Office XP is the first Office product designed to utilize voice recognition technology for the following reasons:

- You can control the Office programs by speaking commands.
- You can dictate your text into Word, Excel, and the other Office programs to make data entry much easier.

You must have a fairly fast computer for the voice commands and dictation to work well. A 650MHz machine would probably be the minimum even though the Office paperwork states that Office XP runs on a machine less than half that speed. For full reliability and accuracy, the faster the better. Even then, dictation is only about 95% accurate. 95% sounds like a lot until you realize that a 1,500-word essay that you dictate will have a total of 75 misspelled words on the average.

> In addition to having a quick computer, you must have a quality microphone and speakers hooked to your computer. A combination microphone and speaker headset is perhaps the best equipment to have when using voice dictation.

When you first use the voice command and dictation features, Office walks you through an equipment test that adjusts your microphone for optimal speaking quality and volume. In addition, you will read some sample text to train Office in your speaking inflections, tone, and style. The initial training is able to generate about an 85% accuracy rate for Office's speech recognition, but as you keep using the product with your microphone, the accuracy will improve and get closer to the 95% to 97% accuracy level.

To issue a menu command using your voice, click the Language bar option titled Voice Command. You then can issue menu commands such as File, Save just by speaking the options. To dictate words and phrases into your Office products, such as a letter in Word, select Dictate on the Language bar, click your mouse pointer where the first word should appear in your document, and begin speaking.

Using Office to Share Information with Others

Although many people will use Office on single-user computers, Microsoft understands that today's office worker needs the ability to share information globally. Today's computers are often networked to other computers, either through a *network*, an Internet connection, or an *intranet* connection.

As long as you use e-mail programs such as Outlook Express, Outlook, Microsoft Exchange, Windows Messaging, Microsoft Mail, or Netscape Messenger, you can create a Word document and send it to users on your mail system. When you send a document, the receivers can read the document and even make changes to the document using Word. Word keeps track of revisions, and each reviewer's notes appear separate from the others. Using Word's Reviewing toolbar that appears when you select Tools, Track Changes, you can accept or reject any of the reviewer's comments after the document gets back to you.

Office enables you to integrate all Office products. Therefore, if you want to send a report with an Excel worksheet graph to someone over the network, embed that graph into a Word document (as explained in Hour 22, "Sharing Information Between Programs") and send the Word document. The graph travels along with the document.

Office supports several document-routing options on the File, Send To menu, and here are the more common ones:

- *Mailing Recipient (for Review)*—a copy of your document to your list of reviewers. Each reviewer can make changes to his copy, and then return the document to you.

- *Routing Recipient*—Sends a single copy of your document to each reviewer in turn. Every subsequent reviewer can read the preceding reviewers' comments and add his own. The document finally gets back to you after the final reviewer makes revisions.

- *Exchange Folder*—Requires Microsoft Exchange on a client/server based network. Sends a copy of your document to a public folder that everyone on your receiver list can read. Posting is useful when you have a company-wide policy or message that you want everyone to read. Your network administrator should be able to help set up a public folder.

Word keeps track of who made each revision. You can have the reviewers make changes to a copy or to the original document. To determine who made a revision, point to the edit and the editor's name appears over the edit, along with the date the edit was made.

If the reviewers insert sound objects into the routed document, they can review the document with speech as well as with editing marks!

Figure 2.8 shows a screen from Word with revision marks. The revisions appear on your screen in color—a different color for each editor who made a revision—so that the revisions are easy to distinguish from the original text. Word's accept or reject Tools, Track Changes menu options enable you to quickly incorporate or delete any and all revisions made by the editing team.

FIGURE 2.8
Revision marks enable a team of editors to revise the same document electronically.

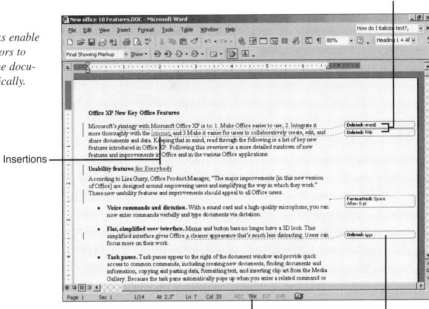

Deletions

Insertions

Indicates revision tracking is on   Revision descriptions

Both Word and Excel currently support revision marks. You can use the Tools, Track Changes menu options to see revision marks, hide revision marks (to see what the document will look like if you incorporate all revisions), and accept or reject revision marks.

> You can right-click a revision mark and view a pop-up menu that enables you to easily accept or reject the revision mark.

Making Office Easier to Use

Several accessibility features make Office easier to use. You will become familiar with many of these features as you work with Office. Following is a sample of some of these features:

- Make toolbar buttons larger so they are easier to find. Right-click on a toolbar and select Customize from the pop-up menu that appears. The Customize dialog box provides access to larger icons on the toolbar buttons.

- The Office programs contain many *AutoComplete* features with which you can begin typing items such as dates, times, days of the week or month, names, and any other AutoText entries you set up. Office completes the entry for you. If you begin typing a month name such as Nov, for example, Word displays a small box with November above your month abbreviation. If you press Enter, Word completes the month name for you! If you type a full month name, such as July, Word offers to complete your entry with the current date, such as July 7, 2002. You can accept the complete date by pressing Enter or ignore it by typing the rest of the sentence as you want it to appear.

- You can rearrange toolbar buttons and customize toolbars so that they contain only the buttons you use most frequently. Office itself analyzes how you use the menus and toolbars and begins to hide any options and buttons you use less frequently to reduce screen clutter. You can always see all menu options and toolbars when you want by displaying a menu for a couple of seconds until the hidden options appear. In addition, you can drag a toolbar left or right to see hidden options. These personalized menus attempt to give you the tools you need when you need them.

- You can assign shortcut keys to just about any task in any Office product. Suppose that you often need to color and boldface an Excel value. Create a shortcut keystroke and press it whenever you want to apply the special formatting.

Get Ready for the Internet and Office

Microsoft did not make Office's Internet interface really stand out; instead, the Internet interface appears as just one of a long line of Office features so that you can access the Internet from within the Office environment. The seamless Web integration lets you get to Internet information much easier than before. The Internet interface between the various Office products differs a little, but the Internet interface is always underneath Office, ready to handle the connection.

The Web Toolbar

All core Office programs contain a Web toolbar that appears when you click a hyperlink inside a document. You can also display the Web toolbar by right-clicking on a toolbar and selecting Web from the list that appears. Alternately, click the Web button to display the Office Web toolbar shown in Figure 2.9. The buttons give you Web access from within an Office program.

FIGURE 2.9

Access the Internet from this Office Web toolbar.

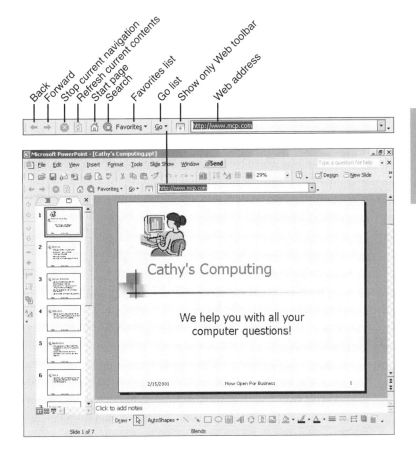

If you're logged on to the Internet when you click a Web toolbar button such as the Start Page button, Office takes you directly to your Start page, substituting your Web browser for the current Office program on your screen. If you're not logged on to the Internet before using the Web toolbar buttons, Office initiates your logon sequence for you.

> If you use Internet Explorer as your Web browser, type the name of any Office data file in the URL Address box and Internet Explorer displays your properly formatted Office data file.

An inserted hyperlink is just one way that you can connect an Office document to the outside, online world. The Office products enable you to create Web pages from data located inside your documents as the next section demonstrates.

If you're giving a PowerPoint presentation and need to reference something on the Web, simply insert a hyperlink to that Web site and click it during the presentation. PowerPoint jumps to the Web and displays the page.

A Web site does not have to exist yet for you to insert a hyperlink to it. For example, you might be creating an in-house reference manual for your company's new Web site. You can insert a hyperlink to an address on your company site before the site actually appears on the Internet.

You can even use the Internet as your Office data repository. Not only can you access the Internet Web pages from the Web toolbar, but you can also edit Web pages as if they were on your own PC. If you want to edit a document located on an FTP or HTTP site, just enter the document's URL when you open the document. You can also save to HTTP and FTP sites by using any of the Office Save commands.

Summary

This hour introduced some of the more interesting features of Office, including the Office Assistant, accessibility features, and clip art files. By routing documents to your co-workers over your network (or over the Internet using Office's built-in Internet support), you can all work on the same documents and track revisions as each of you review Office material.

Hour 3, "Welcome to Word 2002," introduces Word. You'll soon see why Word is considered to be the most powerful word processor available.

Q&A

Q What if I want to use the Office Assistant only when I need help?

A Right-click the Office Assistant to display the pop-up menu and select Hide Assistant. The Office Assistant window disappears. When you want to use the Office Assistant again, click the Standard toolbar's Office Assistant button. You might want to display the Office Assistant's Options dialog box (right-click the Office Assistant and select Options) to change the way the Office Assistant responds to you. The Options dialog box enables you to modify the timing of the Office Assistant's responses.

Q **Why would I** *route* **a document instead of** *sending* **a document if co-workers needed to make revisions?**

A Use the document routing option when you want to send the same document to multiple co-workers and let each co-worker see the revisions made. When you send a document, Office sends a copy to each of the recipients, who then make revisions to that single copy and return it to you. Office users often route when they have more time to wait for revisions and when they want to send a document through a predetermined chain of organizational command.

2

PART II

Processing with Word 2002

Hour

HOUR 3

Welcome to Word 2002

This hour introduces you to Microsoft Word 2002. You will soon see why Microsoft Word is the most popular word processor on the market. With Word 2002, you can create documents of any kind with amazing ease. Word 2002 helps you painlessly create letters, proposals, Web pages, business plans, résumés, novels, and even graphics-based multicolumn publications, such as fliers and newsletters.

The highlights of this hour include the following:

- Why Word is considered the most powerful word processor available today
- How to enter text and navigate through your document
- How Word's advanced AutoCorrection features help eliminate common editing tasks for you

Beginning Words About Word

Given that Word is probably the most advanced word processor ever written for a microcomputer, you might think that Word's interface is complicated.

Although some of Word's more advanced features can seem tricky at first, you'll be using Word's most popular and common features quickly. Microsoft made a huge effort to streamline Word's (and all the Office XP products') interface so that you can get to the most common features without a fuss.

Figure 3.1 shows Word's typical screen during the editing of a document. Your screen might differ slightly depending on the options currently set on your installation.

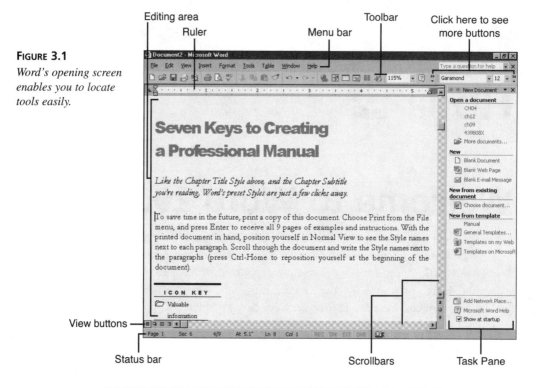

FIGURE 3.1

Word's opening screen enables you to locate tools easily.

You can rest your mouse pointer over any toolbar button until a ScreenTip displays, identifying the button.

The most important area of Word's screen is the editing area. That's where the document you want to edit appears. If the document does not all fit on one screen, you can use the scrollbar to scroll down the page. Word offers several ways to view your document, but you'll almost always work with the normal view (see Figure 3.1) or print layout view (see Figure 3.2). In the normal view, chosen from the View menu or by clicking the

Normal View button in the lower-left part of the screen, more of your document's text fits on the screen than in any other view. In Print Layout view (selected also from the View menu or by clicking the Print Layout button), you gain a better perspective of how your document's text fits onto a printed page, in addition to seeing header and footer text such as page numbers if any appear.

The Task Pane some of your screen's real estate, so you can close the Task Pane by clicking its Close button (the X in the Task Pane's upper-right hand corner). Microsoft added the Task Pane to keep editing tools you might need close by during your editing session. You can always turn the Task Pane back on when you want to utilize it. (Subsequent sections in this and later chapters explore ways to take advantage of the Task Pane.)

The toolbar is actually composed of two separate toolbars next to each other, the Standard toolbar and the Formatting toolbar. Some users prefer these to reside on two separate rows on the screen. You can change to the more common two-row setup by right-clicking the toolbar, selecting Customize, and checking the option marked Show Standard and Formatting toolbars on Two Rows. Figure 3.2 shows how the two-row toolbar separates toolbars into two groups: The top one is the Standard toolbar with typical file and editing commands and the second toolbar is the Formatting toolbar in which common character, paragraph, and document formatting tools await your click.

As with most Office features, several ways exist to perform the same tasks. Use whatever way you prefer. As an example, you can save a mouse click by clicking on either of the two small down arrows (one appears in the middle and one at the right of the single-line toolbar as Figure 3.1 pointed out) and selecting Show Buttons on Two Rows. These arrows are called *Toolbar Options* arrows. The View, Toolbars, Customize menu option also provides the same option.

Traversing the Word and other Office menus is simple. Either press Alt followed by an underlined menu key or point and click with your mouse to open any of the pull-down menus. Office XP features personalized menus that, over time, change as you use Word and the other Office products. The often-used menu commands appear and those you don't use much or at all do not show up when you first display a menu. If you double-click a menu name, keep a menu open for a few moments, or click the arrow at the bottom of a drop-down menu, all of that menu's options appear.

By keeping the most-used commands on the menu and hiding the others (for a short period), Word keeps your screen clutter down but sometimes makes locating a more obscure menu option harder. You can elect to keep the personalized menus on. You also can turn on all menu options at all times (the option set for this book's figures) by selecting Tools, Customize and checking the option labeled Always Show Full Menus.

Standard toolbar
Formatting toolbar   Toolbar Options arrows

FIGURE 3.2

With only minor adjustments, you can change the appearance of your screen to suit your editing preferences.

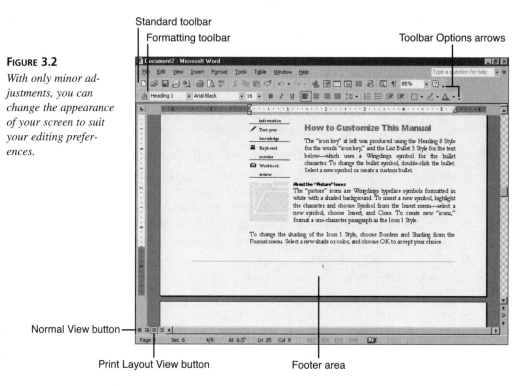

Normal View button

Print Layout View button   Footer area

Documents and Disks

Several ways exist to create new documents. Most of the time to create a new document, however, you will select File, New to display the New Document Task Pane window. You then can click Blank Document to create an empty Word document or select from one of the templates Word offers such as several legal, letters, and fax templates. A *template* is a pre-defined page, sometimes with accompanying artwork, such as a standard letter format or a fax cover sheet that gives your document a pre-defined look.

If you click Templates on Microsoft.com and you have a Web connection, you can select from hundreds of Word templates on Microsoft's Web site. After you select a template, you then just fill in the document's content.

Word hides the Task Pane window after you make a selection from it to give you more editing room. As you work, a different Task Pane might appear to help you with a different feature.

When you are ready to save your document for the first time, select File, Save, and specify a location and filename before clicking Save. After the first time you save a document, you only need to select File, Save (or press Ctrl+S) to update your changes. To save the document using a different name or location, select File, Save As and enter a new name.

Word documents end with the `.doc` filename extension as in `Proposal.doc`. Filenames can have spaces in them. You don't have to type the extension when opening or saving documents; All Office products automatically attach the correct extension.

Once on disk, you can load any document into memory to make further changes or to print the document by selecting File, Open (or pressing Ctrl+O) and selecting the file you want to edit.

Remember that you can use Office XP's Speech Recognition to enter commands in Word as you can all Office XP products. In addition, you can dictate text directly into your document instead of using the keyboard. See the previous hour's lesson for details.

Editing Multiple Documents

If you want to work on two documents at the same time, perhaps to cut and paste information from one into the other, use File, Open to open a second (or even a third, fourth, or more) document. Press Ctrl+F6 to switch between the documents. Your Windows taskbar will show a Word icon for each document. You can switch between documents by clicking the appropriate Windows taskbar icon.

With several documents open, the taskbar can get cluttered with Word icons. You can clean up the taskbar by selecting Tools, Options, View and unchecking the Windows in taskbar option. Your Windows taskbar then shows only one Word session even if you edit multiple documents at the same time in that session.

Select Window, Arrange All to show both (or as many as you currently have open) documents on the screen at the same time.

If you're new to Word or to word processing, master editing with a single document before you tackle multiple documents at once.

Entering and Editing Text

This section reviews fundamental Word editing skills and brings you up to speed even if you are new to word processing. In this section, you learn how to do the following:

- Type text into a document and maneuver around the screen
- Copy, cut, and paste text from one location to another
- Locate and replace text

Entering Text

The blank editing area is where you type text to create a new document. Of course, Word supports more than just text because you can add graphics and even Web page elements to a Word document. The best place to familiarize you with Word, however, is to start with straight text.

Two pointers appear in Word: the mouse's pointing arrow and the insertion point, which is the flashing vertical bar (also called the *text cursor*) that shows where the next character will appear. As you type, remember these basic editing hints:

- Don't press Enter at the end of each line. As you type close to the right edge of the screen, Word automatically wraps the text to the next line for you.
- Only press Enter at the end of each paragraph. Each subsequent press of the Enter key adds an extra blank line before the next paragraph. (If you type a list of items, you would press Enter at the end of each item.)
- If you make a typing mistake, press the Backspace key to erase the last character you typed. Continue pressing Backspace to erase multiple characters. You can also erase any text you've typed, not just the most recent character. If you press one of the arrow keys, you can move the insertion point (the text cursor) all around the document until you get to text you want to erase. At that point, you can press the Delete key to erase whatever character follows the insertion point.

Insert mode is Word's default editing mode. When you are using Insert mode, new text you type appears at the text pointer, pushing existing characters to the right (and down the page if needed). When in *Overtype mode*, new text replaces existing text.

The Word Status bar shows the current insertion mode. If the letters OVR are visible, Word is in Overtype mode. If OVR is grayed out, Word is in Insert mode. You can switch between the two modes by pressing the Insert key.

Not only can you insert text, but Word also enables you to insert blanks. Suppose that you forget a space or want to insert three spaces before the start of a paragraph. You can move the pointer to the place you want the blanks (to the left of text that you want to shift right) by pointing and clicking the mouse pointer to anchor the insertion point in position. Press the Spacebar as many times as you need to shift the existing text right.

Navigating Word Documents

When you first type a document, you might enter the rough draft all at once and edit the text later, or you might be the kind of writer who edits as you go. No matter how you write, you need to be able to move the insertion point around a Word document quickly, locating just the text you want. Often, you navigate through a Word document using these general practices:

- Use the four arrow keys to move the insertion point within the current editing area.
- Click the scrollbars to scroll through the display until you view the text you want.
- Click your mouse pointer anywhere inside the editing area to set the insertion point in that location.
- If you type more text than fits in the editing area, use the scrollbars, arrow keys, PageUp, PageDown, Ctrl+Home, and Ctrl+End keys to scroll to the portions of text that you want to see.

If you open an existing document, press Shift+F5 to jump directly to your most recent edit.

To quickly navigate many pages in a document, press Ctrl+G (the shortcut for Edit, Go To) to display Figure 3.3's Find and Replace dialog box and enter a page number to jump to that page. The Find and Replace dialog box is great for jumping not only to specific page numbers, but also to specific text that you want to read or edit. You will learn more about the Find and Replace dialog box as well as how the Task Pane helps you search for text.

FIGURE 3.3

You can quickly jump to any page.

The navigation skills you learn here also apply to the other Office XP products. Excel, for example, has a similar Find and Replace dialog box.

Selecting Text

Earlier in this hour, you learned how to insert and delete individual characters; you now learn how to select entire sections of text you can move or delete.

When you highlight (*select*) text, you can perform tasks on that selection. For example, you can select two sentences and underline them for emphasis. You can select text using your keyboard or mouse. Table 3.1 shows the mouse-selection operations.

TABLE 3.1   Word Makes Easy Work of Text Selection

To Select	Do This
Any text	Click the mouse on the first character of the text and drag the mouse to the last character. (Figure 3.4 shows a partial paragraph selection.)
A Single Word	Double-click anywhere on the word.
A Sentence	Press Ctrl and click anywhere within the sentence.
A Line	Click the white margin area at the left of the line.
A Paragraph	Double-click the white margin area at the left of the paragraph or triple-click anywhere inside the paragraph's text.
The Entire document	Press Ctrl and click the white margin area at the left of the document's text.

Beginning with Word 2002, you can select multiple occurrences of text by pressing Ctrl before you select text. By using Ctrl, you can select a sentence at the top of your document and one at the bottom at the same time, and then apply a special format to both sentences at once. The next hour's lesson explains how to format selected text.

To select text with your keyboard, move the insertion point to the beginning of the selection, press the Shift key, and move the insertion point to the final selection character. Release the Shift key when you're finished selecting the text.

You can press Ctrl+A to select your entire document.

Selected text

FIGURE 3.4

Select a block of text to edit.

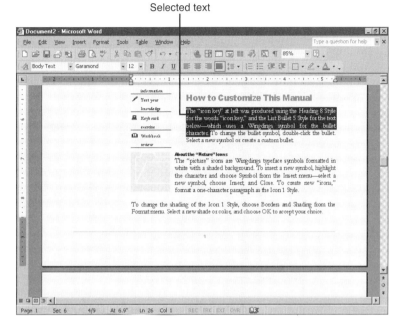

Deleting Text

Press Delete to erase characters to the right of the insertion point. Any characters to the right of the deleted character shift left to close the gap. You can also press Delete to delete selected text. Furthermore, you can press Backspace to erase text characters to the left of the insertion point.

Here's a tip that even advanced Word gurus often forget: Ctrl+Backspace erases the word to the *left* of your insertion point, and Ctrl+Del erases the word to the *right* of your insertion point.

Copying, Cutting, and Pasting

After you select text, you can *copy* or *cut* (move) that text to a different location. One of the most beneficial features that propelled word processors into the spotlight in the 1980s was their capability to copy and move text. In the medieval days (before 1980), people had to use scissors and glue to cut and paste. Now, your hands stay clean.

Windows uses a *clipboard* concept to hold text that you want to cut, copy, or move; and Office takes the concept of the clipboard further with the Office Clipboard. The Office Clipboard is where text resides during a copy, cut, or paste operation. It shows itself in

Office as a Task Pane and is a section of memory that holds text and other document items (even graphics) that you place there. It can hold 24 selected items, and a special Clipboard Task Pane automatically appears as you select text (see Figure 3.5). If you don't want to see the Task Pane when you use the Office Clipboard, click the Task Pane's Options button and select Collect Without Showing Office Clipboard. You can always redisplay the Task Pane by selecting from the View menu.

FIGURE 3.5

The Clipboard Task Pane displays items you've cut or copied.

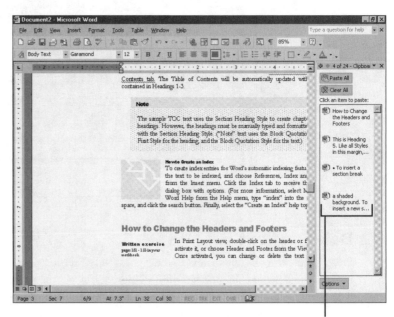

Items you've copied or cut

To copy text or other document elements such as graphics from one place to another, first select the item. Next, copy the selected text to the Office Clipboard by selecting Edit, Copy (you can also press Ctrl+C or click the Copy button). Then, paste the Office Clipboard contents in their new location by selecting Edit, Paste (alternatively you can press Ctrl+V or click the Paste button). You can paste the same text again and again wherever you want it to appear. If you've copied several items to the Office Clipboard (by performing a copy operation more than once during the current editing session), click where the pasted item is to appear in your document and then click the item in the Office Clipboard Task Pane.

When you paste an item into your document, a small Paste Options button (similar to the one on the Paste toolbar button) appears under the pasted text. You can ignore the button by continuing with your typing and the icon goes away. But if you click on the Paste button's drop-down list arrow, Word displays several formatting options that control the way your text will paste into the document.

When you cut text from your document (select Edit, Cut, click the Cut toolbar button, or press Ctrl+X), Word erases the text from your document and sends it to the Office Clipboard where you can paste the Office Clipboard contents elsewhere. In effect, cutting and pasting moves the text. As with copying text, you don't have to paste the most recent item you've copied to the clipboard if you've copied multiple items. Simply click the item you want to paste in the Office Clipboard Task Pane. You can paste the same item into several different locations.

> You can also move and copy by using your mouse. This technique is called *drag and drop*. To use this method to move text, select the text to move and hold the mouse button while dragging the text to its new location. To copy (instead of move) with your mouse, press and hold Ctrl before you click and then drag the selected text. Word indicates that you are copying by adding a small plus sign to the mouse pointer while you are performing the operation.

Finding and Replacing Text

Use Word to locate text for you. When searching through extremely long documents, Word's search capabilities come in handy. Suppose that you are writing a political letter, for example, and you want to correct a congressional district's seat name. Let Word find all occurrences of the word *district* by following these steps:

1. Select Edit, Find or press Ctrl+F to display the Find and Replace dialog box, as shown in Figure 3.6.

FIGURE 3.6

Enter text that you want Word to locate.

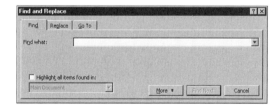

2. Type the word or phrase you want to find in the Find What text box. For example, type District to locate that word. Click Find Next.

3. When Word locates the first occurrence of the search text, it highlights the word.

4. If the selected text is the text you wanted to find, click the Cancel button (or press Escape) to clear the Find and Replace dialog box. Word keeps the selected text highlighted. To remove the selection, press an arrow key or click anywhere in the editing area. If the selected text is not the text you want, click the Find Next button in the Find and Replace dialog box to search for the next occurrence of the text.

A feature new in Word is the find and highlight option. If you click the Find and Replace dialog box's option labeled Highlight All Items Found In, and then click Find All, Word immediately highlights all occurrences of the text. This option is useful when you want to see where all occurrences of text occurs without locating each individual one using the Find and Replace method.

> Be careful, however, because if you click your mouse or press any key other than the mouse buttons and keyboard keys that scroll your document, Word will remove all the highlighted words.

As you probably can guess from the name of the Find and Replace dialog box, Word not only finds, but can also replace text. Suppose that you wrote a lengthy business proposal to an associate whom you thought was named Paul McDonald. Luckily, before you sent the proposal over your corporate network (using Outlook 2002), you realized that Paul's last name is spelled *Mac*Donald.

Use Word to change all names of *McDonald* to *MacDonald* by following these steps:

1. Select Edit, Replace or press Ctrl+H. Word displays the Find and Replace dialog box with the Replace tab displayed.

2. Type **McDonald** in the Find What text box.

3. Press Tab to move the insertion point to the Replace With text box.

4. Type the replacement text (in this case, **MacDonald**).

5. If you want Word to replace all occurrences of the text, click the Replace All button. After Word finishes replacing all the occurrences, it indicates how many replacements were made in a message box.

    If you want to replace only one or a few of the occurrences (for example, there might be another person with the name McDonald in the business plan whose name is spelled that way), click the Find Next button again. Upon finding a match, Word selects the text and gives you a chance to replace it. To skip an occurrence, click Find Next rather than Replace after a match is found that you want to ignore.

6. Press Escape or click Cancel when you are finished.

> If you want to delete all occurrences of a word or phrase, leave the Replace With text box blank before clicking Replace All.

Using the Search Task Pane

Word can display a Search Task Pane that aids you in your search for specific data when that data lies in other documents elsewhere on your computer or on a networked computer. You can even search for email messages using the Search Task Pane. Click the Standard toolbar's Search button to display the Search Task Pane. Figure 3.7 shows the Search Task Pane.

Search pane

FIGURE 3.7

Use the Task Pane when you have several searches to make.

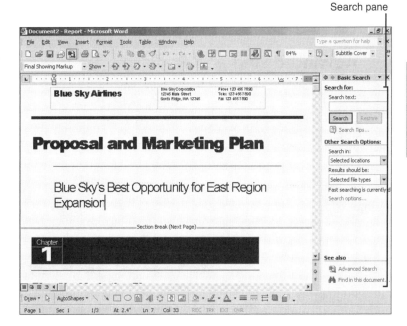

To look for something, type a word or phrase in the Search text box. Open the drop-down list labeled Search In The to select the folder and networked computers (if any are attached) to use in your search. Click the Minus signs next to any item to expand that computer's folder structure. You can limit your search to specific files by selecting file types in the box labeled Results Should Be.

When Word completes the search, a new Task Pane appears that lists the filename of every file found that matches your search. If you open the Search Task Pane and then realize that you want to search within the current document, click the option labeled Find In This Document to show the standard Find and Replace dialog box and enter your search criteria.

Obviously, the scope of the Search Task Pane is generally far greater than that of a single document. With the Find and Replace dialog box you learned about in the previous section, and with the Search Task Pane you learn about here, you now have the tools to search within a file and across a file. Be careful when using the Search Pane and make sure, however, that you are as specific as possible. Otherwise, Word will return a huge list of matching values. If you start a search and realize that too many documents are being listed because your search was not specific enough, click the Stop Search button that appears during the search to halt with the list you have at the time.

Advanced Find and Replace

The Find and Replace dialog box (see the preceding section) contains more buttons. If you want more control over how Word searches for and replaces text, click the More button on either the Find or Replace pages. The dialog box expands to show more options, as Figure 3.8 shows.

After you click the More button and the dialog box expands, the More button becomes a Less button that you can click to return to the simpler Find or Replace pages.

FIGURE 3.8

Advanced options enable you to control your find-and-replace operations.

Advanced options —

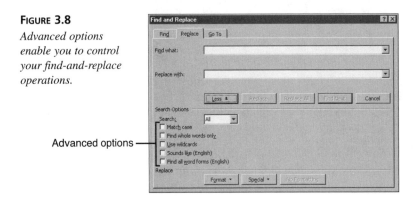

Table 3.2 describes each of the advanced find-and-replace options.

TABLE 3.2 The Advanced Find and Replace Dialog Box Options

Option	Description
Search	Determines the scope of the find and replace. Select All to search the entire document starting from the beginning, Down to search the document from the insertion point's current position down in the document, and Up to search the document from the insertion point's current position up through the document.
Match Case	Finds text only when the text exactly matches the capitalization of your search text.
Find Whole Words Only	Matches only when complete text words match your search phrase. If this box is checked, Word does not consider McDonald a match for McD, for example. If unchecked, McD matches McDonald, McDonald's, and McDonalds.
Use Wildcards	Uses an asterisk (*) to indicate zero or more characters, or a question mark (?) to indicate a single character in your search. If you search for Mc* and click this option, for example, Word matches on Mc, McDonald, and McDonald's. If you search for M?cDonald, Word considers MacDonald a match but not McDonald.
Sounds Like	Bases the match on words or phrases that phonetically match the search phrase but are not necessarily spelled the same way as the search phrase. Therefore, Word would consider both *to* and *too* matches for the search phrase *too*.
Find All Word Forms	Matches on similar parts of speech that match the search phrase. Therefore, Word would not consider the verb color to be a match for the noun color when you check this option.

Word cannot conduct a Word Form search if you have checked either the Use Wildcards or Sounds Like options.

AutoCorrecting and AutoFormatting

Word is smart. Often, Word fixes problems without you ever being aware of them, thanks to Word's *AutoCorrect* feature. As you type, Word analyzes the errors and makes corrections or suggested improvements along the way. If you have selected Tools, AutoCorrect and selected Replace Text As You Type and Automatically Use suggestions from the Spelling Checker options, Word makes spelling corrections as you type.

The Office Assistant is always there to guide you, but AutoCorrect is integral to Word as well as to many of the other Office XP products. If AutoCorrect recognizes a typing mistake, it immediately corrects the mistake.

Following are just a few of the mistakes AutoCorrect recognizes and corrects as you type:

- AutoCorrect corrects two initial capital letters at the beginning of sentences. `LAtely, we have been gone` becomes `Lately, we have been gone`.

- AutoCorrect capitalizes the names of days and months that you forget to capitalize.

- AutoCorrect corrects a sentence that you accidentally type in the Caps Lock key mode. For example, `lATELY, WE'VE BEEN GONE` becomes `Lately, we've been gone`.

- AutoCorrect replaces common symbols' predefined characters. When you type **(c)**, for example, Word converts the characters to a single copyright symbol (©).

- AutoCorrect replaces common spelling transpositions, such as `teh` with `the`.

If AutoCorrect corrects something that you don't want corrected, press Ctrl+Z (Alt+Backspace also works) and AutoCorrect reverses its action. If you type an entry in the AutoCorrect list that you do not want corrected in the future, such as `QBasic` that Word incorrectly changes to `Qbasic`, press backspace as soon as Word first corrects the word. A small bar appears beneath the correction. When you rest your mouse pointer over the bar for a moment, the AutoCorrect option buttons appear so that you can control the way the correction works.

The initial AutoCorrection word list and AutoCorrect options are preset. However, you can add your own frequently misspelled (or mistyped) words to the list. You will most certainly want to add your initials to the AutoCorrect table, for example, so that you need only to type your initials when you want to enter your full name in a document.

To add your own AutoCorrect entries to the list, perform these steps:

1. Select Tools, AutoCorrect Options. Word displays the AutoCorrect dialog box, as shown in Figure 3.9.

2. Type the AutoCorrect shortcut, such as an abbreviation, in the Replace text box.

3. Press Tab.

4. Type the AutoCorrect replacement text in the With text box.

5. Press Enter.

After you enter a new AutoCorrect entry, you can begin using the AutoCorrect feature immediately.

In addition to AutoCorrect entries, Word also automatically formats special character combinations within your document as you type. For example, Word converts common typed fractions, such as 1/2, to their single character equivalent. You can control exactly which *AutoFormat* features Word uses by selecting Tools, AutoCorrect Options and then clicking the AutoFormat As You Type tab.

FIGURE **3.9**

*Add your own
AutoCorrect entries.*

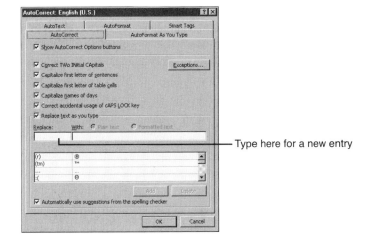

Type here for a new entry

Correcting Mistakes

At any point you can *undo*, or reverse, your most recent edit or edits. Click the toolbar's Undo button. (This performs the same action as selecting Edit, Undo, and is easier to use in most cases.) If you delete a character or even an entire paragraph, for example, click Undo. Word puts the deleted text right back where it was originally!

As you edit documents, Word changes its Edit, Undo menu option to reflect your last change. If you delete text, for example, the Edit menu's first option becomes Undo Clear, indicating that you can undo the clearing of text that you previously performed.

Word keeps track of multiple edits. Therefore, if you realize that the last three modifications you made were wrong, click Undo three times and Word reverses those three edits no matter what they were. If you reverse too many of your changes, just press the Redo toolbar button, and Word replaces the undo—in effect, undoing the undo! It gets confusing. If you click the arrows next to either the toolbar's Undo or Redo buttons, Word displays a list of up to 100 recent changes, which you can choose to undo or *redo as a group from that point forward*.

Initial Spelling and Grammar Correction

As you type, you'll soon notice red and green wavy lines. The red and green wavy lines indicate that Word found a spelling or a possible grammatical error. Word is not perfect, just helpful, and sometimes Word incorrectly flags such errors when they are not really errors. This hour's already up, so for now just understand that the wavy lines mean that possible misspellings or grammar problems occur in your text. In Hour 5, "Managing Documents and Customizing Word 2002," you'll learn how to utilize the spelling and grammar checker.

Summary

This hour introduced Word, Office XP's word processing product. As you saw in this hour, Word makes entering and editing text simple. In fact Word can even correct mistakes as you type. One of Office's many productivity boosters is that all the products in the Office XP suite often work in a similar manner. Therefore, many of the skills you learned in Word this hour carry over to the other products. Furthermore, if you have used Word in the past, you have already seen some of the improvements Microsoft made with Word.

The next hour delves deeper into Word and shows you how to format your document's text. In addition, you see how you can use Word templates and wizards to practically create your documents for you.

Q&A

Q Does it matter whether I press Tab or several spaces when I want to move text to the right?

A In some cases, pressing Tab and the Spacebar several times seem to produce the same visual results, but you should reserve pressing Tab for those times when you want to indent or align several lines of text. You can more easily adjust tab spacing later if you want to change the indention.

Q How can I remove items from the Office Clipboard Task Pane?

A Either click Clear All to erase the entire clipboard or right-click over the Clipboard Task Pane item that you want to remove and select Delete. Remember that if you've hidden the Clipboard Task Pane, you need to select Edit, Office Clipboard to display the Office Clipboard Task Pane once again.

Hour 4

Formatting with Word 2002

This hour demonstrates Word's formatting features, which add style and flair to your writing. Not only can Word help your writing read better, but also it can help your writing look better.

Word supports character, paragraph, and even document formatting. If you don't want to take the time to format individual elements, Word can format your entire document automatically for you. When you begin learning Word, type your text before formatting it so that you get your thoughts in the document while they are still fresh. After you type your document, you can format its text.

The highlights of this hour include the following:

- Which character and paragraph formats Word supports
- Why you should not get too fancy with document formats
- When different views are helpful
- How to see a preview of your printed document

Simple Character Formatting

When you want to make a point, you can *format* your text to modify the way the text looks. The three standard character formatting styles are underline, boldface, and italicized text. Figure 4.1 shows a document with boldfaced and italicized text on the top half and with underlined text on the bottom half.

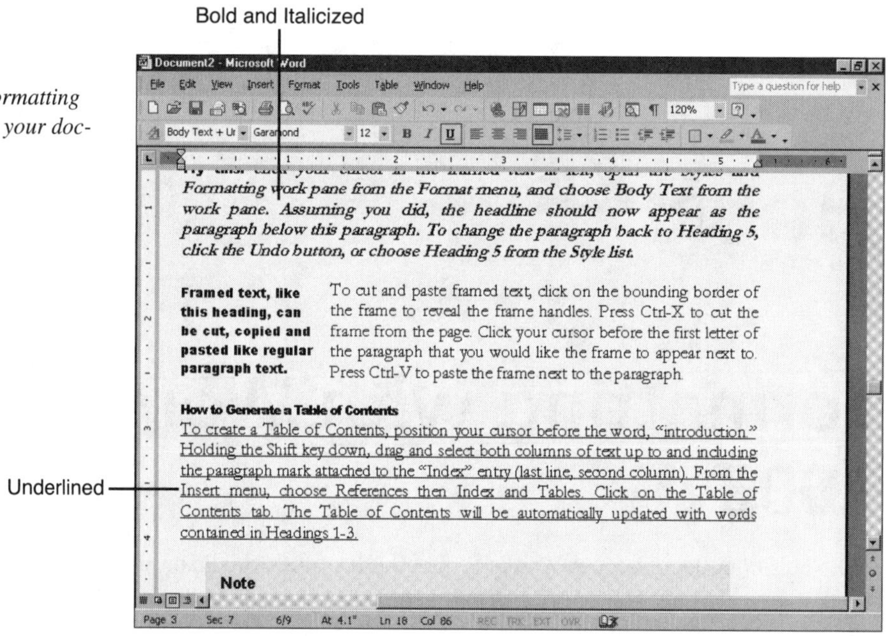

Bold and Italicized

FIGURE 4.1

Character formatting adds flair to your documents.

Underlined

These special formatting styles are called *character formats* even though you can apply them to multiple characters, paragraphs, and complete documents as easily as you can apply them to single characters. The character formatting styles are applied to whatever text you select for the formatting.

Express but don't impress. Too many fonts make your documents look busy and distract the reader from the main ideas in your document.

For example, select the text that you want to format and click the Bold, Italic, or Underline toolbar buttons. Alternatively, you can apply the same commands by pressing Ctrl+B, Ctrl+I, or Ctrl+U. The text you select before applying the format or the text you type after selecting a format style takes on that format. So, to underline a sentence you've already typed, highlight the sentence and press Ctrl+U. To underline the next sentence you want to type, press Ctrl+U before typing the sentence.

Applying Fonts

One of the most common formatting changes you can make is to change the *font*, or typeface, used in your document. A font determines the way your characters look, whether curly or elegant. Fonts have different names, such as Courier New and Times New Roman.

Consider a daily newspaper. The banner across the top of the page probably looks similar to old Gothic letters; the headlines are more standard type. Either might or might not be boldfaced, underlined, or italicized (although a newspaper rarely applies underlining styles). Throughout your paper, the articles might contain the same font as the headline, but the headline font might be larger and heavier than the articles' font.

The size of a font is measured in *points*. One point is approximately 1/72nd of an inch. As a standard rule of thumb, a 10- or 12-point size is standard and readable for most word processing. As you type and move your insertion point throughout a document, Word displays the current font name and size on the Formatting toolbar. To change any selected text's typeface, click the drop-down arrow to the right of the Font box and select a new font. To choose a new size for selected text, use the Font Size drop-down list.

Instead of using the toolbar to apply font and other format changes, you can set formats in the Font dialog box. When you select Format, Font, Word displays the Font dialog box, as shown in Figure 4.2. You can also display the Font dialog box by right-clicking selected text and choosing Font from the pop-up menu.

FIGURE 4.2

The Font dialog box provides many character formats.

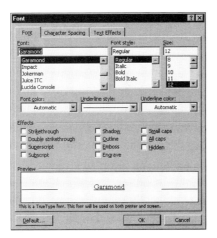

Not only can you set multiple character formats using the Font dialog box, but also Word displays a preview of the font in the dialog box's Preview area. Therefore, you can select various font names, sizes, and styles and see the results before actually closing the dialog box to apply those changes. When the previewed text looks the way you want, select OK to apply those changes to your selected text.

Quickly see a list of to select from by clicking the Font drop-down list arrow to display the Font drop-down list as shown in Figure 4.3. After selecting text, or before typing new text, you can select a new font from this drop-down list. The Font drop-down list shows an example of each font.

Font drop-down list

FIGURE 4.3

Examples of each font appear for you to select.

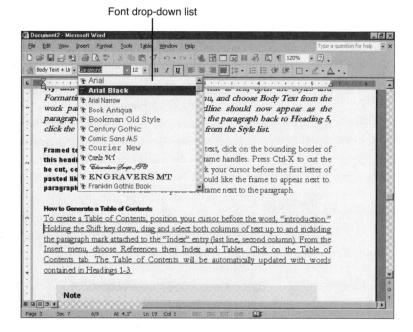

Applying Color

You can change the color of your text. To do this, click the drop-down arrow next to the Font Color toolbar button to see the Font Color palette, as shown in Figure 4.4. Click a color on the palette, to change your selected text to that color.

Use the Formatting toolbar's Highlight button to add color to the area behind your text. The Highlight button works well for marking important text that you want to reference later or emphasize it for other readers. To use the button, select the text and then click the Highlight tool—Word highlights the text as though you marked your screen with a yellow highlighter pen.

FIGURE 4.4

You can change the color of text.

Click to display the Font Color palette.

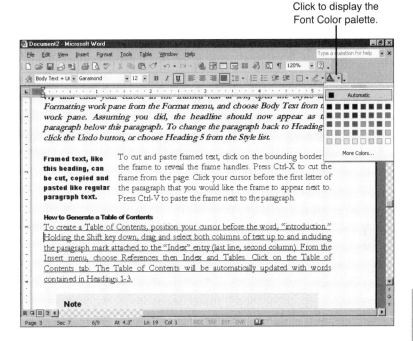

Inserting Numbers and Bullets

Word makes numbered and bulleted lists easy to produce. Assuming that the typical AutoFormat options are set (select Tools, AutoCorrect Options, AutoFormat As You Type and make sure that the options labeled Automatic Bulleted Lists and Automatic Numbered Lists are checked), follow these steps to create a formatted and indented numbered list:

1. Press Tab to start the first numbered item.

2. Type the number and punctuation, such as **1.** (follow the number with a period).

3. Press Tab.

4. Type the text for the first numbered item.

5. Press Enter. Word converts your previous text to a numbered list and starts the next item in the list started by number 2.

   If you don't want the next numbered item that automatically appears, you can click the icon that automatically appears next to the first number to stop the automatic numbering or cancel it altogether for the rest of the document.

6. Keep entering numbered items. When you finish, press Enter without typing any text after a number and Word stops creating the numbered list at that point.

In other words, to create a well-formatted numbered list, just start typing the list! Word formats and numbers your list after you enter the first item.

If you want to convert a series of paragraphs or lines into a numbered list, select the text and then click the Numbering toolbar button. Figure 4.5 shows a numbered list.

FIGURE 4.5

Word helps you create numbered lists.

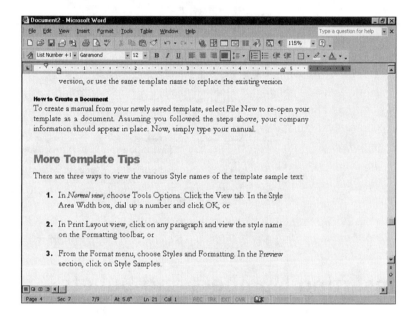

Here's another numbering trick: Before you begin typing the numbered list, click the Numbering toolbar button. Word types the first number for you and inserts a tab. You only have to complete the numbered item. Word continues to add the numbers as you type the list.

One of the best features of Word is that you can delete and insert numbered items from and to numbered lists, and Word automatically renumbers the remaining items.

If you want to create a bulleted list, type the items to be bulleted, select the items, and then click the Bullets button. Again, when you add and delete items, Word automatically adds or removes the bullets.

You can control the size of the bullets as well as the styles used for your bulleted and numbered lists by selecting Format, Bullets and Numbering.

Often, you might want to indent a numbered or bulleted list differently from Word's default location. To do so, simply click on the first number or bullet in the list and Word highlights all the numbers or bullets. Drag the selected list left or right to shift the entire list to another location.

Paragraph Formatting

You can change the format of entire paragraphs of text, such as the line spacing, justification, and indention of text. You can apply that format to selected paragraphs or to all the paragraphs in your document. This section describes the essentials for formatting your paragraphs so that your documents look the way you want them to look.

As with all the formatting commands, you can set up a paragraph format before typing the paragraph and Word applies the format to the newly-typed paragraph. In addition, you can change the format of existing paragraphs of text.

4

Justifying Text

Perhaps the most common way to format a paragraph is to justify it. When you *justify* text, you determine the text's alignment in relation to the right and left margins. Word supports these justification options:

- Left-justification aligns (makes even) text with the left margin.
- Center-justification centers text between the left and right margins.
- Right-justification aligns text with the right margin.
- Full-justification aligns text with both the left and right margins.

The simplest way to justify existing text is to click anywhere inside the paragraph that you want to justify (or select multiple paragraphs if you want to justify several) and then click the toolbar's Align Left, Center, Align Right, or Justify (for full justification) buttons. Before you start a paragraph, you can click at the left, middle, or right of an empty line of text to justify the text that you then type there.

Newspaper, magazine, and newsletter columns are usually fully justified. The text evenly aligns with the left and right margins.

Setting Margins and More

Display the Page Setup dialog box (shown in Figure 4.6), by selecting the File, Page Setup command. In addition, you can double-click the top gray area of the ruler. This dialog box enables you to control your paragraph and page margins. Enter values for your top, bottom, left, and right margins so that your text does not extend past the margin limits.

FIGURE 4.6

The Page Setup dialog box enables you to set margins, page size, and page layout.

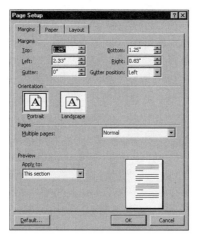

Many printers, especially laser printers, cannot print flush with the edge of the paper. Generally, one-half inch is the minimum margin size these printers allow.

Using Tab Settings

A *tab stop* controls the horizontal placement of text on a line. When you place a tab stop at a particular location on a line, Word moves the insertion point to that point when you press the Tab key. To set tab stop values, click the Tabs command button in the Format, Paragraph dialog box to display the Tabs dialog box, as shown in Figure 4.7. The bottom line is that a tab keeps you from having to press your spacebar many times when you want to insert multiple spaces in your text. In addition, a tab is more accurate when aligning text.

FIGURE **4.7**

The Tabs dialog box enables you to specify multiple tab settings.

Table 4.1 describes each of the options in the Tabs dialog box. After you set tabs, press your Tab key as you enter paragraph text to move the insertion point to the next *tab stop*.

TABLE 4.1   The Tabs Dialog Box Options Determine the Kind of Tab You Require

Option	Description
Tab stop position	Enables you to enter individual measurement values, such as .25" to represent one-fourth of an inch. After you type a value, press Set to add that value to the list of tab settings. To clear a tab stop, select the value and click Clear. Click Clear All to clear the entire tab list.
	Alignment
Left	Left-aligns text at the tab stop (the default).
Center	Centers text at the tab stop.
Right	Right-aligns text at the tab stop.
Decimal	Aligns lists of numbers so that their decimal points align with each other.
Bar	Inserts a vertical bar at the tab stop.
	Leader
None	Removes *leader* characters. A leader is a character that provides a path for the eye to follow across the page within a tab stop. By default, Word displays nothing (blanks only) for tab areas.
....	Displays a series of periods inside the tabs (often used for connecting goods to their corresponding prices in a price list).
-------	Displays a series of hyphens between the tabs.
_____	Displays a series of underlines between the tabs.

Later in this hour, the section titled "Making the Ruler Work for You" explains how to use the ruler to set and adjust tab settings.

Setting Indentation and Spacing

If you need to change *indentation* (the space between the page margin and where the text aligns) or *line spacing* (the amount of blank space between lines), select Format, Paragraph to display the Paragraph dialog box, as shown in Figure 4.8.

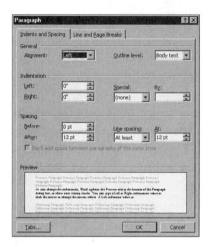

You can type a Left or Right indentation value or click the arrows to change the current values. A Left indention value indents not only the first line of a paragraph, but also the entire paragraph's left margin. A Right indention value indents from the right. You can set off a particular paragraph from surrounding paragraphs, such as a quoted paragraph, by indenting the paragraph by specifying either a Left, Right, or Full (using both) indention value. As you change the indentation, Word updates the Preview area at the bottom of the Paragraph dialog box to show your setting results.

> Do not use the spacebar to indent text on multiple lines because the text will not align properly. Use tab stops to ensure that text aligns at the tab.

You can determine how indentation applies itself to the paragraph by clicking the Special drop-down list arrow and then choosing (None), First Line, or Hanging. If you leave (None) selected, Word indents the complete paragraph by the Left and Right indentation values that you supply. If you select First Line, Word uses the value in the By field to indent only the first line of the selected paragraph. If you select Hanging, Word will indent all the lines of the paragraph except the first line.

If you indent the first line or apply a hanging indent, your Left and Right indentation values still apply to the entire paragraph. The First Line and Hanging Indent values specify the *additional indenting* you want Word to perform on the first or subsequent paragraph lines.

The Spacing section enables you to specify exactly how many points you want Word to skip before or after each paragraph. You can also request that Word double-space, triple-space, and perform other multi-spacing options by changing the value under Line Spacing.

Increase or decrease a paragraph's indentation by clicking the Decrease Indent and Increase Indent buttons on the Formatting toolbar.

Making the Ruler Work for You

As you specify indentation and tab information, the ruler updates to indicate your settings. Not only does the ruler show settings, but you can also make indentation and tab changes directly on the ruler without using dialog boxes.

Figure 4.9 shows the ruler's various tab stops and indentation markers. Click anywhere on the ruler to add a tab stop after you select the appropriate tab from the tab selection area. To remove a tab, drag the tab stop down off the ruler into the document area before releasing the mouse. By dragging an indentation handle, you can change a paragraph's indentation on-the-fly.

4

You can double-click the gray bar across the top of the ruler to display the Page Setup dialog box.

Inserting Line and Page Breaks

Lines and pages do not always break the way you need them to because they break according to Word's default. For example, you might want to end a page early because you want to insert a chart at the top of the next page or start a new chapter. Or, perhaps you want to put a sentence on a line by itself to make it stand out from the surrounding text. The Format, Paragraph dialog box's Line and Page Breaks page enables you to control the way your document's lines and pages start and stop. When you click the Paragraph dialog box's Line and Page Breaks tab, Word displays the settings shown in Figure 4.10.

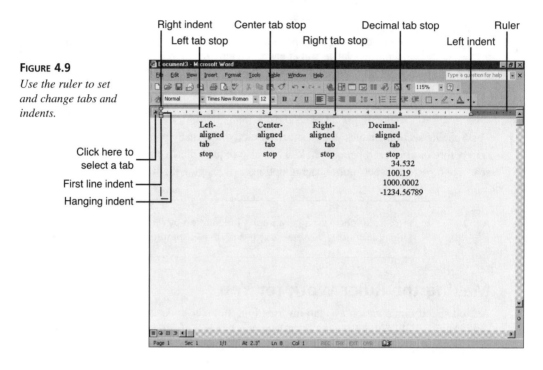

FIGURE **4.9**

*Use the ruler to set
and change tabs and
indents.*

Here's a quick run-through of the options: A *widow* is the last line of a paragraph that
prints at the top of the next page, and an *orphan* is the first line of a paragraph that prints
at the bottom of a page. Usually, widowed and orphaned lines look incomplete. If you
click the Widow/Orphan control option, Word adjusts page breaks, if necessary, so that
two or more paragraph lines always begin a page and so that two or more paragraph lines
always end a page.

The Keep Lines Together check box ensures that a page break never splits the selected
paragraph. The Keep with Next check box ensures that a page break never appears
between the current paragraph and the next. The Page Break Before check box forces a
page break before the selected paragraph even if a page break would not normally appear
for several more lines.

By enabling the Suppress Line Numbers check box, law pleadings and other documents
with line numbers will not print the lines on the selected paragraph lines. If you have set
up automatic hyphenation, the Don't Hyphenate option deactivates automatic hyphenation for the selected paragraph.

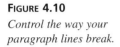

FIGURE 4.10

Control the way your paragraph lines break.

Viewing Your Document's Formatting

You can view the existing format on text that you've already typed. Click anywhere within a paragraph and press Shift+F1. The mouse pointer changes to a question mark. When you click over text, Word displays all the information about that selected text, including the character and paragraph formatting applied, inside the Reveal Format Task Pane. This feature is neat! (Figure 4.11 shows an example.) To get rid of the formatting description, click the Task Pane's Close button.

4

FIGURE 4.11

You can find out a lot about formats!

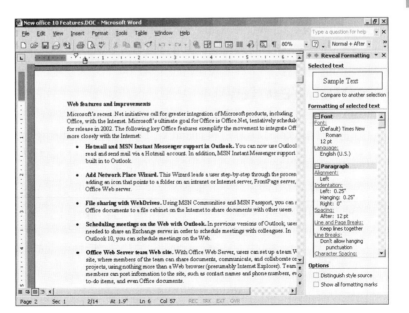

Formatting with Styles

A *style* is a collection of character and paragraph formats you can apply to selected text. Each Word document includes several default styles, and you can modify those and add your own. Each style has a name. Word comes with several styles, and you can also create your own.

Click the drop-down arrow on the Style box. (You might have to click the More Buttons button at the right of the toolbar to see the Style box drop-down list arrow.) You will see the names of the document's styles. After you select a style, Word applies it to the current paragraph and subsequent paragraphs that you type.

If you want to change a style's formatting or create a new style, select Format, Styles and Formatting to show the Styles and Formatting Task Pane. (You can also click the Styles and Formatting button to display the Task Pane.) To modify the current style, click on a style and open the style's drop-down list to choose Modify. If you want to create a new style, click the New Style button.

Suppose that you routinely write résumés for other people. You might develop three separate sets of character and paragraph formats that work well, respectively, for the title of a résumé and an applicant's personal information and work history. Instead of defining each of these formats every time you create a résumé, format a paragraph with each style and store the styles under their own names (such as Résumé Title, Résumé Personal, and Résumé Work). The next time you write a résumé, you need only to click the Style box's drop-down list arrow and select Résumé Title from the style list. When you then type the title, the title looks the way you want it to look without your having to designate any character or paragraph format.

Format Painter

Word's *Format Painter* feature too-often goes ignored but provides one of the easiest ways to replicate any kind of character, paragraph, or other style throughout your document. After you format text the way you want, you no longer have to apply the set of formatting commands to format another area of your document the same way. Instead, you use the Format Painter to, well, *paint* the format where you want to apply it.

Suppose that your document contains several passages of quoted text throughout. Where the quoted passages appear, you want to separate it from the surrounding text by indenting, italicizing, and applying a special font to those quoted passages. All you need to do is apply the formatting to one of the passages and paint the rest as follows:

1. Click anywhere within the formatted passage.

2. Click the Format Painter button. Your mouse pointer changes to a brush icon.

3. Select the next quoted paragraph by clicking and dragging the brush until you've selected the entire text to format.

4. Release the mouse button. Word formats the second paragraph the same as the first. All margins, indents, tab stops, and character and paragraph styles now apply to both paragraphs.

To paint several non-consecutive paragraphs throughout your document, click on the paragraph that contains the style you want to select and then double-click the Format Painter button. When you click on subsequent text to convert the style to the original paragraph's style, the Format Painter remains active. Keep clicking on paragraphs to format. Press Esc when you format the final paragraph to deactivate the Format Painter.

The choice of creating a special quoted passage style versus applying the Format Painter depends on your preferred way of working. If you take the time to create a quoted paragraph style, you only then need to select that style before typing the next passage, or apply that style to the already-selected passages. The Format Painter feature allows you to format several areas of text the same without requiring that you first create a style, but the Format Painter requires a little more work each time you use it than simply selecting a style from the Style drop-down list box.

4

Preview for Printing

In the previous hour's lesson, you saw how the Normal view differs from the Print Layout view. The Normal view provides a larger editing area but in the Print Layout view, your onscreen document looks closer to the way it will appear when you eventually print the document. Some people prefer to use the Print Layout view if they use headers and footers. These items otherwise remain hidden while working inside the Normal view during an editing session.

Print Preview shows how your document will look on paper. Select File, Print Preview to display the preview screen. By default, Word shows you how the current page will look on the printed page. As Figure 4.12 shows, you can click Print Preview's Multiple Pages button to display several pages. You get a bird's-eye view of your printed document, which enables you to predict print format problems without wasting time or paper. Although you cannot edit text inside the Print Preview, you can drag the ruler's left and right symbols to change the margins of the page.

Click the Close button or press Esc to exit Print Preview.

Multiple Pages   Margin markers

FIGURE 4.12

View how your printed document's pages will look.

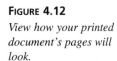

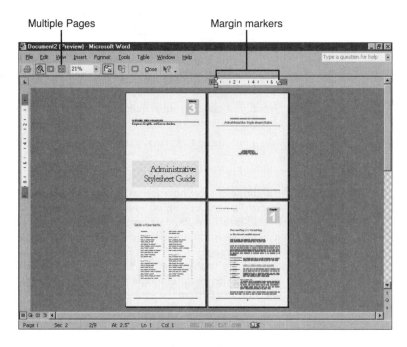

If you want a closer view of your document in Print Preview, click the magnifying glass mouse pointer anywhere on the preview screen to take a closer look at that section of the printed page.

Controlling View Size

A full page probably won't entirely fit on your screen. You can adjust the amount of text that you see by changing the size of the displayed document. When you need to see as much of your document as possible, select View, Full Screen. Word hides the toolbars, Status bar, and Menu bar to give more screen real estate to your document. Click the Close Full Screen button or press Esc to return to the preceding viewing state.

You can also determine just how much of your document will fit on your screen by selecting from the Zoom dialog box (shown in Figure 4.13). Select View, Zoom to display this. The Zoom dialog box enables you to adjust the display size of your characters onscreen so that you can see more text on the screen. If your margins and font size make your document's text wider than your screen size but you want to see entire lines, shrink the percentage shown in the Zoom dialog box to squeeze more text on to your screen. You can enable Word to adjust the size to fill your entire screen by selecting the Page Width option.

FIGURE **4.13**

Display as much of your text as you need to.

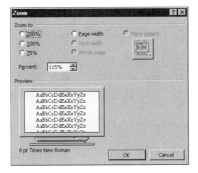

A Word About Word's Wizards

This hour has discussed various ways to format text within your documents. Word's wizards, however, help you create documents with much of the formatting and styles already in place, ready to use. When you select Zoom dialog box Zoom dialog box File, New and click the General Templates hyperlink, Word displays a list of wizards and templates from which you can select.

4

Templates contain formatting that you can use, as well as automated buttons that you can click to format certain text elements. Wizards are more interactive and produce more customized documents than do templates.

For example, select File, New to display the New Document Task Pane. Select the General Templates hyperlink. Click the Publications tab, and double-click the Brochure Wizard icon. Word walks you through a step-by-step procedure to create a brochure. Obviously, Word does not know the specific text you'll use in the brochure, but Word's wizard will set up a standard template-based style for the brochure's headlines, titles, column placement, and font. You then can add the specific text and format the brochure further to match your needs.

Word Themes

A *theme* is a set of predefined and unified elements that often appear in documents. Here are some of the elements defined within a theme:

- Background colors
- Heading and regular paragraph styles
- Horizontal lines
- Web hyperlinks
- Bulleted and numbered lists
- Table borders and colors

Notice that some of the theme elements apply to documents you create for Web pages, graphic presentations, and reports. In a nutshell, a theme is like a personality that your document takes on.

When you use a template or a template-based wizard to create a document, Word adds the template's formatting and styles to the blank document. When you apply a theme to a document, every theme-defined element within your document changes instantly—even after you've completed the document.

To apply a theme, either before, during, or after you create a document, select Format, Theme. Word displays the Theme dialog box such as the one in Figure 4.14.

FIGURE 4.14

A theme changes elements within your document.

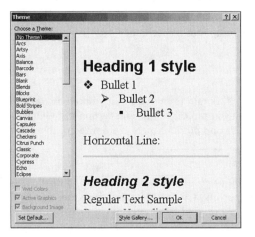

Many themes are tied to standard styles that are available within all Word documents, such as Heading 1 (for major headlines), Heading 2 (for titles), and regular text. If you utilize styles, you will learn which styles are most beneficial to your work and you'll begin to apply those styles to your documents to maintain a uniform appearance. For example, you can apply the Heading 1 style to your themed document's major title or headline, and later you could apply a different theme. Word will then update your headline to match the new theme.

Styles, Templates, or Themes?

Word and the other Office products offer so many choices; even Office gurus get confused. A *style* is a specific set of formats you can apply to text. A template is a pre-defined set of styles that you request when you first create a document. Until you change one of the specific template styles, that style will apply to any text that uses the style. If you want to change the look of a document that you create with a template (or with a template wizard), you must redo all the styles by hand.

A *theme* is a pre-defined set of styles for a document. When you change an existing document's theme (or apply a theme to a document that never had one), Word does all the work for you by reformatting all the theme's pre-defined styles. You can change a theme over and over until your document looks the way you want.

Summary

This hour explained the various format options available to Word users. Keep your audience in mind; don't overdo formats or your documents will look cluttered. Keep your documents readable as you format.

You can apply the character formats to individual characters as well as to selected text or even the entire document. Paragraph formats control the spacing and justification of paragraphs. By using styles, templates, and themes, you help streamline the overall uniform look and personality of your documents.

The next hour moves into document management and Word customization. Depending on how you use Word, you might want to change the way Word behaves in certain situations—and you will learn how to do just that.

Q&A

Q How can I type an italicized paragraph?

A Before typing the paragraph, set up the formatting. If you want to italicize a word, phrase, or an entire document that you are about to type, press Ctrl+I (or click the Formatting toolbar's Italic button) before you type, and Word will italicize the text as you type it.

Q How can I see my entire page on the screen at once?

A If you have an extremely high-resolution monitor and graphics adapter card, you can probably see an entire document page when you select the full-screen view with View, Full Screen. If you want to see the toolbars, menu, and Status bar,

4

however, you probably have to adjust the display by selecting View, Zoom. After you display the Zoom dialog box, click the Page Width option to enable Word to fit the text within your screen width, or you can control the width using the Percent option. The only other way to see an entire page is to select File, Print Preview to enter the Print Preview mode; in Print Preview mode, you can make simple margin adjustments but no text changes.

HOUR 5

Managing Documents and Customizing Word 2002

This hour teaches you how to work more globally with your documents than the previous two hours. Instead of concentrating on specific editing skills, you learn how to manage your document properties. Word manages your documents well and tracks changes that are made to the document. This tracking really comes in handy if you work in a group environment.

The proofing tools in Word are powerful and work as you type. You learned a little about the spelling checker in Hour 3, "Welcome to Word 2002," but in this hour you'll learn to control the spell checker as well as use Word's grammar, hyphenation, and synonym features.

The highlights of this hour include the following:

- What document properties are
- Where to locate and change a document's properties
- How to use the spelling and grammar checkers
- Why you need to proof documents manually despite the proofing tools in Word
- How to customize Word to behave the way you want

Understanding Document Properties

Each Word document (as well as the other Office XP documents) has properties. A *property* is information related to a particular document, such as the author's name and creation date. If you do not specify properties, Word adds its own to your document. You see the Properties dialog box when you select File, Properties (see Figure 5.1).

FIGURE 5.1

You can track your document's properties.

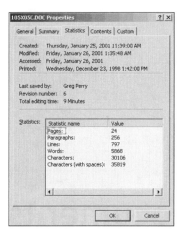

The pages in the Properties dialog box provide the following information:

- *General*—Contains the document's file information, including the date and time you created, last modified, and last accessed the document.
- *Summary*—Tracks a document title, author (name to which software is registered by default), keywords, and comments you enter about the document.
- *Statistics*—Tracks the document's numeric statistics, such as character, word, page counts, and total editing time.
- *Contents*—Describes the parts of your document, such as the header, body, and footer.
- *Custom*—Keeps track of customized information that you specify and want to track. You can use this page to monitor customized properties such as the department responsible for creating or maintaining the document, the name of a project group that works on the document, and the person responsible for typing the document's information.

As you add items to the Properties Custom dialog box page, indicate the item's data type (such as text or date) so that Word can properly format the

> property value that you want to track. The Custom page is great for using in departments in which many people see and edit the same set of documents.

Some properties are available elsewhere in Word. You can find a document's statistics, such as word and paragraph counts, for example, by selecting Tools, Word Count. Often, you can select from a menu option more quickly than you can display the document properties.

A new feature in Word 2002 is the addition of the Word Count toolbar. When you select Tools, Word Count and click the Show Toolbar button, Word displays a floating toolbar that enables you to keep track of the word count as you type. Every time you click the Word Count's Recount button, the word count is recalculated. The Word Count toolbar can also display a count of the lines, pages, and paragraphs depending on your selection.

> If you create numerous documents and continually search through your files for particular ones, consider adding search keywords to the Properties Summary page. Then, you can more quickly find that document using the Advanced Search option in the Open dialog box.

Using Word's Advanced Proofreaders

Word offers these proofreading features for your writing:

- *Spell checker*—Checks your document's spelling either from beginning to end after you finish creating your document or while you type.

- *Grammar checker*—Checks your document's grammar either from beginning to end or as you enter text into the document.

- *Thesaurus*—Provides synonyms for the selected word.

- *Hyphenation*—Automatically hyphenates words at the end of lines, when appropriate, either from beginning to end or as you enter the text into the document.

5

> Word's built-in proofreading tools do not eliminate your proofing responsibilities! No matter how good Word is, Word cannot match human skills when deciphering the written language. Word's spell check has no problem with this sentence, for example:
>
> *Wee road two the see too sea the waives.*
>
> The proofreading tools work only as guides to find those problems you might have missed during your own extensive proofing.

Another important reason to learn the proofreading tools is that the other Office products use similar features. Therefore, after you learn how to use Word's proofreading tools, you also know how to use the tools for an Excel worksheet or an Access database.

Using the Spell Checker

By default, Word automatically checks your spelling and your grammar as you type your document. You can turn off this option (or turn it back on if it's off) by selecting Tools, Options, Spelling and Grammar. Click the options labeled Check Spelling As You Type and Check Grammar As You Type. Any time you see red wavy underlines or green wavy underlines as you type, Word is letting you know about a possible spelling problem (the red line) or grammar problem (the green line).

Occasionally, you will be typing text inside Word (and the other Office products) and a blue dotted line will appear beneath the word. The blue line indicates a *smart tag*, which often is a proper name or date. You will learn more about smart tags in Part V, "Organizing with Outlook 2002." The smart tags indicate actions that you might want to perform on the tagged word or phrase, such as add a person to your Outlook contact list.

Depending on the options you (or someone else) have set, your version of Word might not check both spelling and grammar as you type. Therefore, if you don't see any wavy lines, you should check your document's spelling and grammar after you have typed the document so that you don't miss anything. In addition, you might not see wavy lines if Word's AutoCorrect feature automatically replaced all your misspellings with corrected entries.

To turn on and off the Check Spelling As You Type option, choose Tools, Options, and then click the Spelling & Grammar tab. On that page, check the Check Spelling As You Type check box.

When you see a red wavy line, you can correct the problem in these ways:

- Edit the misspelling manually.
- Right-click the misspelling to display the pop-up menu shown in Figure 5.2. Word offers you the following options:
  - *Suggested corrections*—Word displays a list of possible spellings at the top of the pop-up menu. When you select one, Word replaces the incorrect spelling with your selected word.
  - *Ignore All*—Ignore all subsequent similar misspellings (in case you want to type foreign words or formal names, but you don't want to add those words to Word's spelling dictionaries).

- *Add to Dictionary*—Add the word to Word's dictionary so that Word no longer flags the word as misspelled.

- *AutoCorrect*—Select AutoCorrect and choose a correct word to add the misspelling to the AutoCorrect entries so that Word subsequently corrects the word for you on-the-fly.

- *Language*—Specify a different language dictionary to use (useful if you write for the medical or a technical community and you maintain several dictionaries for each subject).

- *Spelling*—Display Word's more comprehensive Spelling dialog box, as shown in Figure 5.3.

FIGURE 5.2
Right-click to select your spell-correction choice when Word finds a misspelling.

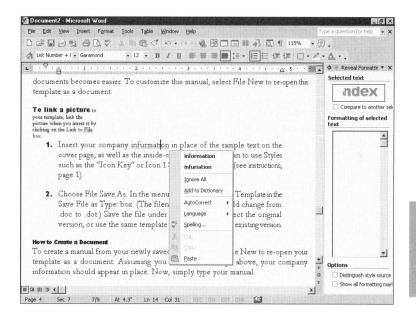

Word enables you to easily remove words that you accidentally add to your spelling dictionary. Select Tools, Options and click the Spelling & Grammar tab. Click the Custom Dictionaries button. Select the dictionary from which you want to delete (most probably the Custom dictionary, which is the default unless you have created a new customized dictionary), and then click the Modify button. Word displays the dictionary's words in a text box so that you can delete the word or words you no longer want. (You can also edit any existing words or add new words.) Click the Save toolbar button. You must also turn on automatic spell checking by displaying the Spelling & Grammar page once again, clicking the option labeled Check Spelling as You Type, and then clicking OK in each of the displayed dialog boxes.

- Ignore the misspelling and leave the red wavy line.
- Ignore the misspelling, but check the entire document's spelling after you finish typing the document.

FIGURE 5.3

The Spelling dialog box offers more options than the pop-up menu.

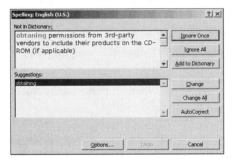

The Spelling dialog box appears when you click the pop-up menu's Spelling option. In addition, the dialog box appears when you select Spelling and Grammar from the Tools menu. Table 5.1 lists the options in the Spelling dialog box.

 When you check the spelling of your document by choosing Tools, Spelling and Grammar, Word checks from the cursor's current position down to the end of your document. Word then shows a message box asking if you want to check starting at the beginning of the document. If you want Word to check your entire document's spelling in one step (assuming that you have turned off the automatic spell checking that occurs as you type), move your cursor to the top of your document (by pressing Ctrl+Home) before launching the spelling check to check from the beginning to end of the document in one step.

TABLE 5.1   The Spelling Dialog Box Options Provide Spelling Services

Option	Description
Ignore Once	Tells Word to ignore this misspelling but continues to flag the misspelling in the future if it occurs.
Ignore All	Tells Word to ignore all occurrences of this misspelling in this document.
Add to Dictionary	Adds the word to Word's spelling dictionary.
Change	Corrects only this occurrence of the misspelled word.
Change All	Corrects all occurrences of this misspelled word.

TABLE 5.1 continued

Option	Description
AutoCorrect	Adds the misspelling and selected correction to your collection of AutoCorrect entries. You can also select AutoCorrect Options to add the correction to your list of AutoCorrect entries so that Word corrects the spelling automatically in subsequent editing sessions.
Options	Displays the Spelling & Grammar options page (shown in Figure 5.4) you can use to modify the behavior of the spelling and grammar checker.

FIGURE 5.4

Change the Spelling & Grammar options in this dialog box.

Using the Grammar Checker

When you see a green wavy line beneath a word, Word is warning you about a possible grammar problem. Figure 5.5 shows the pop-up menu Word displays when you right-click a green wavy-lined word.

If you don't want Word to flag possible grammatical problems as you edit your document, select Tools, Options, Spelling and Correction and uncheck the option labeled Check Grammar As You Type. Word will not mark grammar problems as you enter text. However, after you finish your document, select Tools, Spelling & Grammar (F7 is the shortcut key) to check the grammar for your entire document. You might want to keep Office Assistant turned on if you check grammar all at once. Microsoft added a lot of plain-spoken, grammar-correcting advice to the Office Assistant's repertoire of helpful topics.

Although many people consider the Office Assistant a nuisance, the Office Assistant shines when used in conjunction with the grammar checker.

FIGURE 5.5

*Word displays a pop-
up menu when you
right-click a word with
a green wavy under-
line.*

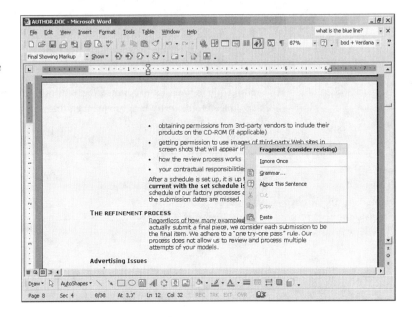

As with the spelling pop-up menu, you can replace a grammar problem with the suggested word or words, ignore the suspected problem (just because Word indicates a problem does not necessarily mean that one exists), or you can start the full grammar-checking system to correct that problem as well as the rest of the document.

When you check a document's grammar from the Tools, Spelling & Grammar option (to check the entire document) or by selecting the full grammar check from the pop-up menu, Word displays the same Spelling & Grammar dialog box you see when you check for spelling only. As Figure 5.6 shows, however, the Office Assistant can chime in with its advice as well.

Using Automatic Hyphenation

As long as you turn automatic hyphenation on from the Tools, Language, Hyphenation menu option, Word can hyphenate your text as you type, or you can manually hyphenate your entire document. Word supports three kinds of hyphens:

- *Regular hyphens*, which Word uses to break words at the end of lines (when needed) to maintain proper document formatting. You must turn on automatic hyphenation by selecting Tools, Language, Hyphenation and checking the option labeled Automatically Hyphenate Document.

- *Optional hyphens*, which break special words (*AutoCorrect* becomes *Auto-Correct*, for example) only if those words appear at the end of lines. (Press Ctrl+Hyphen to indicate where you want the optional hyphen as you type the word.)

- *Nonbreaking hyphens*, which keep certain hyphenated words together at all times; if the hyphenated name *Brian-Kent* appears at the end of a line and you want to prevent Word from breaking apart the names at the end of a line, for example, press Ctrl+Shift+Hyphen.

FIGURE 5.6

Select your grammar-correction choice when Word finds a problem.

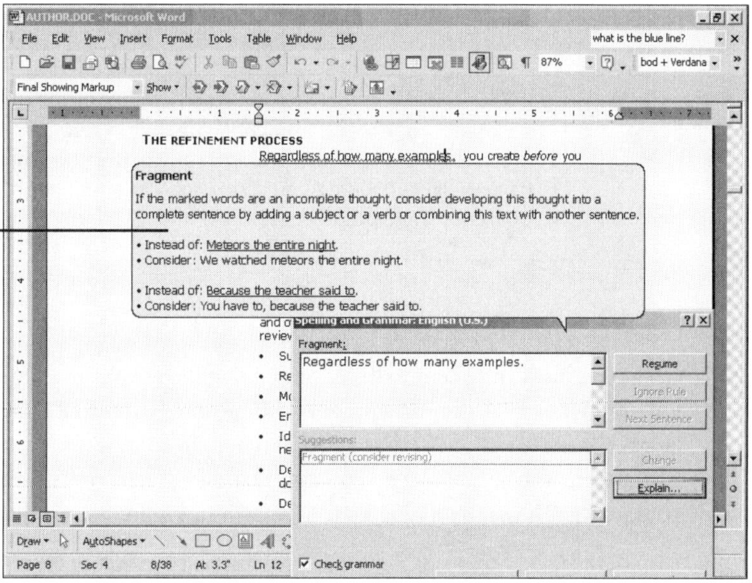

Office Assistant offers advice

You need to indicate optional and nonbreaking hyphens only when you type special words that Word would not typically recognize, such as company names and special terms.

The area that Word checks for possible hyphenation, toward the end of a line, is called the *hyphenation zone*. You can adjust the size of the hyphenation zone so that Word inserts a hyphen closer to or further from the right edge of the line. Select Tools, Language, Hyphenation to display the Hyphenation dialog box, as shown in Figure 5.7. The Hyphenation zone field enables you to determine the amount of space between the end of a line's last word and the right margin. A higher value reduces the number of hyphens that Word adds. If you want to keep the hyphenation to a minimum, consider limiting the number of consecutive lines that Word can hyphenate at one time by specifying a value in the Limit consecutive hyphens to text box.

FIGURE 5.7

Specify automatic hyphenation to let Word do the work.

5

To hyphenate your document manually after you have created it, select Tools, Language, Hyphenation and click Manual. Word prompts for your approval at each hyphen location.

If you want to stop Word from hyphenating particular paragraphs, select those paragraphs, and then select Format, Paragraph, click the Line and Page Breaks tab, and check the Don't Hyphenate option.

> If you export your document text to another program (such as to a Web page), do not have Word hyphenate your document. The target system that produces the final output should control the hyphenation, if possible. If you have Word hyphenate your document, hyphens might appear in the middle of lines if the typesetter fails to eliminate all of Word's hyphens.

Using the Thesaurus

When you just can't seem to think of a particular word, type a *synonym* which is a different word whose meaning is similar to the meaning you want. Then, solicit Word's thesaurus for a suggestion. To see a list of synonyms, first click anywhere in the word and then choose Tools, Language, Thesaurus. Alternatively, press Shift+F7. Either way, Word displays the Thesaurus dialog box, as shown in Figure 5.8.

FIGURE 5.8

Find synonyms fast.

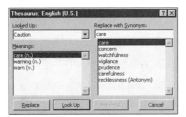

From the Thesaurus dialog box, you can select a replacement word. Word automatically replaces the original word with the replacement as soon as you click Replace. Alternatively, use the replacement word list to look up additional synonyms. If you cannot find a good synonym for dissolve but one of the replacement words for *dissolve* is *liquefy*, for example, look up synonyms for *liquefy*. Do so by selecting the *liquefy* entry in the Thesaurus dialog box and clicking Look Up. Through this link of related words, you might find the synonym for which you are looking.

Simple Translation

Word provides simple translation of words, phrases, and even your entire document. Depending on which dictionaries were installed on your system, you can translate between your default language and several others such as Spanish and French.

To translate, highlight a word or phrase, right-click over the selection, and select Translate from the pop-up menu. Word displays the Translate Task Pane. (If you want to translate a word not found in your document, you can enter the word to translate at the top of the Translate Task Pane window.) Select the translation you desire from the Dictionary list, such as English to Spanish, and click the Go button. Word translates the text and displays the result in the Results area.

Computer translation is helpful but certainly not guaranteed to be 100% accurate. So many idioms, phrases, and word combinations exist that computer technology simply cannot yet translate perfectly. In addition, be warned that the first time you use translation, Word pauses and installs the feature. Depending on the options you chose when you installed Office, you might need your Office CD-ROM for the install procedure.

Customizing Word to Work for You

If you don't like the way Word does something, you can usually customize Word to act the way you want. The Tools menu contains options that enable you to customize Word:

5

- *Customize*—Enables you to change the layout of Word's toolbars and menus
- *Options*—Enables you to control the behavior of most of Word's automatic and manual editing features

Using the Customize Features

Figure 5.9 shows the dialog box that appears when you select Tools, Customize. (Your Customize dialog box might show a different set of checked options from the figure's.)

The Toolbars page enables you to specify exactly which toolbars you want to see, if any, during your editing sessions. Too many toolbars can clutter your screen and take away editing space, but different toolbars are useful at different times. Display the Tables and Borders toolbar, for example, any time you want to create or edit tables in your documents. (The toolbar selection is also available from the View, Toolbars menu option.)

Most people modify the options on the Commands page when they want to add or remove an item from the menus in Word. To do this, select the menu from the Categories list and Word displays that menu's items in the Commands list. You then can change a menu label or add one from the list.

FIGURE 5.9

Customize toolbars and menus.

The Options page includes controls that enable you to increase the size of the toolbar icons to read them more easily, to determine whether you want to see ScreenTips, and to determine whether you want shortcut keys attached to those ScreenTips. From the Options page of the Customize dialog box, you can control the way Word displays menu options and the two most common toolbars, the Standard and Formatting toolbars.

Using the Options Settings

You can choose Tools, Options to display the Options dialog box. This dialog box is the Library of Congress of Word options. Using the Options dialog box, you can modify the behavior of these Word features:

- *View*—Changes the way Word displays documents and windows.
- *General*—Determines colors, animation, behavior, and the measurement standard (such as inches or centimeters).
- *Edit*—Changes the way Word responds during your editing sessions.
- *Print*—Determines several printing options.
- *Save*—Specifies how you want Word to save document changes.
- *Spelling & Grammar*—Lists several spell-checking and grammar-checking settings that you can change. This is one place where you can turn these options on or off.
- *File Locations*—Enables you to set disk drive locations for common files.
- *Compatibility*—Lists a plethora of options you can change to make Word look and feel like other word processors, including previous versions of Word.
- *User Information*—Holds name, initials, and address of the registered party for use with document summaries and automatic return addresses.

- *Security*—Enables you to specify passwords for encryption and for the sharing of the document.

- *Track Changes*—Determines the format Word uses when you make changes to documents in a group environment or when you want to track several revisions for the same document. (Word can keep track of multiple versions of a document.)

Summary

This hour explained how to better manage your Word documents through the use of document properties. The document properties contain count statistics as well as other pertinent information that stays with your documents. If you work in an office environment, the properties help maintain order when many people edit the same document.

Part of managing your documents is proofing them to make them more readable and correct. The proofing tools in Word include a spell checker, grammar checker, hyphenation capabilities, and thesaurus. Although these tools don't replace human proofreading, they can help you locate problems.

Finally, you can customize almost any part of Word. This hour gives you just a glimpse of the many modifications that can be made to Word's settings. Take the time to peruse the pages inside the Options dialog box. Even advanced Word users forget some of the options that can make their editing lives simpler. Check these Options dialog box screens frequently as you learn Word, and you will make Word work the way you want it to.

The next hour wraps up Word as you learn about its more advanced capabilities.

5

Q&A

Q Does Word update my document-property values for me?

A In some cases, Word updates your document's property values. As you type words into your document, for example, Word updates that document's word count. You must specify other user-specific properties, such as the document-search keywords and comments.

Q Why should I wait until after I create a document to proof it?

A Most Word users prefer to turn on the automatic spell checker but wait until their document is finished before hyphenating and checking the grammar. During the editing process, edits frequently change hyphenation locations; depending on your computer's speed, Word might slow down considerably to update changed hyphens when you change lines. Additionally, the grammar checker has to work constantly as you create your document, not only slowing down your edits but also indicating bad grammar in the places where you might be typing rough-draft material.

Q Should I modify Word settings if several people use the same computer?

A If you share a computer with others, you should not customize Word without telling the others what you have done. As a group, you might determine that certain Word options are better defined than others, but be sure to make customization changes only with the consent of others. Otherwise, the next person who uses Word might think Word no longer can check spelling, when in fact you have only turned off the spell checker temporarily.

HOUR 6

Advanced Word 2002

This hour wraps up our Word coverage by giving you an idea of Word's uncommon features and advanced capabilities. Despite being advanced, these features are not difficult to use.

You will find a lot of tidbits throughout this chapter that you will use as you write. From inserting special characters to creating multiple-column newsletters, Word offers something for everybody's writing needs.

The highlights of this hour include the following:

- How to type special characters that don't appear on your keyboard
- How to insert the date, time, and page numbers in your documents
- When to add AutoText entries and when to add AutoCorrect entries
- How to prepare tables in your documents
- How to convert a single-column document into multiple columns
- What headers, footers, footnotes, and endnotes are all about

Using Special Characters

Symbols are special characters that don't appear on the standard keyboard, such as ¿ and £. To enter special symbols, select Insert, Symbol to display the Symbol dialog box, shown in Figure 6.1.

Click here to display a list of other
character sets with symbols.

FIGURE 6.1

*Find a symbol you
want to insert.*

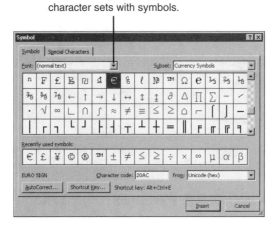

If you don't see the symbol you want to insert, select a different font from the Font drop-down list. Many fonts, such as *WingDings*, supply special symbols from which you can choose.

> If you find yourself inserting the same symbol over and over again, consider adding that symbol to your AutoCorrect list. Click the Insert, Symbol dialog box's AutoCorrect button to see the AutoCorrect dialog box (in which Word has already inserted the symbol). Type the AutoCorrect entry that you will use to produce the special symbol, press Enter, and you have created the AutoCorrect entry for that symbol.

You can assign a shortcut key to any symbol. Click the Symbol dialog box's Shortcut Key button, type a shortcut keystroke (such as Alt+Shift+S), and press Enter. Word then assigns that shortcut keystroke to the special symbol. Subsequently, you won't have to display the Symbol dialog box to insert special symbols, but will only have to press the appropriate keystroke.

Many special characters already have AutoCorrect and shortcut-key entries. If you want to see these predefined symbols, click the Symbol dialog box's Special Characters tab to display the Special Characters page, as shown in Figure 6.2. Scroll through the list to see which symbols already have a keyboard shortcut assigned.

Figure 6.2

Word comes predefined with many shortcuts for symbols.

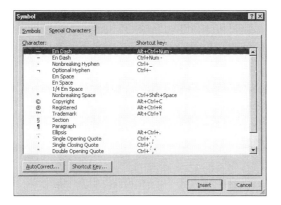

Inserting Dates and Page Numbers

In addition to special characters, you can insert the date and time at the cursor's current position. To do this, select Insert, Date and Time, and then click the date and time format from Word's selection list. If you click the Update Automatically option, Word constantly updates the date and time. If you leave the Update Automatically option unchecked, Word maintains the original date and time in the document.

Press Shift+Alt+D to insert the date at the cursor's location.

If you want Word to insert page numbers at the top or bottom of the document's printed pages, select Insert, Page Numbers. Word displays the Page Numbers dialog box. Select from the Position list to indicate whether you want the page numbers to appear at the top or bottom of the document pages. In addition, you can control the left, center, right, or inside facing page alignment from the Alignment list box.

6

Word can format page numbers in several formats, such as 1, Page 1, -1-, Roman numerals, and even letters of the alphabet. Click Format to select from the various page-number format options.

Inserting Pictures, Video Clips, and Sounds

A *clip* (also called a *clip file*) is an image, audio, or video file that you can add to your documents to spruce them up. To add a clip to a document, select Insert, Picture, From File to display the Insert Picture dialog box. Locate the image on your disk and click Insert to insert the image. The Insert Picture dialog box shows a small, thumbnail sample of your graphic image.

If you often insert the same image or video clip, consider adding the clip to your Office *Media Gallery*. The Media Gallery is a repository of graphic images, sounds, and videos you add to your Office documents. The Media Gallery makes common clips easy for you to find, thus eliminating the need for you to search your disk drive every time you want to insert a clip.

To add a clip to your Media Gallery, perform these steps:

1. Display the Media Gallery by selecting Insert, Picture, Clip Art. Word displays the Insert Clip Art Task Pane. As you familiarize yourself with the Media Gallery and add clips and graphics to the gallery, you will begin to utilize the Insert Clip Art Task Pane's search features to more quickly locate the media object you want to insert.

2. Click the Media Gallery link at the bottom of the Task Pane. (Many other clips are available online if you click the Media Gallery Online link.)

3. Click the Office Collections option to display a list of pictures, video clips, and sounds that come with Office. When you click on a category, the Media Gallery displays all items from that category as shown in Figure 6.3.

4. Select the image or clip to insert into your document.

FIGURE 6.3

Select an image or clip to add to your document.

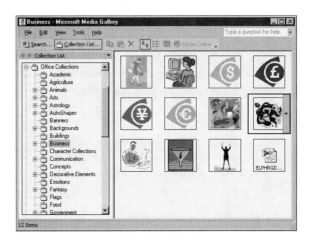

You can display inserted graphic images from the Print Layout view or from the Print Preview screen. If you insert a sound or video clip, Word places an appropriate icon at the location. When you or someone else views your document in Word (or on the Internet even if you create Web pages inside Word), that clip plays.

Watercolor Pictures

A *watermark* is a faded graphic image that appears behind text in a document. With Word, a watermark can appear in color (assuming that you have a color printer) or appear in a grayscale tone. Watermark images are so faded they do not interfere with the text in any way. Yet, a watermark image does lightly appear in the background on the page and prints behind the text. Some of the Office themes contain such watermark images.

A watermark might be a company logo or a design that adds personality to your printed documents. To add a watermark, select Format, Background, Printed Watermark. Click the Picture watermark option and then click Select Picture. Choose an image and click Insert. Word inserts the watermark behind your document's text.

Inserting Scanned and Digital Camera Images

Technology is rapidly changing, and Office does its best to keep up with that hurried pace. You can easily insert images that you scan on a scanner or take with a digital camera. Office makes inserting pictures from these devices as easy as inserting graphics from a file.

For example, suppose that you want to scan a child's drawing to insert into a letter to relatives. Simply select Insert, Picture, From Scanner or Camera. Word displays a scanner collection dialog box or digital camera dialog box from which you can control your scanner or digital camera's transfer of the picture to your document.

Creating and Using AutoText Entries

6

In addition to AutoCorrect, *AutoText* also enables you to quickly insert completely formatted multilined text. AutoText is often called *boilerplate text*, which is a publishing term used for text that appears frequently.

Suppose, for example, that you often place your boldfaced, 16-point, name and address centered across the top of your personal letters. Instead of typing and formatting this text each time you need it, follow these steps to add the text as an AutoText entry:

1. Type and format the text you want to add to the AutoText entries. Make sure that it is exactly as you want it to be reproduced.

2. Select the text.

3. Select Insert, AutoText, AutoText. Word displays the AutoText page, which shows the AutoText entries currently in effect, as shown in Figure 6.4.

FIGURE 6.4

Adding an AutoText entry makes subsequent typing easier.

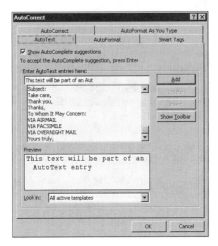

4. Type an abbreviation for the AutoText entry in the field labeled Enter AutoText Entries Here. You can either type this text to activate the AutoText entry, or you can select from the available options listed.
5. Press Enter.

When you subsequently type the AutoText entry's abbreviation and press F3, Word replaces the abbreviation with your expanded formatted AutoText entry. AutoText entries require the F3 keystroke. Nevertheless, AutoText entries can be more complex and longer than AutoCorrect, which allows only 255 characters.

After you create an AutoText entry, check the Show AutoComplete check box on the AutoText dialog box before closing the dialog box. Afterwards, when you type that AutoText entry's abbreviation, a ScreenTip appears that shows your entry beneath the abbreviation. If you press Enter at that point, Word replaces your abbreviation with the expanded entry so that you don't have to press F3. If you want to ignore the AutoText instead, just keep typing and the ScreenTip will go away.

If you use the predefined AutoText entries often, consider adding better shortcuts. Add a second Created on AutoText entry called cron, for example, so that you don't have to type as much to enter the AutoText in your document. To add a cron entry that mimics that of Created on, type **Created on** and press F3 to display the current entry. Highlight the expanded words and select Insert, AutoText, AutoText. Type the new name, **cron**, and click Add to add the new entry.

Adding Tables to Your Documents

Word's report-creation power shines when you see how easily you can compose customized tables of information in Word documents. *Tables* are collections of information organized in rows and columns. Tables might contain numbers, text, even graphics, or combinations of any of these. Each row and column intersection is called a *cell*. As you begin to use both Word and Excel, you might want to embed part of an Excel's worksheet into a Word table. Embedded worksheets enable you to report financial data from within Word. (Hour 7, "Excel 2002 Workbooks," introduces Excel.)

Creating a New Table

To create a new table, perform these steps:

1. Select Table, Insert, Table. Word displays the Insert Table dialog box, as shown in Figure 6.5.

FIGURE 6.5

Use the Insert Table dialog box to prepare the new table.

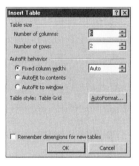

2. Specify the number of columns and rows your table will need. You can change these values later if you need to. Estimate on the high end, however, because it is easier to delete additional rows and columns than to add them.

3. Enter a column width, or leave the Column Width field set to Auto if you want Word to guess the table's width. You can change a table's column width at any time—even after you enter data. You can request that Word automatically adjust each column's width to the widest data in the column by selecting the AutoFit to Contents option. The AutoFit to Window option adjusts the column widths equally within the table's size if you resize the window that holds the table.

4. When creating your first table, press Enter or click OK. After you get used to creating tables, you can click the AutoFormat button to select from a list of predefined table formats, as shown in Figure 6.6.

6

FIGURE 6.6

Word can format your table automatically.

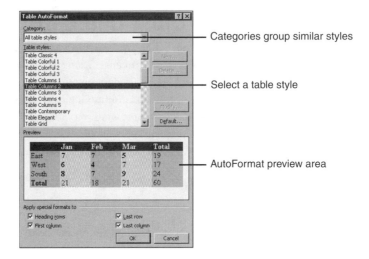

Categories group similar styles

Select a table style

AutoFormat preview area

5. Click OK (or press Enter) to close the Insert Table dialog box. Word creates your table and outlines the table's cells in a grid format.

> Word contains another tool that helps you build more customized tables. You can draw your tables by clicking the Insert Table toolbar button and dragging the resulting table of cells down and to the right until you have outlined the table size you prefer. In addition, you can draw tables freehand using the Word tools available (described later this hour in a section entitled "Drawing Tables Freehand").

Traversing the Table

One of the easiest ways to enter data in a table's cell is to click the cell (which moves the cursor to the cell) and type. As you type past the cell's right margin, Word wraps the cell and increases the row height (if needed) to display the complete cell contents.

When you begin typing data, notice that Word's automatic formatting might not match the table's data; perhaps one of the columns is too narrow or too wide. Use your mouse to adjust the size of a row or a column's width by clicking and dragging one of the table's four edges in or out. You can also expand or shrink individual columns and rows by dragging their edges.

Although you can click a cell with your mouse every time you want to enter or edit the contents of that cell, the cursor-movement keystrokes come in handier because you can traverse the table without ever removing your hands from the keyboard. Table 6.1 describes how to traverse a table's rows and columns.

When you move your cursor to a table's row or column edge, Word changes the mouse pointer to a table-adjuster cursor. When the mouse cursor changes, you can drag your mouse to resize the column or row.

TABLE 6.1   Moving Around a Table

Press This...	To Move the Table's Cursor Here
Tab	The next cell
Shift+Tab	The preceding cell
Alt+PageUp	The column's top cell
Alt+PageDown	The column's bottom cell
Alt+Home	The current row's first cell
Alt+End	The current row's last cell

To select a row or column, click the margin to the left of the row or in the area above the column. The Table, Select menu also provides a row and column selection option if you find that easier to use. When you select a column or row, Word highlights the selected item. After Word selects a row or column, you can drag your mouse down, up, left, or right to select additional rows or columns.

Inserting New Columns and Rows

Not creating enough rows or columns for your table is one of the first table problems you will encounter. To insert or delete rows or columns, select a row or column and right-click your mouse in the margin to the left of the row or directly above the column. The menu that appears enables you to add rows or columns.

Suppose that you need to insert a column. Select the column that will appear after the new column by pointing above the column until the mouse pointer changes to a down arrow. Select multiple columns by dragging your mouse to the right after you have selected one column. Right-click your mouse to display a pop-up menu. The menu will differ, depending on whether you have selected a row or column first. Select Insert Columns, and Word inserts a new column to the left of the selected column. The right-click menu also contains a Delete Columns command. Keep in mind that the Table, Insert menu provides additional row and column insertion options that you can explore.

6

After you create a simple table, click in the table and then select Table, Table AutoFormat to select a style, such as a shaded style. Word will format your table professionally.

Drawing Tables Freehand

As you have seen, the Tables menu option gives you complete control over tables you create. Word goes one step further to help you create exactly the table you want. The Standard toolbar's Tables and Borders button enables you to draw tables freehand the way you might draw using a pencil and paper. The Tables and Borders button enables you to quickly draw tables that don't necessarily have an equal number of columns for each row.

Follow these steps to use the Tables and Borders button:

1. Click the location in your document where you want the new table.

2. Click the Tables and Borders button. (You might have to click the More Buttons toolbar button first to locate the Tables and Borders button on your toolbar.) Your mouse pointer turns into a pencil shape, and the Tables and Borders toolbar appears.

3. Click and drag the pencil pointer diagonally down and across the page. A rectangular table outline appears. When you release the mouse, the outline becomes your table's outline.

4. Continue adding rows and columns by dragging the mouse. Notice that you can draw (by dragging) a partial row or partial column. If you draw a row or column you don't want, click the Tables and Borders Eraser tool and drag over the table lines you want to delete.

After you have drawn the table's basic outline, use the Border Color, Outside Border, and Shading Color tools to modify the table's colors. The remaining tools enable you to modify the table many ways, including

- Merging two or more cells into one
- Splitting long cells into multiple cells
- Changing a cell's text alignment (as you might do with border columns)
- Equally distributing columns or rows within an area
- Sorting (alphabetically or numerically) cells within a selected row or column
- Summing a selected row or column automatically

Creating Multiple Columns

When you want to create newspaper-style columns—such as those that appear in newsletters and brochures—configure Word to format your text with multiple columns. You can assign multiple columns to the entire document or to only a selected part of your document. Figure 6.7 shows a document with three columns and a single column at the top for the title area. Generally, you should type your document's text before breaking the document into multiple columns.

FIGURE 6.7

You can use multiple columns for brochures and other pamphlets.

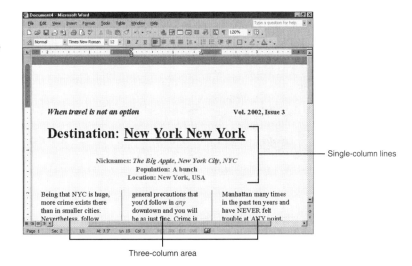

When you want to set multiple columns, follow these steps:

1. Select the text you want to convert to multiple columns. If you want to select your entire document, press Ctrl+A.

2. Select Format, Columns to display the Columns dialog box shown in Figure 6.8.

Click to determine columns

FIGURE 6.8

Set up multiple columns with the Columns dialog box.

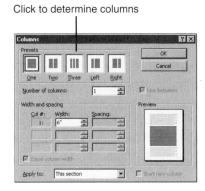

6

3. In the Presets area, click the column format you want and then enter the number of columns you want to produce.

4. In the Width and Spacing area, adjust the column width and spacing between columns or accept Word's default. Generally, the default measurements work well. As you adjust the columns, Word updates the Preview area to give you an idea of the final result.

5. If you want a line between the columns, click the option labeled Line Between.

6. When you click OK, Word formats your selected text into multiple columns.

To add multiple columns quickly and let Word handle the spacing (which Word generally does well), select the text that you want to format into multiple columns and then click the toolbar button's Columns button. Drag your mouse to the right to select the number of columns (from one to four). When you release the mouse, Word formats the multiple columns.

If you format your document into multiple columns that are fully-justified, you will probably need to hyphenate the document. Thin, justified columns often contain a lot of extra spaces that Word inserts to maintain the right-justification. You might want to select File, Print Preview to see how your overall document looks with the narrow columns before printing.

Creating Headers and Footers

A *header* is text that appears at the top of each page (or the pages you select, such as all even pages) in your document. A *footer* appears at the bottom of your pages. You might want to add page numbers to the top or bottom of a document, and you can do so from the header or footer area. You don't have to add headers and footers to each page—Word enables you to type them just once, and it automatically adds them to each page.

To add a header or footer, follow these steps:

1. Select View, Header and Footer to display the Header and Footer toolbar, and display an entry area in which you can type the header and footer text. Figure 6.9 shows a document that displays this toolbar and the Header entry area in a document.

2. Type your header text. If you want to type footer text, click the toolbar's Switch Between Header and Footer button to display the footer entry area and type your footer text. If you want to add page numbers, the date, or time to your header or footer text, click the appropriate buttons on the Header and Footer toolbar.

3. Click the Close button to anchor the header or footer in your document.

Header entry box

FIGURE **6.9**

Use the Header and Footer toolbar to develop your document's header and footer.

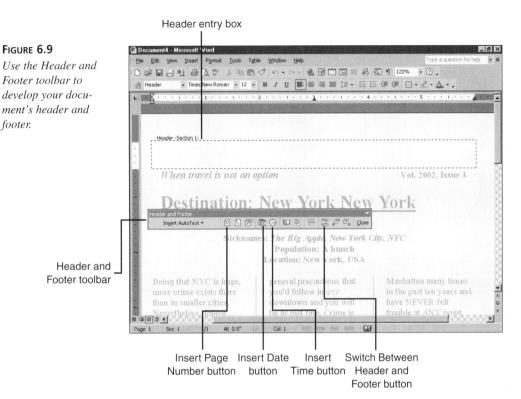

Header and Footer toolbar

Insert Page Number button   Insert Date button   Insert Time button   Switch Between Header and Footer button

Word normally dims header and footer text so that you can easily distinguish between the header, footer, and the rest of your document. You can see these items when editing your document within the Print Layout view, but they remain dimmed while in Normal view. If you want to specify that the header (or footer) are to appear only on certain pages such as odd- or even-numbered pages, select File, Page Setup, Layout and check the Different Odd and Even or Different First Page check box. You must be in the Print Layout view to see headers, footers, footnotes, and endnotes in their proper places on the page.

If you want to edit a header or footer, display your document in Print Layout view and then double-click the dimmed header or footer text. Word opens the Header and Footer toolbar and enables you to edit the header or footer text.

Adding Footnotes and Endnotes

A *footnote* differs from a footer in that a footnote appears only at the bottom of the page on which you include it. Word inserts a footnote reference in the text where you choose

6

to insert the footnote. If you later add text to the page so that the footnote reference moves to the next document page, Word automatically moves the footnote as well. Therefore, the footnote always appears on the same page as its reference. *Endnotes* are footnotes that appear at the end of your document rather than at the bottom of each page.

To insert a footnote, follow these steps:

1. Select Insert, Reference, Footnote. Word displays the Footnote and Endnote dialog box shown in Figure 6.10. Click the option you want to add, Footnote or Endnote.

FIGURE 6.10

Add footnotes and end-notes with this dialog box.

2. If you want Word to number the footnote (or endnote) sequentially starting with 1, click Insert. If you want to use a different symbol for the number, click the Symbol button, choose a symbol, and then select that symbol from the Custom Mark text box.

3. Click Insert to add the footnote. Word adds a separating line between your document and the note, adds the reference number to your document text where you inserted the footnote, and places the cursor at the bottom of the page next to the footnote reference number.

4. Type the footnote (or endnote) and click your mouse on the body of the document to resume editing.

Remember that you must display the Print Layout view to see headers, footers, footnotes, and endnotes in their proper places on the page.

Summary

This hour wrapped up this book's discussion of Word. You learned how to add the document extras that often turn simple writing into powerful cross-referenced published works.

If you need to display tabular information, let Word create and format your tables so that your data presentation looks clean. In addition, multiple columns work well for newsletters and brochures to keep the reader's attention.

To speed up your writing, use as many AutoCorrect and AutoText entries as you can. If you repeatedly type a phrase, sentence, or block of information, that text is a good candidate for AutoCorrect or AutoText.

Hour 7 introduces you to Excel 10. As you will see, Excel enables you to present numeric data as professionally as Word presents your documents.

Q&A

Q Should I use AutoText or AutoCorrect?

A You must decide how much formatting and effort the boilerplate text requires. If you need to type the same text often but the text consists of only a word or two and requires no special formatting, use AutoCorrect (Tools, AutoCorrect). With AutoCorrect, Word makes changes for you as you type the AutoCorrect abbreviations. (Be careful not to create AutoCorrect entries from common words, or Word might replace text that you don't always want replaced.) If the text is lengthy or requires special formatting that spans multiple lines, however, add the text as an AutoText entry. After you type the AutoText abbreviation, press the F3 key to expand the abbreviation into the formatted full text. Keep in mind that AutoCorrect imposes a 255-character limit on entries you make there.

Q Why can't I see my headers and footers while editing my document?

A Perhaps you are displaying your document in Normal view. Select View, Print Layout to see headers and footers in their correct positions on the page.

Q What is the difference between a table and a document formatted with multiple columns?

A Both tables and multicolumn documents have multiple columns. The multicolumn document, however, is useful when you want to create a newspaper-style document with flowing columns of text and graphics. Tables have both columns as well as rows, making cells at each row and column intersection for specific data. A multicolumn document might contain a table in one of its columns.

Use tables when you want side-by-side columns of related information. Use multiple columns when you want your text to snake from the bottom of one column to the top of another.

6

PART III

Computing with Excel 2002

Hour

HOUR 7

Excel 2002 Workbooks

This hour introduces you to Excel 2002, Microsoft's spreadsheet program. Microsoft Excel is to numbers what Word is to text; Excel has been called a *word processor for numbers*. With Excel, you can create numerically based proposals, business plans, business forms, accounting worksheets, and virtually any other document that contains calculated numbers.

If you are new to electronic worksheets, you will probably have to take more time to learn Excel's environment than you had to learn Word's. Excel starts with a grid of cells in which you place information. This hour takes things slowly to acquaint you with Excel and explains the background necessary for understanding how an Excel working area operates.

The highlights of this hour include the following:

- What worksheets and workbooks are
- How to enter various kinds of Excel data
- How to navigate in an Excel worksheet

Starting Excel

When you start Excel, you'll see a screen similar to the one in Figure 7.1.

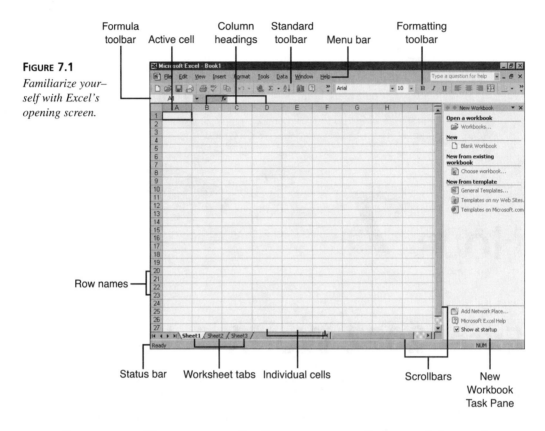

FIGURE 7.1
Familiarize your-self with Excel's opening screen.

Formula toolbar Active cell   Column headings   Standard toolbar   Menu bar   Formatting toolbar

Row names

Status bar   Worksheet tabs Individual cells   Scrollbars   New Workbook Task Pane

Understanding Worksheets and Workbooks

Excel enables you to create and edit worksheets that you store in workbooks. Typically, people work with a single worksheet, (sometimes called *spreadsheets* or just *sheets*). A *worksheet* is a collection of rows and columns that holds text and numbers as you see in Figure 7.1. Typically, Excel helps users prepare financial information, but you can manage other kinds of data in Excel, such as a project timeline. If your project requires multiple closely-linked worksheets, you can store the worksheets in one large workbook file. A *workbook* is a collection of one or more worksheets stored in the same file. A company with several divisions might create a workbook with annual sales for each division, and each division might be represented with its own tabbed worksheet inside the workbook.

Anytime you create, open, or save an Excel file, you are working with a workbook. Often that workbook contains only one worksheet. When that's the case, the terms work-sheet and workbook are basically synonymous. To open a new Excel worksheet (in a new workbook), select File, New to display the New Document Task Pane, which is virtually identical to Word's New Document Task Pane that you learned about in Hour 4, "Formatting with Word 2002."

All Excel files end in the .xls filename extension. Your workbook name is the Excel name you assign when you save a file. You can save Excel worksheets and workbooks in HTML and other formats (such as Lotus 1-2-3 for compatibility and older versions of Excel). When you save your worksheet as an HTML file, you then can embed your worksheet data inside a Web page. To save your work, select File, Save, name your Excel workbook and specify the location, and click OK. To load an existing Excel file, use File, Open.

A worksheet is set up in a similar manner to a Word table, except that Excel worksheets can do much more high-end, numeric processing than Word tables can.

Initially, blank Excel workbooks contain three worksheets named Sheet1, Sheet2, and Sheet3, as shown at the bottom of Figure 7.1. When you click a sheet's tab, Excel brings that sheet into view. Again, most of the time you'll stick with one worksheet file per workbook, so you'll typically never have to click on the secondary worksheet tabs to bring the other worksheets into view.

You can give your worksheet a name other than Sheet1. Doing so is a good idea to help you keep track of what data is on each worksheet. Right-click the worksheet tab labeled Sheet1, select Rename from the shortcut menu, and enter a different name. By giving your worksheet a meaningful name, such as 2002 Payroll, you can more easily distinguish that worksheet from others that you might use later.

Each worksheet column has a heading; heading names start with A, B, and so on. Each row has a heading, starting with 1, 2, and so on. The intersection of a row and column, called a *cell*, also has a name that comes from combining the column number and row name, such as C4 or A1. A1 is always the top-left cell on any worksheet. The gridlines throughout the worksheet help you to distinguish between cells.

No matter how large your monitor is, you will see only a small amount of the worksheet area. Use the scrollbars to see or edit information in the off-screen cells, such as cell M200.

Every cell in your workbook contains a unique name or address to which you can refer when you are tabulating data. This name is called the *cell reference* and is unique for each cell in the worksheet. The *cell pointer* (the cell with the dark border around it, the active cell that will receive the next character that you type) indicates the active cell, and you learn to select multiple cells later this chapter. The cell pointer's location, or cell

7

reference, appears at the left of the Formula bar. (Some refer to cell reference as the *cell address*.) In Figure 7.1, the box reads A1 because the mouse pointer is in cell A1.

When you move your mouse pointer across Excel's screen, notice that the pointer becomes a cross when you point or click over a cell. The cross returns to its pointer shape when you point to another part of Excel such as a toolbar or Task Pane.

Figure 7.2 shows a worksheet used to create an invoice for a company. Excel's automatic calculation features are perfect for applications, such as invoices, that require totals. With Excel's advanced formatting tools, your worksheets don't have to look as though they conform to a rigid row-and-column grid system.

Many of Excel's tools and options are similar to Word's, so you already understand many of them. This applies as well to the basic features in each of the Office products.

FIGURE 7.2

Your Excel worksheets don't have to appear dull and boring.

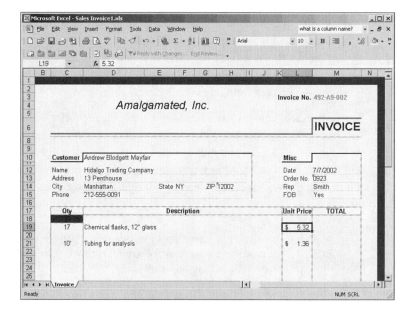

Entering Worksheet Data

Often, entering worksheet data requires nothing more than clicking the correct cell to select it and then typing the data. The various kinds of data behave differently when entered, however, so you should understand how Excel accepts assorted data.

Excel can work with the following kinds of data:

- *Labels*—Text values such as names and addresses, as well as date and time values

- *Numbers*—Numeric values such as 34, –291, 545.67874, and 0

- *Formulas*—Expressions that compute numeric results (some formulas work with text values as well)

Excel also works well with data from other Office XP products as well as integrate into the online Internet world by supporting hyperlinks that you can embed into your worksheets. Additionally, you can *import* (transfer) data from other non-Microsoft products, such as Lotus 1-2-3.

Entering Text

If you want to put text (such as a title or a name) in a cell, just click the cell to select it and then type the text. By default, Excel left-justifies the text in the cell. As you type, the text appears both in the cell and in the Formula bar (see Figure 7.3). Remember that the Name Box to the left of the Formula bar displays the name of the cell into which you are entering data. When you press Enter, Excel moves the cell pointer down one row. In addition to pressing Enter, you can click the Enter button (indicated by a green checkmark) to the right of the Name Box to keep the current cell selected or press one of the arrow keys or the Tab key to move the cell pointer to a different cell adjacent to the current one.

Press Tab to move the cell pointer to the right or the arrow keys to move the cell pointer in any direction after you enter data.

As you type text into a cell, you can press the backspace to erase what you've typed before anchoring the contents in the cell with Enter or another cursor-movement key. If you press Esc or press the Cancel button at any point during your text entry but before you move to another cell, Excel erases the text you typed in the cell and restores the original cell contents. In addition, you can click the Undo button or press Ctrl+Z to back up to a cell's previous state.

When you create a new worksheet, the cell sizes take on the width and height size specified by the template you specify or by the default template if you don't specify a different one. If the width of your text is greater than a cell's original width, Excel does one of two things depending on the contents of the next cell to the right:

- If the adjacent cell is empty, Excel displays the entire contents of your entry, with the overflow spilling into the next cell to the right.

7

- If the adjacent cell contains data, Excel truncates (cuts off) the wide cell to show only as much text as fits in the cell's width. Excel does not remove the unseen data from the cell; however, if the adjacent cell contains data, it always displays instead.

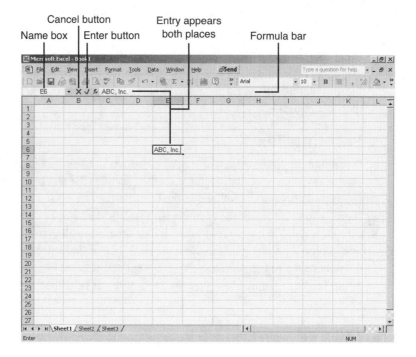

FIGURE 7.3

Excel might or might not display all a cell's contents.

Figure 7.4 shows two long labels in cells C5 and C10. The same label, which is longer than standard cell width, appears in both cells. Because no data resides in D5, Excel displays all the contents of C5. The data in D10, however, overwrites the tail end of C10. C10 still contains the complete label, but only part of it is visible.

> You can increase and shrink the width and height of columns and rows by dragging the right edge of a column heading or the bottom edge of a row heading. If you drag the right edge of column D to the right, for example, all rows in the entire column D widen.

Excel usually recognizes any entry that begins with an alphabetical character as text. Some textual data, such as price codes, telephone numbers, and ZIP Codes, can fool Excel into thinking you are entering numeric data because of the initial numeric value.

As you see in the next section, Excel treats numeric data differently from text data when you type the data into cells. If you want Excel to treat a number (such as a ZIP Code) as a text entry so that calculations are not performed on the cell, precede the contents with a single apostrophe ('). For example, to type the ZIP Code 74137, type '74137; the apostrophe lets Excel know to format the value as text.

No data in
D5 to overwrite C5

FIGURE 7.4

Excel might or might not display all of a cell's contents.

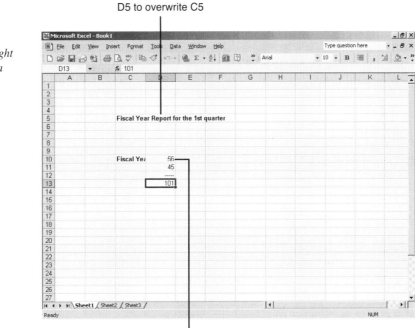

Cell D10 overwrites
part of C10

When you enter what would otherwise be a valid number, but use the apostrophe prefix, Excel places a small green triangle in the cell's upper-left corner. This triangle is a small warning that cautions you about the apostrophe where possible numeric data should appear. If you click the cell, Excel displays an icon you can click to open a pop-up menu with the following options:

- Convert to Number—Converts the number to a numeric format by removing the apostrophe (you would choose this if you accidentally typed the apostrophe or changed your mind later).

- Help on this error—Displays online help about entering numeric and text data.

- Ignore Error—Keeps the apostrophe and removes the green triangle tag.

7

- Edit in Formula Bar—Places the value in the Formula bar with the insertion point text cursor at the end of the data so that you can edit the data.

- Error Checking Options—Displays the Options dialog box, shown in Figure 7.5, from which you can change the way Excel reacts to a possible data-entry error such as numeric values that you enter with an apostrophe.

- Show Formula Auditing Toolbar—Displays a toolbar with which you can trace all cell references related to a formula to help you repair formulas that don't produce the results you expect them to.

FIGURE 7.5

Specify how you want Excel to handle common errors.

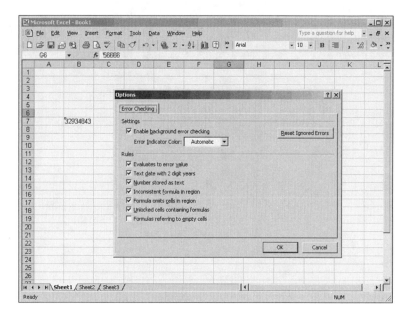

Entering Numbers and Formulas

Excel accepts numeric values of all kinds. You can type positive numbers, negative numbers, numbers with decimal points, zero-leading numbers, numbers with dollar signs, percent signs, and even *scientific notation* (a shortcut for writing extremely large and small numbers).

If you type a number but see something similar to 3.04959E+16 appear in the cell, Excel converted your number to scientific notation to let you know that the cell is not wide enough to display the entire number in its regular form. Excel does not extend long numbers into adjacent cells. Excel converts all numbers that contain more than 12 digits to scientific notation.

Excel right justifies numbers inside cells. You can change the format for a single cell, group of cells, or for the entire worksheet, as you will see in Hour 9, "Using Excel 2002."

Perhaps the most important task in learning Excel is mastering formulas. You never have to do math in Excel because Excel does it for you. The trick is getting your formulas correct. Hour 8, "Reconstructing and Editing Excel 2002 Worksheets," explains the ins and outs of Excel formulas. Later in this lesson, you get a chance to create a simple worksheet. As you will see, if your data changes, Excel automatically recalculates the entire worksheet for you. Therefore, once you create a worksheet and enter all the formulas, you can concentrate on the data and let Excel do the calculating.

Entering Dates and Times

Excel supports almost every national and international date and time format. Excel uses its AutoFormat feature to convert any date or time value that you type to a special internal number that represents the number of days since midnight, January 1, 1900. As with all Office 10 products, Excel automatically displays all dates the user enters with four-digit year values by showing the full year. Although this strange internal date representation of days since 1-1-1900 might not make sense now, you use these values a lot to compute time between two or more dates. You can easily determine how many days an account is past due, for example, by subtracting the current date from the cell in the worksheet that contains the due date.

 Excel uses a 24-hour clock to represent time values unless you specify a.m. or p.m. To convert p.m. times to 24-hour times, add 12 to all time values after 12:59 p.m. Thus, 7:54 p.m. is 19:54 on a 24-hour clock.

You can type any of the following date and time values to represent 6:15 p.m., July 4, 1976, or a combination of both 6:15 p.m. and July 4, 1976:

```
July 4, 1976
4-Jul-76 6:15 p.m.
6:15 p.m.
18:15
07/04/76 18:15
07-04-76 18:15
```

If you enter any of these date and time values, Excel converts them to a shortened format (such as 7/4/76 18:15). You can enter a date, a time value, or both. The shorter format often helps worksheet columns align better.

7

Navigating in Excel

Your mouse and arrow keys are the primary navigation keys used to move from cell to cell. Unlike Word, which uses an insertion point, Excel uses a cell pointer to show you the currently *active* cell. The active cell has a darkened border around it and accepts whatever data you enter next. As you press an arrow key, Excel moves the cell pointer in the direction of the arrow to a new cell, making the new cell the active one.

If you work with a rather large worksheet, you might find the Go To command useful. Press F5 to display the Go To dialog box where you can select a range of cells that you might have previously named or type a cell reference value such as **C141** to jump to that cell.

Table 7.1 lists the most commonly used navigational keystrokes used within a worksheet. Use your mouse to scroll with the scrollbars. To scroll long distances, press Shift while you scroll with the mouse.

TABLE 7.1   Using the Keyboard to Navigate Excel

Press This Key...	To Move
Arrow keys	The direction of the arrow one cell at a time.
Ctrl+Up arrow, Ctrl+Down arrow	The topmost or bottommost cell that contains data, or if at the end of the range already, the next cell that contains data.
Ctrl+Left arrow, Ctrl+Right arrow	The leftmost or rightmost cell that contains data, or if at the end of the range already, the next cell that contains data.
PageUp, PageDown	The previous or next screen of the worksheet.
Ctrl+Home	The upper-left corner of the worksheet cell A1.
End, Arrow	The last blank cell in the arrow's direction.
Ctrl+PageUp, Ctrl+PageDown	To next or previous worksheet within current workbook.

A Quick Practice

The next hour's lesson, "Editing Excel Worksheets," presents the details of creating, editing, and understanding specific areas of an Excel worksheet. For practice, however, work through the following steps to try Excel now. To do so, you will create a simple test-tracking worksheet for a professor. By working with a hands-on example now, you'll have a better feel for the overall Excel concept as you work the rest of this section of the book.

Follow these steps to create your first worksheet:

1. Select File, New and select Blank Workbook from the New Worksheet Task Pane to create a new workbook.

2. Click on cell C4 to move the cell pointer there and make it the active cell. The cell name, C4, appears in the Formula bar.

3. Type **Student Gradebook**. The text is wider than the cell, but Excel extends the text label over into the right cell (D4).

4. Click on cell B6 and type **Name**.

5. Press Tab to move the cell pointer to C6. (You can also click in C6 or press the Right Arrow key to move the cell pointer to C6.)

6. Enter the labels **Test 1**, **Test 2**, **Test 3**, and **Average** in cells C6 through F6.

7. Move to B8 and enter these values across row 8: **Mary Bee**, **77**, **89**, and **86**. (The 86 ends up in cell E8.)

8. Enter these values underneath the previous ones to add the second row of data for your worksheet: **Paul North**, **89**, **87**, and **94**.

9. Enter the following data for the next row: **Terry Smith**, **93**, **100**, and **95**. Notice that cell B10 is not wide enough to hold Terry Smith's entire name. As soon as you enter data in C10, the right portion of Terry Smith's name is truncated. You will fix this problem in a moment.

10. Enter the following for the row 11: **Sue Willis**, **64**, **79**, and **83**.

11. Type **Class Average:** in cell D13 (the label will fill into E13). Your worksheet should resemble the one in Figure 7.6.

The worksheet requires some formatting to look better, but you've already used Excel to enter text and numbers. The averages now need computing via a formula. Additionally, a little formatting would greatly improve the look. Follow these steps to complete the worksheet:

1. Move the cell pointer to F8 and type this: **=(C8+D8+E8)/3**. Then press the Down Arrow to move to cell F9. Notice that Excel computed the average of Mary Bee's test scores. You just entered a formula that requests the average. The formula tells Excel to add the contents of cells C8, D8, and E8, and then divide the sum by 3. Several methods exist for creating such a formula, and you'll learn even better ways throughout the next three hour's lessons.

2. Excel is smart and guesses at a lot of tasks to make life easier for you. Instead of typing the same formula all the way down column F, you only need to copy and paste the formula you just entered to F9, F10, and F11 to calculate the other three student averages. Click on cell F8 (the cell to copy) and press Ctrl+C to copy the cell to the Clipboard. Excel highlights the cell to show the selection.

3. Click cell F9 and do this: hold down the Shift key while pressing Down Arrow twice. Excel highlights three cells. These cells are the target of your copy.

7

Name box   Formula bar

FIGURE 7.6

You are on your way to creating your first Excel worksheet!

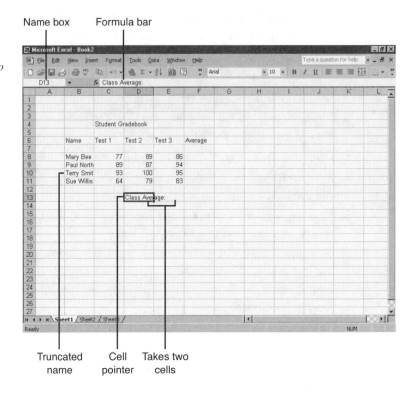

Truncated   Cell   Takes two
   name   pointer   cells

4. Press Ctrl+V (or select Edit, Paste) to paste the Clipboard contents into the high-lighted cells. When you do, Excel instantly updates the averages for the remaining three students. Excel even changes the formula you copy to reflect the new row numbers. This is called *relative cell referencing* because the formulas are copied relative to their new location. You can ignore the Paste icon that Excel displays after the paste. Beginning with Office XP, when you paste data into a document, the Paste icon appears and enables you to modify the way the paste is performed. You could, for example, elect to paste the formula as text and if you did, the result would not show in the cell but the formula itself would.

> If Excel refused to change the row numbers when you copied the formula from F8, all four students would reflect Mary Bee's average. You can click on cell F10 and look at the formula in the Formula bar (beneath the Standard toolbar) to see that all references are now made to row 10 and no longer to row 8 even though you copied the formula from row 8. Fancy? You bet.

5. You now must compute the average for the class. That's simple, just type the following formula in cell F13: **=(F8+F9+F10+F11)/4**. The class average appears instantly. Your worksheet now looks like the one in Figure 7.7.

FIGURE 7.7

Excel calculates all the averages for you.

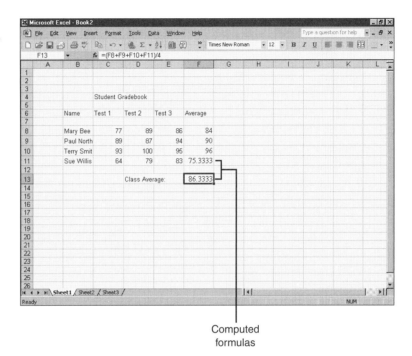

Computed
formulas

Now that you've finished entering text, numbers, and formulas, you can improve a worksheet's look with a little formatting. In addition, you might be interested in knowing how Excel can improve upon the functionality of the worksheet. If you insert new rows into the worksheet, by inserting blank rows, Excel will change the average calculations at the end of the displaced student rows to reflect their new row location. You also can insert new columns in case the students take additional tests and the formulas update to reflect new column names.

One problem exists, however, with the formulas in their present state. If you add additional tests, you will have to change each calculated average to reflect the additional test scores. As you might expect, Excel supports other ways to enter formulas so that the formulas update automatically even if you add new test columns. You'll learn about some of these features as you progress through the next two hours.

7

For now, follow these steps to complete the worksheet's format:

1. Although you will often format individual cells, you can use Excel's AutoFormat feature to create an interesting worksheet look. Select the entire Student Gradebook table by clicking on cell B4 and dragging your mouse to cell F13 to highlight the entire table.

2. Select Format, AutoFormat to display the AutoFormat dialog box.

3. Scroll down to the Colorful 2 format and select it. Instantly, Excel makes your table appear as though you slaved away for an hour over a hot computer!

4. The two average calculations produce answers with too many decimal places for this worksheet. You should format the numbers so that they show only two decimal places. Highlight cells F11 through F13 by clicking and dragging your mouse.

5. On the Formatting toolbar, you'll see a comma (,) that indicates, with the ScreenTip pop-up description, that it is called the Comma Style button. Click the Comma Style toolbar button and Excel changes the two cells to look better, displaying only two decimal places. (You might have to click the far right toolbar button that shows additional options if you do not see the Comma Style button.) As Figure 7.8 shows, your Student Gradebook worksheet now looks truly professional. Excel even increased the Student Name column so that plenty of room exists for each name.

FIGURE 7.8

Your simple worksheet now looks more exciting.

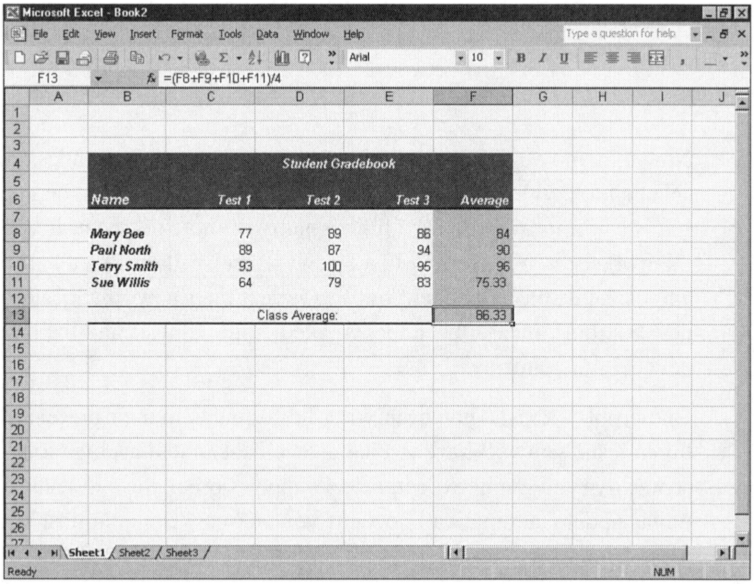

6. Rename the worksheet name by right-clicking over the Sheet1 tab name at the bottom of the screen, selecting Rename, and type **Grades**. Don't worry about naming the other two worksheets because they are not being used at this time.

> By default, Excel creates new workbooks with three worksheets. You can remove extra worksheets by right-clicking over any worksheet tab and selecting Delete. In addition, you can insert additional worksheets by right-clicking over a tab and selecting Insert from the shortcut menu. Excel will display Insert window, and you then can select Worksheet to insert a blank worksheet. When you insert new worksheets, Excel inserts a new worksheet to the left of the one on which you right-clicked.

7. You can save your creation by selecting File, Save and entering a name such as **Gradebook** for the document name. Excel automatically appends the .XLS filename extension if you do not supply it. You've just saved a workbook with three worksheets, but only one has anything valid in it, the first one with the name of Gradebook.

Now that you've got some hands-on experience with Excel, you're ready to master some of the more detailed aspects of the program. The next hour takes you through a more involved look at formulas and cell data.

Summary

This hour introduced Excel, and covered elements on Excel's application screen. It also explained the concept of workbooks and worksheets. The workbook files contain your worksheets, and your worksheets hold data, such as numbers and labels. As you see throughout this part of the book, Excel supports a tremendous number of formatting options so that you can turn your numeric data into eye-catching, appealing output.

Although Excel works best with numeric data, Excel works with text (called labels) such as names, addresses, titles, dates, and time values. The true power of Excel shows itself in its manipulation of numeric data. Excel works with formulas that you enter as well as several internal functions that perform calculations. In the next hour's lesson, you will learn more about how to specify formulas to produce accurate results.

7

Q&A

Q I'm not good at math. Can I use Excel?

A Don't worry: Excel does all the calculating. Your job is to place the numeric data on the worksheets so that Excel can do its thing. You also must specify formulas so that Excel can compute results for you. Many people use Excel for common household actions, such as tracking exercise routines and grocery lists. Excel is not just for accounting and mathematical applications. You learn in the next hour how to specify formulas. There, you will see that Excel provides a lot of help along the way and can even guess at many calculations, such as totals, that you routinely need in your worksheets.

Q Do I always enter the time along with the date?

A You can enter a time value, a date value, or both. Excel turns the information into an internal shortened format. (You can change the display format if you want to make the data look better.) If you don't enter a date with a time value, Excel accepts the time value only and tracks just the time. If you enter a date, Excel tracks only the date.

HOUR **8**

Restructuring and Editing Excel 2002 Worksheets

This hour teaches you how to manage your Excel 2002 worksheets as well as organize them to make them work more effectively for you. You will be surprised how Excel helps maintain your formulas when you modify worksheets. Understanding ranges is critical if you want to really master Excel. Therefore, be sure that you master this hour. You will use range names and references in Excel formulas and functions.

In addition to the editing tools, you also learn how to format worksheets to make them look better. This hour teaches the formatting essentials, so you will be ready for the fancy stuff in the next hour.

The highlights of this hour include the following:

- How to insert and delete rows and columns
- How to work with ranges of cells
- When range names are important
- How to write formulas so that they compute in the order you want them to
- How to format cells to add eye-catching appeal to your worksheet

Worksheet Editing

Some of the most important Excel skills you can learn are editing skills. Entering numeric data is error-prone at its best; the faster you edit cell values accurately, the faster you complete accurate worksheets. The following sections show you the primary editing techniques Excel provides.

Selecting Cells

You can select a cell, a row of cells, or a column of cells just by clicking and dragging your mouse. As you drag your mouse, Excel selects a rectangular region, called a *range*. You notice as you drag your mouse that Excel displays the number of rows and columns you have selected. You see the message 10R X 4C appear in the toolbar's Name Box as you select 10 rows and 4 columns, for example. When you release your mouse, Excel displays the selection's upper-left corner cell name inside the Name Box as Figure 8.1 shows.

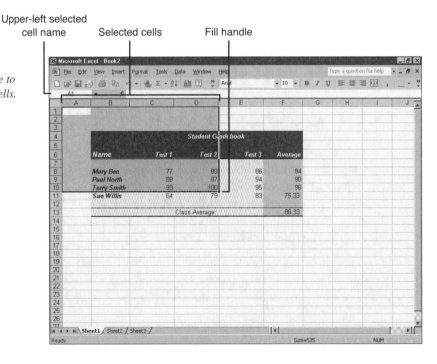

FIGURE 8.1

Drag your mouse to select multiple cells.

Not only can you select an adjacent rectangular region of cells, but you can also select non-adjacent regions. Select the first area, and then press Ctrl while you click another cell and drag the mouse to select the second region. The highlighted selection appears in both places on your screen. Remove any selection (either adjacent or non-adjacent) by clicking your mouse on any cell or by pressing an arrow key.

Editing Cell Contents

Much of your Excel editing requires that you correct numeric data entry. Of course, if you begin to type a number (or a formula) into a cell but realize you have made a mistake, press Backspace to erase your mistake or press the arrow keys to move the cell pointer back over the entry to correct something.

If you have already moved to another cell when you recognize that you have entered an error, quickly correct the mistake as follows:

1. Move the cell pointer to the cell you need to correct (click the cell to move the pointer there).

2. Press F2, which is the standard Windows editing shortcut key. (If you have still got your hand on the mouse, you can double-click the cell to edit the cell's contents.) You know Excel is ready for your edit when you see the cell pointer appear in the cell.

3. Use the arrow keys to move the cell pointer from the end of the cell to the mistake.

4. Press the Insert key to change from Overtype mode to Insert mode or vice versa. As with Word, Overtype mode enables you to write over existing characters, whereas Insert mode shifts all existing characters to the right as you type the correction.

5. Press Enter to anchor the correction in place.

If you want to reverse an edit, click the Undo button. To reverse an undo, click the Redo button. As you can see, after you have mastered one Office product (as you have Word), you know a lot about the other products.

Inserting and Deleting

As you saw in the preceding hour, you edit Excel worksheets somewhat differently from Word documents, even though both programs perform tasks in a similar manner and with similar menu commands and dialog boxes. The nature of worksheets makes them behave differently from word processing documents. The next few sections explain how to insert and delete information from your worksheets.

Inserting Entire Cells

Inserting cells, as opposed to inserting data inside a cell, requires that the existing worksheet cells move to the right and down to make room for the new cell. Perhaps you created a worksheet of employee salaries and failed to include the employees who work at another division. You can easily make room for those missing entries by inserting new cells. You can insert both new rows and new columns in your worksheets.

When you want to insert a cell into an existing worksheet, you will perform these steps:

1. Select the cell that should appear *after* the inserted cell.
2. Select Insert, Cells to display the Insert dialog box.
3. Click either the Shift Cells Right option or the Shift Cells Down option to determine the direction of the shift. The shift makes room for your new cell.
4. Click OK to begin the shift.

You can use the mouse to cells right or down to make room for new data by utilizing the *fill handle*, the small black box that appears in the bottom-right corner of a cell. (Figure 8.1 shows the selected range's fill handle.) Press Shift and drag the cell's fill handle (or the selection's fill handle if you have selected a group of cells) down or to the right. Excel grays out the areas that are left blank by the shifting.

Inserting Rows and Columns

To insert a row or column (and thus move the other rows down or other columns to the right), perform these steps:

1. Select the row or column that appears *after* the inserted rows or columns by clicking its header to select the entire row or column. If you want to insert more than one row or column, select that many existing rows or columns by dragging the row or column selection.
2. Select Insert, Rows or Insert, Columns. Excel shifts the existing rows or columns to make room for the new empty row or column. Instead of selecting from the menu bar, you can point to the selected row or column and display the shortcut menu shown in Figure 8.2 by right-clicking the mouse to insert the new row or column. (Excel inserts multiple rows or columns if you first selected more than one row or column.)

Deleting Rows and Columns

You can use the Delete dialog box not only to delete cells, but also to delete entire rows and columns.

To delete a row or column, perform these steps:

1. Select a cell in the row or column you want to delete.
2. Select Edit, Delete to display the Delete dialog box.
3. Select either the Entire Row or Entire Column option.
4. Click OK to perform the deletion. Excel shifts columns to the left or shifts rows up to fill in the missing gap.

FIGURE 8.2

The shortcut menu offers insert, delete, and several other options.

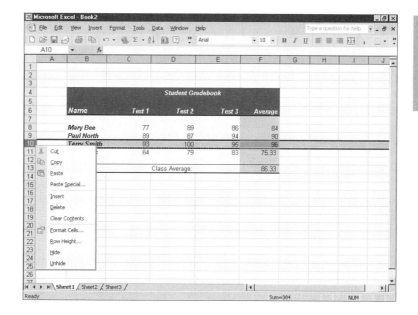

8

If you want to delete multiple rows or multiple columns, select cells from each column or row you want to delete before displaying the Delete dialog box.

Deleting rows and columns differs from deleting specific contents inside cells. When you want to erase a cell's specific contents, the other cells to the right and below that cell don't shift to fill in the empty space. To erase a cell's contents, click on the cell to move the cell pointer there and press F2 to edit the cell's contents. Press Backspace to erase the cell. Even quicker, you can press Ctrl+X or select Edit, Cut to remove the contents and send them to the Office Clipboard where you can paste them elsewhere or ignore them.

Working with Worksheet Ranges

A *range* is a group of cells. A selected group of cells comprises a range. A range is always rectangular, and it might be a single cell, a row, a column, or several adjacent rows and columns. The cells within a range are always contiguous, but you can select multiple ranges at the same time. You can perform various operations on ranges, such as moving and copying. If, for example, you wanted to format a row of totals in some way, you would first select the range that includes the totals and then apply the format to that range.

Figure 8.3 shows three ranges on a worksheet. You can describe a range by the cell reference of the upper-left cell of the range (the anchor point) and the cell reference of the
lower-right cell of the range. As you can see from Figure 8.3, multiple-celled ranges are
designated by listing the *anchor point*, followed by a colon (:), followed by the range's
lower-right cell reference. Therefore, the range that begins at B3 and ends at F4 has the
range of B3:F4. To select more than one range, in case you want to apply formatting to
different areas of your worksheet at once, hold Ctrl while selecting the ranges.

FIGURE 8.3

*Three ranges appear
on this worksheet.*

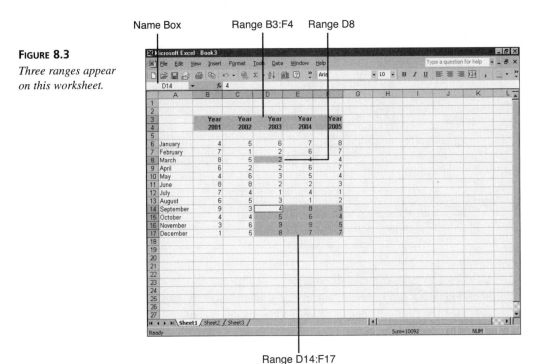

Name Box   Range B3:F4   Range D8

Range D14:F17

You will work quite a bit with ranges. One of the ways to make your worksheets more
manageable is to name your ranges. Range names are far easier to remember than using
range references. You might assign the name *Titles* to your column titles, for example,
Months to your column of month names, and so on.

To name a range, perform these steps:

1. Select the cells that you want to include in the named range.

2. Click the Name Box at the left of the Formula bar (the text box that displays cell
   references).

3. Type the range name. The name can be as long as 255 characters and the first character must be a letter or the underscore character. The rest of the name can contain letters, numbers, a period, and the underscore character but no spaces or other special characters such as a question mark. The name cannot be the same as a possible cell reference, so R2D2 would not count as a valid range name.

4. Press Enter. When you subsequently select the range, you will see that Excel displays the *range name* rather than the range reference in the Name Box.

Range names are easier to remember than range references. If you create a payroll worksheet and assign the names GrossPay, NetPay, HoursWorked, TaxRate, and PayRate to the ranges holding that data, for example, you never again have to type the range references. When you want to move or copy one of the ranges or use the range as a formula, just refer to the range name and let Excel figure out the correct references. You learn how to use ranges (including range names) in formulas in the section called "Using Formulas."

> Here's an even better reason to name ranges: If you move a range, Excel moves the name with the cells! If you tracked range references and not names, you often must track down the latest references when you refer to the range. By naming ranges, you never have to worry about keeping track of references because the names won't change even if the references do.

> Use meaningful names. Although AAA works as a name for a column of net sales figures, NetSales makes a lot more sense and is easier to remember.

If you create a large worksheet and you need to return to a named range to make some changes, click the Name Box's drop-down list box arrow and select the name. Excel instantly displays and selects that range for you.

Using Formulas

Without *formulas*, Excel would be little more than a simple row and column-based word processor. When you use formulas, however, Excel becomes an extremely powerful time-saving planning, budgeting, and general-purpose financial tool.

On a calculator, you typically type a formula, and then press the equal sign to see the result. In contrast, all Excel formulas *begin* with an equal sign. For example, the following is a formula:

=4*2-3

The asterisk is an operator that denotes the times sign (*multiplication*). This formula requests that Excel compute the value of 4 multiplied by 2 minus 3 to get the *result*. When you type a formula and press Enter or move to another cell, Excel displays the result, not the formula, on the worksheet.

As Figure 8.4 shows, the answer 5 appears on the worksheet, and you can see the cell's formula contents right on the Formula bar area. When entering a formula, as soon as you press the equal sign, Excel shows your formula on the Formula bar as well as in the active cell. If you click the Formula bar and then enter your formula, the formula appears in the Formula bar as well as in the active cell. By first clicking the Formula bar before entering the formula, however, you can press the left and right arrow keys to move the cell pointer left and right within the formula to edit it. When entering long formulas, this Formula bar's editing capability helps you correct mistakes that you might type.

The cell's formula appears here

The formula's answer appears here

FIGURE 8.4

Excel displays a formula's result on the worksheet.

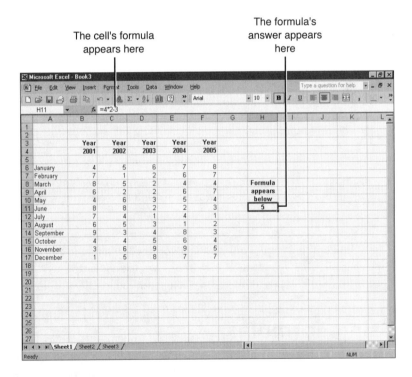

Excel's Primary Math Operators

Table 8.1 lists the primary math operators you can use in your worksheet formulas. Notice that all the example formulas begin with the equal sign.

TABLE 8.1   The Primary Math Operators Specify Math Calculations

Operator	Example	Description
^	=7 ^ 3	Raises 7 to the power of 3 (called *exponentiation*)
/	=4 / 2	Divides 4 by 2
*	=3 * 4 * 5	Multiplies 3 by 4 by 5
+	=5 + 5	Adds 5 and 5
-	=5 - 5	Subtracts 5 from 5

You can combine any and all the operators in a formula. When combining operators, Excel follows the traditional computer (and algebraic) *operator hierarchy* model. Therefore, Excel first computes exponentiation if you raise any value to another power. Excel then calculates all multiplication and division in a left-to-right order (the first one to appear computes first) before addition and subtraction (also in left-to-right order).

The following formula returns a result of 14 because Excel first calculates the exponentiation of 2 raised to the third power, and then Excel divides the answer (8) by 4, and then multiplies the result (2) by 2, and finally subtracts the result (4) from 18. Even though the subtraction appears first, the operator hierarchy forces the subtraction to wait until last to compute.

```
=18 - 2 ^ 3 / 4 * 2
```

If you want to override the operator hierarchy, put parentheses around the parts you want Excel to compute first. The following formula returns a different result from the previous one, for example, despite the same values and operators used:

```
=(18 - 2) ^ 3 / 4 * 2
```

Instead of 14, this formula returns 2,048! The subtraction produces 16, which is then raised to the third power (producing 4,096) before dividing by 4 and multiplying the result by 2 to get 2,048.

Using Range Names in Formulas

The true power of Excel shows when you use cell references and range names in formulas. All the following are valid formulas. Cell references or range names appear throughout the formulas.

```
=(SalesTotals)/NumOfSales
=C4 * 2 - (Rate * .08)
=7 + LE51 - (Gross - Net)
```

When you enter formulas that contain range references, you can either type the full reference or point to the cell reference. If you want to include a complete named range in a formula (formulas can work on complete ranges, as you see later this hour), select the entire range and Excel inserts the range name in your formula. Often, finding and pointing to a value is easier than locating the reference and entering it exactly.

If, for example, you are entering a formula, when you get to the place in the formula that requires a cell reference, don't type the cell reference; instead, point and click on the cell you want to use in the formula, and Excel adds that cell reference to your formula. If you have entered a formula such as =7 +, instead of typing a cell reference of LE51, you can point to that cell and press Enter or type another operator to continue the formula. Immediately after typing the cell reference for you, Excel returns your cell pointer to the formula (or to the Formula bar if you are entering the formula there) so that you can complete it.

After you assign a name to a range, you don't have to remember that range's reference when you use it in formulas. Suppose that you are creating a large worksheet that spans many screens. If you assign names to cells when you create them—especially to cells that you know you will refer to later during the worksheet's development—entering formulas that use that name is made easier. Instead of locating that cell to find its address, you need only to type the name when entering a formula that uses that cell.

Relative Versus Absolute Cell Referencing

When you copy formulas that contain cell references, Excel updates the cell references so that they cite *relative references*. For example, suppose that you enter this formula in cell A1:

`=A2 + A3`

This formula contains two references. The references are relative because the references A2 and A3 change if you copy the formula elsewhere. If you copy the formula to cell B5, for example, B5 holds this:

`=B6 + B7`

The original relative references update to reflect the formula's copied location. Of course, A1 still holds its original contents, but the copied cell at B5 holds the same formula referencing B5 rather than A1.

An absolute reference is a reference that does not change if you copy the formula. A dollar sign ($) always precedes an absolute reference. The reference B5 is an absolute reference. If you wanted to sum two columns of data (A1 with B1, A2 with B2, and so on) and then multiply each sum by some constant number, for example, the constant number could be a cell referred to as an absolute reference. That formula might resemble this:

`=(A1 + B1) * $J$1`

8

J1 is an *absolute reference*, but A1 and B1 are relative. If you copied the formula down one row, the formula would change to this:

```
=(A2 + B2) * $J$1
```

Notice that the first two cells changed because when you originally entered them, they were relative cell references. You told Excel, by placing dollar signs in front of the absolute cell reference's row and column references, not to change that reference when you copy the formula elsewhere.

$B5 is a partial absolute cell reference. If you copy a formula with $B5 inside the computation, the $B keeps the B column intact, but the fifth row updates to the row location of the target cell. If you type the following formula in cell A1:

```
=2 * $B5
```

and then copy the formula to cell F6, cell F6 holds this formula:

```
=2 * $B10
```

You copied the formula to a cell five rows and five columns over in the worksheet. Excel did not update the column name, B, because you told Excel to keep that column name absolute (it is always B no matter where you copy the formula). Excel added 5 to the row number, however, because the row number was relative and open to change whenever you copied the formula.

The dollar sign keeps the row B absolute no matter where you copy the formula, but the relative row number can change as you copy the formula.

The bottom line is this: Most of the time, you use relative referencing. If you insert or delete rows, columns, or cells, your formulas remain accurate because the cells that they reference change as your worksheet changes.

Copying Formulas

Excel offers several shortcut tools that make copying cells from one location to another simple. Consider the worksheet in Figure 8.5. The bottom row needs to hold formulas that total each of the projected year's 12-month values.

How would you enter the total for column B in cell B19? You could type the following formula in cell B19:

```
=B6+B7+B8+B9+B10+B11+B12+B13+B14+B15+B16+B17
```

Better ways exist to total a column of numbers, but for now this will suffice. Beginning with Excel 2002, as you enter formulas, Excel color codes cells that you refer to as you type the formula. Therefore, if you were to create Figure 8.5's worksheet and start typing

=B6+B7+ into the total area, Excel colors each cell starting with B6, as well as that cell reference in the formula, a unique color. By color coding the cells to match the formula references, you'll more easily be able to spot mistakes in long formulas.

FIGURE 8.5

A total row is needed for the project's yearly values.

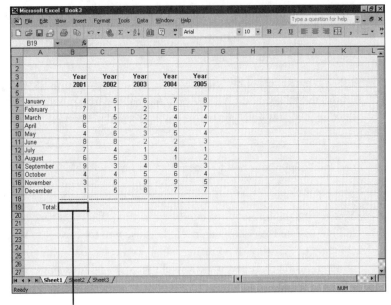

This column needs a total

After you have typed the formula in B19, you then *could* type the following formula in cell C19:

=C6+C7+C8+C9+C10+C11+C12+C13+C14+C15+C16+C17

You then could type the values in the remaining total cells. Instead of doing all that typing, however, copy cell B19 to cell C19. Hold Ctrl while you drag the cell edge of B19 to C19. When you release the mouse, cell C19 properly totals column C! Press Ctrl and copy C19 to D19 through F19 to place the totals in all the total cells. The totals are accurate, as Figure 8.6 shows.

After you drag one or more cells to fill data in other cells, Excel displays the AutoFill Options button at the right of the fill that you can click to specify how you want the new cells to be formatted (the same as the original cell or without bringing the original cell's format to the new ones). Generally, the default fill method works well and you'll often never click the AutoFill Options button to change the way Excel completed your cells.

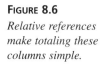

FIGURE 8.6

Relative references make totaling these columns simple.

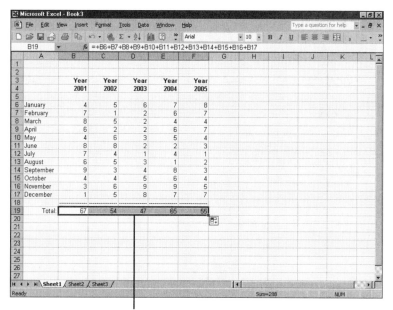

These were copied from B19

Recalculating Worksheets

After you set up formulas, your job is done; Excel's job has just begun, however. If you change any value in the worksheet, Excel recalculates all formulas automatically! Therefore, Excel keeps your worksheet fresh and accurate as you modify values. You can use the same worksheet each month and change only the monthly data. If you leave the formulas intact, Excel computes and displays the correct answers.

You can turn off the automatic recalculation and manually recalculate when ready if you use a slow computer and want to save time when editing a large worksheet. Select Tools, Options and click the Calculation tab. Click the Manual option to force manual recalculation. If you now change the data, Excel does not recalculate your worksheet until you press F9 (the Calculate Now shortcut key).

Working with Functions

The previous sections explained how to enter a formula once, using relative cell referencing, and copy that formula to other cells. Although you only have to type the formula one time, this kind of totaling formula is tedious to type and introduces greater chance for error:

`=B6+B7+B8+B9+B10+B11+B12+B13+B14+B15+B16+B17`

Fortunately, Microsoft includes several built-in *functions* that perform many common mathematical calculations. Instead of writing a formula to sum a row or column of values, for example, use the Sum() function.

Function names always end with parentheses, such as Average(). A function accepts zero or more *arguments*, and an argument is a value that appears inside the parentheses that the function uses in some way. Always separate function arguments with commas. If a function contains only a single argument, you do not use a comma inside the parentheses. Functions generally manipulate data (numbers or text), and the arguments inside the parentheses supply the data to the function. The Average() function, for example, computes an average of whatever list of values you pass in the argument. Therefore, all the following compute an average from the argument list:

```
=Average(18, 65, 299, $R$5, 10, -2, 102)
=Average(SalesTotals)
=Average(D4:D14)
```

> When you begin to enter a formula, ScreenTips pop up after you type the formula's name to help guide you through the formula's required contents.

As with many functions, Average() accepts as many arguments as needed to do its job. The first Average() function computes the average of seven values, one of which is an absolute cell reference. The second Average() function computes the average of a range named SalesTotals. No matter how many cells comprise the range SalesTotals, Average() computes the average. The last Average() function computes the average of the values in the range D4 through D14 (a columnar list).

The following formula computes the average of seven arguments, one of which (F14) is a cell reference, and one of which (R5) is an absolute cell reference:

```
=Average(18, F14, 299, $R$5, 10, -2, 102)
```

The Sum() function is perhaps the most common function because you so often total columns and rows. In the preceding section, you entered a long formula to add the values in a column. Instead of adding each cell to total the range B6:B17, you could more easily enter the following function:

=Sum(B6:B17)

If you copy this Sum() function to the other cells at the bottom of the yearly projections, the total appears at the bottom of those columns.

8

> When you insert rows within the Sum() range, Excel updates the range
> inside the Sum() function to include the new values.

Use AutoSum for Efficiency

Before looking at a table of common functions, Excel helps you with summing functions
by analyzing your selected range and automatically inserting a Sum() function if needed.
Here's how to do that:

1. Select the range that you want to sum. If you want to sum the months over the projected years for this hour's sample worksheets, for example, select the row with the
   January label, as shown in Figure 8.7.

2. Click the AutoSum toolbar button. Excel guesses that you want to sum the selected
   row and inserts the Sum() function in the cell to the right of the row.

3. Make any edits to the summed value if Excel included too many or not enough cells.
   You can click the cell and press F2 to edit the sum. Usually, no edits are required.

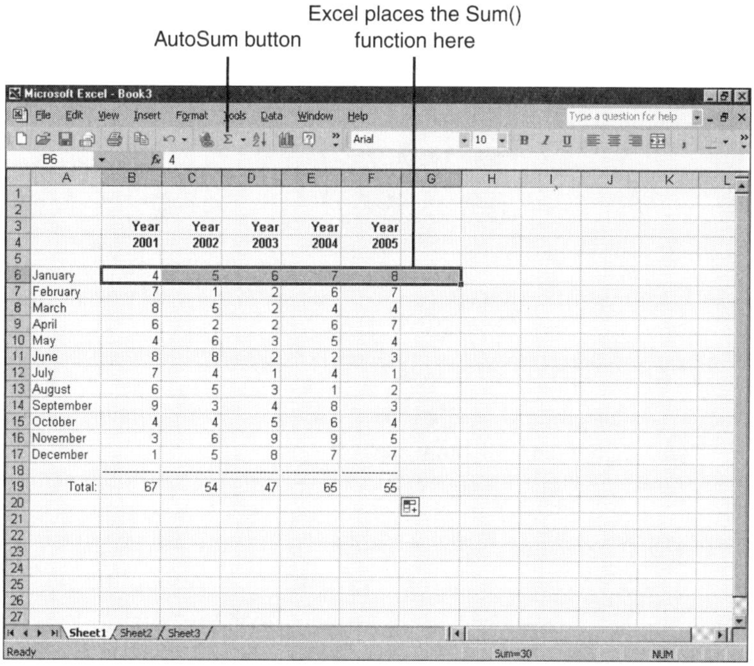

FIGURE 8.7
*Getting ready to
request a sum.*

AutoSum button

Excel places the Sum()
function here

After Excel generates the Sum() function, you can copy the cell down the rest of the column to add the monthly totals. However, can you see another way to perform the same monthly totals with one selection? Select the *entire set* of monthly values with one extra blank column at the right (the range B6:G17). Excel sees the blank column and fills it in with each row's sum when you click AutoSum. You now can select the new column of totals and let AutoSum compute them. Figure 8.8 shows the result of the new sums after you add underlines and a title to the row.

FIGURE 8.8

AutoSum in action.

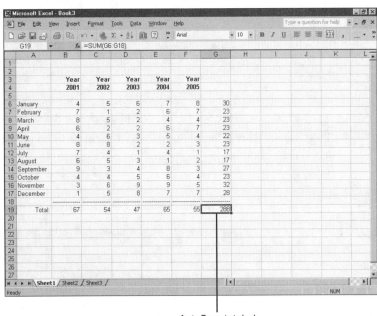

AutoSum totaled
the entire column

Common Functions

Functions improve your accuracy. If you want to average three cell values, for example, you might type something such as

`=C2 + C4 + C6 / 3`

This formula does not compute an average! Remember that the operator hierarchy forces the division calculation first. If you use the Average() function, as shown next, you don't have to worry as much about the calculation's hierarchy.

`=Average(C2, C4, C6)`

8

Another advantage of using functions is that you can modify them more easily than long calculations. If you want to include another cell value into the previous average, for example, you only need to add the extra cell to Average(); if you use a formula, you must remember to change the 3 to 4.

Table 8.2 describes common Excel built-in functions that you find a lot of uses for as you create worksheets. Remember to start every formula with an equal sign and to add your arguments to the parentheses, and you are set!

TABLE 8.2 Common Excel Functions

Function Name	Description
Abs()	Computes the absolute value of its cell argument. (Good for distance- and age-difference calculations.)
Average()	Computes the average of its arguments.
Count()	Returns the number of numerical arguments in the argument list. (Useful if you use a range name for the argument list.)
CountBlank()	Returns the number of blank cells, if any exist, in the argument range. (Useful if you use a range name for the argument list.)
Max()	Returns the highest (maximum) value in the argument list. (Useful if you use a range name for the argument list and you need to pick out the highest value.)
Min()	Returns the lowest (minimum) value in the argument list. (Useful if you use a range name for the argument list and you need to pick out the lowest value.)
Pi()	Computes the value of mathematical pi (requires no arguments) for use in math calculations.
Product()	Computes the product (multiplicative result) of the argument range.
Roman()	Converts its cell value to a Roman numeral.
Sqrt()	Computes the square root of the cell argument.
Stdev()	Computes the argument list's standard deviation.
Sum()	Computes the sum of its arguments.
Today()	Returns today's date (requires no arguments).
Var()	Computes a list's sample variance.

Excel supports many functions, including complex mathematical, date, time, financial, and engineering functions. Click F1 or type a question in the Ask a Question box for Help to supply more details on all the functions you can use.

Advanced Functions

Some of the functions require more arguments than a simple cell or range. Excel contains many financial functions, for example, that compute loan values and investment rates of return. If you want to use one of the more advanced functions, click on an empty cell and select Insert, Function or click the Insert Function button to display the Insert Function dialog box, as shown in Figure 8.9.

FIGURE 8.9

Let Excel help you enter complex functions.

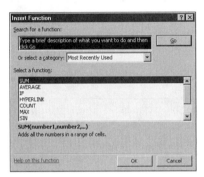

You can select from a category of functions in the drop-down list box or describe what you want to do at the top of the dialog box and let Excel locate a function that might work. When you decide on a function (you can simply scroll the list of function names at the bottom of the dialog box and select one), Excel displays an additional dialog box with text box areas for each of the function arguments, such as the one shown in Figure 8.10. As you continue entering arguments that the function requires, Excel builds the function in the cell for you. As you get more proficient, you no longer need the help of the Insert Function dialog box as often.

FIGURE 8.10

You can quickly enter arguments in the Function Arguments dialog box.

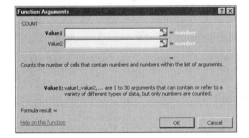

Introduction to Worksheet Formatting

It is now time to show you how to pretty things up. This hour is about to come to a close, but you still have time to learn some cell-formatting basics and you can continue with Excel's more advanced formatting features in the next hour's session.

8

Justification

Excel right-justifies numbers (and formulas that result in numbers) and left-justifies text labels. You don't have to accept Excel's default justification, however. To left-, center-, or right-justify the contents of any cell (or range), select the cell (or range) and click the Align Left, Center, or Align Right toolbar buttons. Using these buttons, you can center titles above columns and adjust your numbers to look just right.

Excel offers a trick that even some Excel gurus forget: If you want to center a title above several columns of data, type the title in a cell above the data. If you cannot center the title over the values by clicking the Center toolbar button, select all the cells around the title so that you have selected as many columns as there is data. Click the Merge and Center toolbar button. Excel centers the title, even though the title resides in a single cell, across the entire column selection.

Row and Column Height and Width

As you learn more formatting tricks, you will need to adjust certain row and column widths and heights to hold the newly formatted values. To adjust a row's height, point to the line that separates the row number from the previous row. When the mouse pointer changes to a double-pointing arrow, drag the row's top edge up or down. In the same manner, to change the width of a column, point to the column heading's right edge and drag your mouse left or right. Sometimes large titles need the larger row heights.

In the same manner, to change the width of a column, point to the column name's left or right edge and drag your mouse left or right. Excel adjusts the column width to follow your mouse movement. When you release the mouse, Excel anchors the new column width where you left it.

If you shrink a column width so that the column can no longer display numerical data, Excel displays pound signs (#####) to warn you that you need to widen the column. Your data is still stored in the cell—it just cannot be displayed.

To adjust the column width so that the column (or range of columns) is exactly large enough to hold the largest data value in the column, select the column (or columns) and double-click the right edge of the column heading. Excel adjusts the column to hold the widest data in the column.

Font Changes

Feel free to change the worksheet's font to add appeal. Simple font changes, such as bold-facing, italicizing, and underlining, greatly improve the look of titles. The Bold, Italic, and Underline toolbar buttons add the proper formatting to your selected cell or range.

If you select Format, Cells and click the Font tab, Excel displays the Font dialog box (virtually identical to that of Word's), in which you can select a new font name and size. As Figure 8.11 shows, simple font changes can make a big improvement on otherwise dull worksheets.

FIGURE 8.11

Already this worksheet looks better.

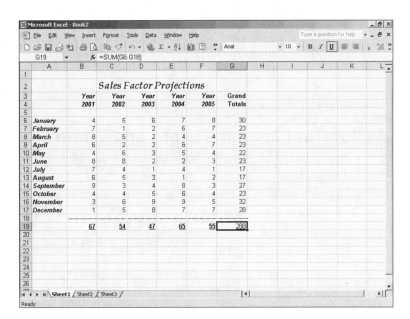

Of course, you can use the Font and Font Size toolbar buttons to change a typeface or size without displaying the Font dialog box.

Making Format Changes

Now that you have mastered Excel basics, it's time to learn the general format categories Excel uses for worksheet data. Table 8.3 describes each of the format categories. Unless you change the default settings, Excel uses the General format for data of all kinds.

TABLE 8.3   Excel's Fundamental Formats

Format Name	Description
General	The numeric data has no special formatting and generally appears exactly the way you enter the data.
Number	You can set the number of decimal places Excel displays for all numeric values.
Currency	Displays a dollar sign and two decimal places for dollar amounts.
Accounting	Aligns currency and decimal points in a column.
Date	Displays date and time values as values whose formats you can change.
Time	Displays only the time portion of a date and time value.
Percentage	Displays a percent sign. If you type 50 into the cell, Excel changes your value to 50%. You can set the number of decimal places Excel displays in the percent.
Fraction	Displays numbers as fractions (great for stock quotes).
Scientific	Uses scientific notation for all numeric values.
Text	Formats *all* data as text. Great for ZIP Codes that are all numbers but that you never use for calculations.
Special	Formats ZIP Codes, phone numbers, and Social Security numbers.
Custom	Lets you define your own cell format. You can decide whether you want to see the plus or minus sign, and you can control the number of decimal places.

Format a selection by choosing Format, Cells and clicking the Number tab to display the formats shown in Table 8.3. If you select the Time format from that list, you must select one of the Time format display variations so that Excel knows how you want the time displayed.

You can also right-click the selection and select the Format Cells command from the shortcut menu. When you do, you see the Format Cells dialog box. You can use this dialog box to assign the formats directly to your data.

As you saw at the end of the previous hour, you can also use Excel's autoformatting capabilities to easily add style to your worksheet. The next hour covers AutoFormat in more detail.

Several Formatting toolbar buttons exist that enable quick formatting of cells using the most common format styles. If you select a cell or a range of cells, you can change the selection's format more quickly with a toolbar button than with the Format, Cells dialog box. Not all Excel's formats are available through the toolbar, but these are: Currency Style, Percent Style, Comma Style, Increase Decimal (to increase the number of decimal places), and Decrease Decimal (to decrease the number of decimal places).

Summary

This hour extended your knowledge of worksheets by giving you more editing tools with which to insert and delete columns, rows, and cells. After you name important worksheet ranges, you won't have to track specific references in your worksheet; the name is easier to remember, and Excel changes the range if you insert data in or delete it from the range.

One of the most powerful aspects of worksheets is their recalculation capability. If you change data or a formula, Excel recalculates the entire worksheet as soon as you make the change. You are always looking at the computed worksheet with up-to-date information, no matter what kind of data changes you make. When you use formulas, you not only improve your worksheet accuracy, but also you finish your worksheets faster.

The next hour picks up where this one leaves off, going into formatting in more detail. Additionally, you see that graphics spruce up your worksheet and are easy to produce.

Q&A

Q Why would I ever use absolute cell referencing?

A Relative cell referencing seems to make the most sense for the majority of worksheets. If you have to rearrange your worksheet, your relative cell reference updates as well. Absolute references are great when a formula points to a single cell, such as an age or pay value, that rarely changes. You could use dollar signs to anchor the cell reference in the formula that uses that cell, but keep the other references relative in case you need to copy the formula around the worksheet.

Q What's the difference between the formatting you get by clicking the Center toolbar button and the formatting you get by clicking the Merge and Center button?

A If you need to center the contents of one cell, both buttons perform the same task. If want to center data (such as a title) above a range of cell columns, however, select the range the centered cell is to go over and click Merge and Center; Excel completes the centering across the multiple columns.

HOUR 9

Using Excel 2002

This hour teaches you how to improve the accuracy of your worksheet data. You can easily edit cell contents with the tools Excel 2002 provides.

After you master worksheet editing skills, you are then ready to see how Excel's AutoCorrect feature and the spelling checker work to improve the accuracy of your worksheets. Excel can also enter values for you. When you ask Excel to fill in a series of cell values, it uses some intuitive guesswork to complete any series that you begin. If you often enter a special series of numbers or labels, you can teach Excel to recognize that series. This eliminates typing when you use the series again.

The highlights of this hour include the following:

- Why the spelling checker and AutoCorrect are important to numeral-based worksheets
- How Excel fills series in for you
- When (and how) to teach Excel a new series
- How to find and replace worksheet data
- How to print worksheets more effectively
- How to use comments to describe a cell

Spell Checking

No worksheet program included a spelling checker before Excel. After all, worksheets are for numbers, right? Of course, the primary purpose for worksheets is formatting, arranging, and calculating numbers. Numbers without titles, however, are worthless in most instances. You have to present your numeric data in such a way that the worksheet users understand the significance of your data. Given the amount of text you enter on your worksheets, a spelling checker makes sense. You can only wonder why worksheet makers did not add spelling checkers long before Microsoft added one to Excel.

You can check your worksheet's spelling, do one of the following:

- Click the Spelling toolbar button
- Select Tools, Spelling from the menu
- Press F7, the Spelling shortcut key

Unlike Word, Excel does not include a grammar checker or a synonym finder. Rarely do you include complete sentences on a worksheet, so the grammar checker would be wasted overhead in most cases.

The spelling checker in Excel is the same one that Word uses (see Hour 5, "Managing Documents and Customizing Word 2002," for a quick review). The spelling checker does not check every worksheet in your workbook, but only the current worksheet active on your screen. If Excel finds an error, you can choose to correct, ignore, or add the error so that the word no longer appears as an error (as might be the case for proper names).

AutoCorrect Worksheets

Use AutoCorrect as you type Excel entries just as you used AutoCorrect in Word. When you type an abbreviation for an AutoCorrect entry, Excel converts that abbreviated form to the complete AutoCorrect entry for you when you press the spacebar or move the pointer to another cell.

Word, Excel, and all the other core Office products share the same AutoCorrect and spelling dictionaries. Therefore, when you make changes and additions in the AutoCorrect or spelling dictionaries of Word or Excel, the other products recognize those changes.

To add AutoCorrect entries, perform the same steps that you do with Word, namely use the Tools, AutoCorrect Options menu to display the AutoCorrect dialog box and add your entries there.

Finding and Replacing Data

Like Word, Excel contains a powerful search-and-replace operation that can search your worksheet for values and replace those values if needed. Although Word users often use Word's search-and-replace, the feature gets less use in Excel. Nevertheless, the feature is extremely beneficial for worksheets. Imagine that you have a worksheet that tracks the payroll for your company, and the minimum wage increases. Instead of laboriously changing each and every cell that includes the minimum wage, you can use Excel's find-and-replace feature to quickly update the data.

The find-and-replace feature in Excel works a little differently from that in Word. The numeric nature of Excel requires a different type of find and replace. Therefore, read this section even if you have mastered the find-and-replace feature in Word.

You display the Find and Replace dialog box by choosing Find on the Edit menu. Alternatively, you can press Ctrl+F. Figure 9.1 shows the Find and Replace dialog box in Excel, after clicking the Options button to show extra details.

FIGURE 9.1

You can use Excel's Find and Replace dialog box to look for text or numbers.

You can request that Excel search by rows or columns. If your worksheet is generally longer than wide (as most are), select By Columns to speed your search. Select the Match Case option if you want Excel to match the uppercase and lowercase letters in your search exactly.

Use Formulas if you are searching for part of a formula (you learn all about formulas in the next hour), use Values if you want Excel to search only the calculated cells (not within formulas), and use Comments if you want Excel to search through cell comments. Generally, you are searching through formulas, so Excel makes Formulas the default search target.

The Match Entire Cell Contents option indicates to Excel that a cell must contain your entire Find value and nothing else before a proper match will be made.

If you want Excel to replace the found value with another value, select the Edit, Replace command to display the Replace page of the Find and Replace dialog box, as shown in Figure 9.2.

FIGURE 9.2

Let Excel replace values for you.

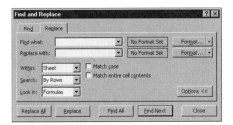

Enter the text you want Excel to locate in the Find What field and type the text you want to replace that with in the Replace field. Click the Replace All button if you want Excel to replace all occurrences of the found text. (Be sure that you want to replace all occurrences, or you'll possibly overwrite data unexpectedly.) Otherwise, click Find Next to find the next matching value and, if that is a value you want to replace, click Replace. If it is not a value you want to replace, click Find Next to locate the next occurrence.

> If you want to find or replace within a limited worksheet range only, select the range before conducting the find or replace operation.

Reviewing Cut, Copy, and Paste in Excel

If you have mastered the Copy, Cut, and Paste commands in Word, those commands in Excel will be a breeze for you. As with Word and the other Office products, Excel uses the Office Clipboard to hold data that you are copying, cutting, and pasting from within or between worksheets. Alternatively, if you open two workbooks at the same time and display both on your screen (by selecting Window, Arrange), you can easily copy, cut, and paste between the two workbooks by dragging content from one worksheet to the other.

To copy data from one location to another, select the cell or cells you want to copy and click the Copy toolbar button (or press Ctrl+C) to copy the worksheet contents to your Clipboard. The contents stay in the original location because you elected to copy and not cut the cells. To paste the Clipboard contents to another location, click the cell to indicate the upper left corner of the target range. Then, click the Paste toolbar button (or press Ctrl+V). Excel overwrites the target cells with the pasted contents, so be sure of the paste target when you paste Clipboard data.

As with all Office products, you can send up to 24 distinct items to the Office Clipboard and paste one or more of the copied items into your worksheet. When you copy or cut more than one worksheet item to the Office Clipboard, the Clipboard Task Pane window appears to display the Office Clipboard contents. You can paste any of the Office Clipboard Task Pane's items to your worksheet. As with Word and the other Office products, you can copy and paste text, numbers, formulas, pictures, Internet hyperlinks, and Media Gallery clips. The Clipboard Task Pane appears by default. However, if its display has been turned off, you can redisplay it by choosing Edit, Office Clipboard.

9

You can continue pasting the copied item to other worksheets as long as you keep selecting a target location and pressing Ctrl+V.

Excel supports drag-and-drop editing, so after you select the cells to copy, press Ctrl and drag the selection to its new location. You must drag the selection by pointing to one of the selection edges; if you attempt to drag from the center of a range, Excel modifies which cells are selected. When you release your mouse button and the Ctrl key, Excel pastes the contents to the target location. Of course, drag-and-drop editing works only when you can see both the source and the target copy and paste locations.

To cut contents and place them elsewhere, just select the cells that you want to cut and click the Cut toolbar button (or press Ctrl+X). Excel removes the selection from its original location and places the selection on your Clipboard. You then can paste the Clipboard contents elsewhere. In effect, cutting and pasting performs a movement of the selected data. If you want to move the selection with your mouse, drag the selection without first pressing Ctrl as you did when copying the contents.

If you want to drag and drop data between two workbooks' worksheets but you only have one worksheet displayed, press the Alt key before dragging your selection. When you drag the selection over the target worksheet's tab, Excel opens that worksheet, and you can drop the dragged contents to the open worksheet.

Clearing Data

Because of the nature of worksheets, erasing worksheet data differs from erasing word-processed data. Other information on the worksheet can heavily depend on the erased data, as you saw in the previous hour's lesson. When you want to erase a cell's or selection's contents, first decide which of the following kinds of erasure you want to perform:

- Erase the selection and send the contents to the Clipboard (as you learned in the previous section).
- Clear only a portion of the selection, such as its formatting, comment, or contents.
- Completely erase the selection and all formatting and notes attached to the selection.
- Erase the selected cells and their position so that other cells in the row move left or cells below move up.

> A worksheet's cell contains a lot more than just the numbers and text that you see on the worksheet screen. Not only can the cells contain formulas and comments, but also they often rely on other cells for information. Therefore, when you want to erase the selection, you must keep in mind how the selection affects other worksheet areas.

If you want to delete only the selected cell's data, press Delete. Excel retains any formatting and comments that you had applied before you deleted the data.

If you want to more selectively erase a cell, select the Edit, Clear command and select from one of the four options listed here:

- The All option deletes the entire selection, including the contents, format, and attached comments (but not the actual cell).
- The Formats option erases only the selection's format; you can get rid of a cell's special formatting and revert to a general format without changing or erasing the actual contents of the cell.
- The Contents option deletes the cell data but leaves the formatting and comments intact.
- The Comments option deletes any special comments that appear in the selected cells.

> Reverse an accidental deletion with Undo (Ctrl+Z).

To remove the selected cells as well as their contents and close the gap left by the deleted selection, select Edit, Delete to display the Delete dialog box, as shown in Figure 9.3. Select Shift Cells Left or Shift Cells Up so that Excel knows how to close the gap that the deletion leaves.

FIGURE 9.3

*You can delete cells
and move all other
cells over those deleted
cells.*

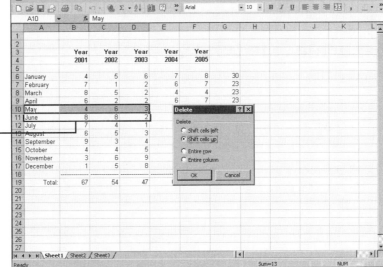

Use the Delete dialog
box to remove cells

Speed Data Entry

Excel can often predict what data you want to enter into a worksheet. By spotting trends in your data, Excel uses educated guesses to fill in cell data for you. Excel uses *data fills* to copy and extend data from one cell to several additional cells.

One of the most common data fills you perform is to use Excel's capability to copy one cell's data to several other cells. You might want to create a pro forma balance sheet for the previous five-year period, for example. You can insert a two-line label across the top of each year's data. The first line would contain five occurrences of the label Year, and the second line would hold the numbers 2001 through 2005. To use the data fill feature in Excel to create the five similar labels, perform these simple steps:

1. Click the B3 cell to move the cell pointer there.
2. Type **Year**. Don't press Enter or any cell-moving keys after you type the label.
3. Locate the cell's fill handle in the lower-right hand corner.
4. Drag the fill handle to the right across the next four columns. As you drag the fill handle, Excel displays the pop-up label Year indicating the value that will be automatically entered in the new cells.
5. Release the mouse button. Excel fills all five cells with the label.

If you drag the fill handle down, Excel copies the label down the column. Although the Edit, Fill command performs the same function as the fill handle, dragging the fill handle is much easier than selecting from the menu. Ctrl+D performs the same operation as Edit, Fill, Down.

Smarter Fills with AutoFill

Even if the only fill Excel performed was the copying of data across rows and columns, the data fill would still be beneficial. Excel goes an extra step, however: It performs smart fills with a feature known as *AutoFill*. AutoFill is perhaps the single reason why Excel took over the spreadsheet market a few years ago and has been the leader ever since. When you use AutoFill, Excel examines and completes data you have entered.

The five-year pro forma period you were setting up in the preceding section included the years 2001 through 2005, for example. You can type **2001** under the first Year title and type **2002** under the second title. Select *both* cells, and then drag the fill handle right three more cells. When you release the mouse button, you see that Excel properly fills in the remaining years (as shown in Figure 9.4).

FIGURE 9.4

Excel's AutoFill feature knew which years to fill.

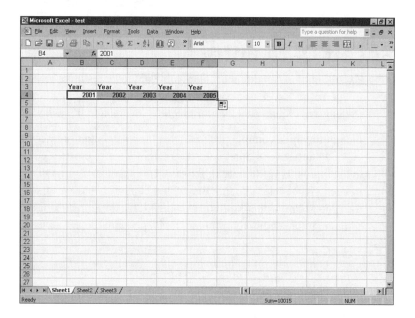

 If you had selected only one cell, Excel would have copied that cell's contents across the worksheet. Excel needed to see the two selected cells to notice the trend.

The years in Figure 9.4 don't exactly align under the titles in the first row, but you can use the text-alignment commands you learned in Hour 8, "Restructuring and Editing Excel 2002 Worksheets," to make your titles line up. Select the year titles and then click the Align Right toolbar button to right-align the years so that they appear directly above the year values.

Excel offers even better tools for automatic cell filling than the drag-and-fill method you just saw. If you want to use AutoFill to increment cells by a single number, as you are doing with the years, you don't really need to select two cells first. If you select any cell that contains a number, press Ctrl, and drag the fill handle, Excel adds a one to each cell to which you extend. Therefore, you could fill four years from 2002 through 2005 just by pressing Ctrl before you dragged the first year's fill handle to the right.

As you know, Excel works with text as well as with numeric values. AutoFill recognizes many common text trends, including the following:

- Days of the week names
- Days of the week abbreviations (such as Mon, Tue)
- Month names
- Month abbreviations (such as Jan, Feb)

Suppose that you want to list month names down the left of the pro forma sheet, starting in cell A5, because you need to report each month's totals for those five years. All you need to do is type **January** for the first month name, and drag that cell's fill handle to the twelfth cell below. Figure 9.5 shows the result.

FIGURE 9.5

Let Excel fill in the series of month names.

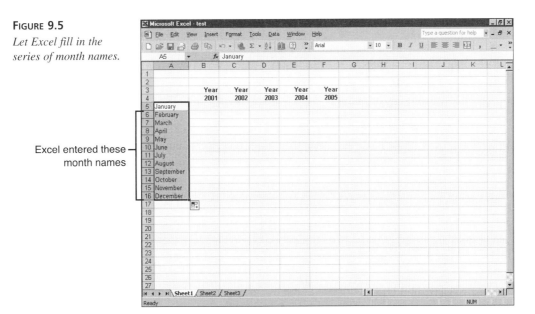

Excel entered these month names

Design Your Own Fills

In addition to using AutoFill to quickly enter the month and weekday names and abbreviations, Excel can fill in any list of values. You can create a new, customized list with values that you often use. For example, you can create a custom list for the employees in your department or for products you sell. After you have shown Excel the new list, anytime you type the first value and drag that cell's fill handle in any direction, Excel fills the remaining cells with your list.

To add your own Custom list to Excel's repertoire of lists, perform these steps:

1. Select Tools, Options.
2. Click the Custom Lists tab to display the current AutoFill lists in effect.
3. Click the Add button.
4. Type your list of values for AutoFill. If you have six departments, you might enter something similar to Dept 1, Dept 2, Dept 3, Dept 4, Dept 5, and Dept 6. Press Enter after each value. Your screen should resemble Figure 9.6.

FIGURE 9.6

*Teach Excel new
Custom list entries.*

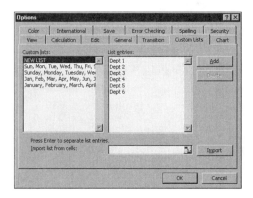

5. Click OK to add your list to AutoFill's current list.

The next time you type the label **Dept 1** in a cell and drag the fill handle to the right or down the worksheet, Excel fills in the remaining departments. If you fill only four cells, Excel uses the first four values. If you fill six or more cells, Excel fills all six departments and starts repeating the department names for any number over six.

If you enter a series in a worksheet, and then decide that the series would make a great AutoFill list (in case you want to add the list to another worksheet), Excel doesn't make you re-enter the list. Just select the entire list by dragging the mouse pointer through the list. When you open the Custom Lists dialog box, click Import to add the selected range to the AutoFill entries.

AutoFill is fine for a typical range of titles and for a series of a dozen or fewer entries, but some data series include numerous entries. When you want to enter a larger number of values in a series, perform these steps:

1. Type the first value of the series in the first cell.

2. Select the cell and all subsequent cells that will receive the rest of the series.

3. Select Edit, Fill, Series to display the Series dialog box.

4. Select Rows if you have selected cells from a row or Columns if you have selected cells from a column.

5. Select the type of series you are entering. (Table 9.1 describes each of the four types from which you can choose.)

6. Select the subtype. If the Type is Date, select a Date unit. If the series is a series of months, for example, check Month.

7. Enter the Step value, which describes how each value in the series increases or decreases.

8. Enter the Stop value if necessary (you rarely need to enter one). If you want to enter a series that increases every three months, for example, you check the Month option, and type **3** for the Step value, Excel will know the final month and you won't need to enter it.

    Although you won't need to indicate to Excel where to stop in most instances, a Stop value is useful if you check the Trend option in the Series dialog box. Excel starts with your initial selected value (if numeric) and estimates the values between that starting value and the Stop value that you supply.

9. Click OK to create and enter the series of values.

TABLE 9.1   Types of Series

Series Name	If You Type...	Excel Can Complete With
Linear	0	1 2, , 3, 4, 5
	-50, 0, 50, 100	150, 200, 250
Growth	2, 4	8, , 16, 32, 64
	10, 100	1000, 10000
Date	1-Jan, 1-Apr	1-Jul, , 1-Oct, 1-Jan
AutoFill	Acctg-101, Acctg-102	Acctg-103, , Acctg-104
	Year '96	Year '97, Year '98

A Word About Printing

As with the other Office XP products, select File, Print to display the Print dialog box for your printer. You can select the number of copies and other print options depending on what features your printer supports. You might want to choose File, Print Preview to display a print preview before printing. This ensures that the printed worksheet looks the way you prefer.

Excel supports a new feature, called *Intelliprint*, that suppresses the printing of extra, blank worksheet pages that often appear because of the way a worksheet happens to appear on the printed page.

Adding Comments

You can insert *comments* in a cell. The comments act like yellow sticky notes onscreen, except that the notes in Excel aren't in the way when you don't want to see them. The comments don't appear in the cell; when you insert a comment, Excel indicates that the comment resides within the cell by flagging the cell's upper-right corner with a red triangle. When you point to the cell, Excel displays the attached comment.

To attach a comment to a selected cell, select Insert, Comment or right-click over a cell and select Insert Comment. Excel opens the box shown in Figure 9.7. Type your comment in the box and press Enter. Excel automatically places your name at the beginning of the comment (assuming that you entered your name when you installed Office). The name indicates who added the comment in case you work in a multiple-user environment. (You can erase the name if you don't want to see it.) You can leave co-workers notes if you edit worksheets as a team. You can also leave yourself a note to fill in data that you might get from an outside source later.

If you select a group of cells and attach a comment, Excel attaches the comment only to the upper-left cell in the selection. Excel cannot attach a comment to an entire selection, only to individual cells.

The earlier section in this hour, "Clearing Data," tells you how to remove comments you no longer need.

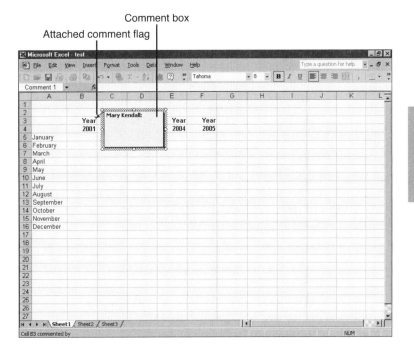

Figure 9.7
Comments help document the worksheet cells.

Summary

Excel's Copy, Cut, and Paste commands work much the same as the corresponding operations in Word. This hour focused more on the differences than similarities between the products. Worksheet data differs from a word processor's, and you must handle certain kinds of Excel deletions differently from Word deletions. Remember that deletions in Excel might affect other cells or formulas and result in erroneous data.

This hour taught you how to speed up your data entry by using AutoFill and AutoCorrect. After you teach Excel your own special series, Excel fills in that series of values for you. Although accuracy is more important than speed, you will welcome the speedy data-entry tools Excel provides.

Now that you have covered the groundwork, you are ready to learn about Excel's powerhouse worksheet formatting features.

Q&A

Q How do I know whether Excel can fill a series I have started?

A Enter the first couple of values, select the cells, and drag the selection's fill handle to the right or down, depending on your desired fill direction. As you drag the fill handle, Excel shows, in a ScreenTips-like pop-up box, which values will fill in the series. If Excel does not recognize the series, the pop-up values won't be correct. You then can teach Excel the new series as explained in this hour or enter the remaining values by hand. In many instances, you will be surprised at the power of Excel; if the first two values in your series are 10 and 20, for example, Excel guesses that you want to extend the series by 10s.

Q Why does Excel sometimes select additional cells when all I want to do is extend a series?

A You are dragging the cell's contents, *not* the fill handle. Be sure that you drag the fill handle when you want Excel to complete the series. If you drag with one of the cell's straight edges rather than its fill handle, Excel attempts to move the cell contents from their original location to your dragging target; therefore, be careful that you have grabbed the fill handle when you are ready for the fill.

HOUR 10

Formatting Worksheets to Look Great

This hour continues your Excel 2002 tutorial by explaining how to format your worksheet with professional styles. The AutoFormat feature in Excel quickly formats your worksheet within the boundaries you select. If you want to format your worksheet by hand, the formatting commands you learn in this hour will enable you to pinpoint important data and highlight that data. Others can then look at your worksheets and easily find your highlighted information.

The highlights of this hour include the following:

- What AutoFormat can do with your worksheets
- How to apply custom formats to selected cells
- How special orientation and wrapped text can improve your worksheet's appearance

AutoFormatting Worksheets

Before diving into additional formatting commands, remember that the AutoFormat feature in Excel converts an otherwise dull worksheet into a nice-looking, professional one. You saw how simple it is to use AutoFormat in Hour 7, "Excel 2002 Workbooks," when you applied an AutoFormat to the simple gradebook worksheet you created.

As you work in Excel, remember that a worksheet's presentation is almost as important as the data within the worksheet. If your worksheet needs sprucing up, try using AutoFormat because it gives a good-looking, consistent dimension to your entire worksheet. After AutoFormat completes, your worksheet will have a uniform appearance. You can then add finishing touches to the worksheet, such as highlighted totals that you want to make stand out.

To use AutoFormat, select the data in your worksheet that you want to format. AutoFormat works on selected cells, so you will need to select your worksheet data first. Select Format, AutoFormat to display the AutoFormat dialog box, as shown in Figure 10.1.

FIGURE 10.1
Let AutoFormat improve your worksheet.

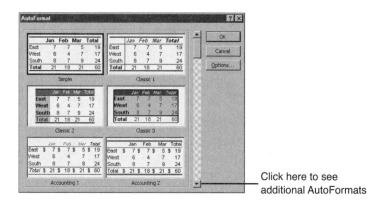

Click here to see additional AutoFormats

Scroll through the AutoFormat samples and choose any format. When you click OK, Excel applies the format to your selected worksheet cells. Figure 10.2 shows that AutoFormat knows to highlight totals and also knows to separate headings from the data detail.

To omit certain AutoFormat format styles, click the Options button in the AutoFormat dialog box to check or uncheck styles. You can keep AutoFormat from changing your worksheet's font, for example, by unchecking the Font option that appears.

FIGURE **10.2**

AutoFormat improved the appearance of this worksheet.

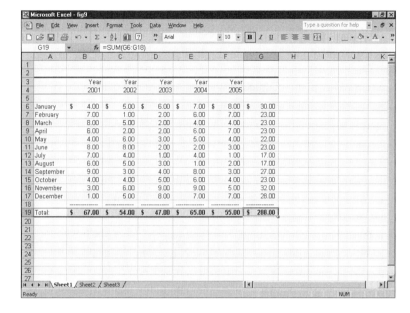

Modifying Styles

Suppose that you often print worksheets to fax to others, and your fax requires boldfaced worksheets so that the recipients can read the numbers. Instead of changing your worksheet text to boldface before faxing the worksheet, you can make boldface the default font style. Excel enables you to change several of the font defaults. So, if you find yourself applying the same font style over and over, consider making that style part of Excel's default style.

To modify the default style, follow these steps:

1. Select Format, Style to display the Style dialog box, as shown in Figure 10.3.

FIGURE **10.3**

You can change any named style.

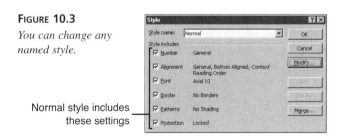

Normal style includes
these settings

2. Select the default style, Normal, from the Style Name drop-down list box. (The *Normal style* is probably already the style you see when you open the dialog box.)

3. To change the Normal style, click the Modify button. Excel displays the Format Cells dialog box, as shown in Figure 10.4, from which you can modify the named style.

FIGURE 10.4

The Format Cells dialog box allows you to modify any format currently set.

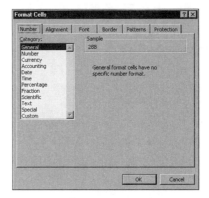

4. Indicate the changes you want to make to the style in the Format Cells dialog box. When you're finished, click OK to close the Format Cells dialog box.

5. Click OK to close the Style dialog box. Excel applies your style to the selected cells. If you made changes to the Normal style, Excel automatically uses that format on future worksheets unless you modify the format or style.

If you plan to create additional worksheets that are similar to the one you just created, consider saving the worksheet as a template. To do this, choose File, Save As and then select Template on the Save As Type list. When you are ready to create the next similar worksheet, load the template; your formats will already be in place.

Additional Formatting Options

Many of Excel's formatting features are identical to Word's, such as boldface, italics, underline, font color, and fill color (the cell's background color). In addition, you now know how to change the alignment for a range. Excel supports several special formats that go further to improve the look of your worksheets. AutoFormat uses some of these special formats, and you can create your own styles that use these formats as well.

The following sections briefly introduce you to these Excel formatting options, which provide you with additional ways to add impact to your worksheets. You can change any of these formats in the Format Cells dialog box. Open the Format Cells dialog box by selecting Format, Cells, or by pressing Ctrl+1.

Special Alignment

Not only can you left-justify, center-justify, right-justify, and justify across selected cells, you can also orient text vertically or to whatever slant you prefer. When you click the Format, Cells, Alignment tab, Excel displays an Orientation box inside the Alignment page, shown in Figure 10.5, in which you can adjust text orientation.

FIGURE 10.5

Align text with the Format Cells dialog box Alignment page.

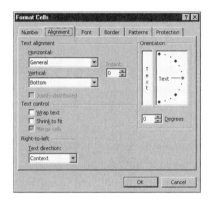

When you click the Alignment page's first orientation text box (the text box with the word Text dropping down the screen), Excel changes all selected cells to vertical orientation. If you want to slant text, such as titles, select a different Degrees value or click the rotating text pointer to the slant you desire. When you click OK, Excel rotates the selected text to your chosen angle. Figure 10.6 shows an example of slanted titles produced by selecting a negative 45-degree angle on the Alignment page of the Format Cells dialog box. The text prints at an angle as well.

If you need to include a lot of text in one or more cells, you already know that Excel either truncates the text or pours the cell's contents into the next cell to the right, depending on whether the adjacent cell includes data. Excel offers several other cell-overflow options as well.

When a cell includes a lot of text, select the Wrap Text option on the Alignment page of the Format Cells dialog box. Excel wraps the text within the cell's width, increasing the cell (and, therefore, row) height to display all the wrapped text. If you click the Shrink to Fit option, Excel decreases the cell's font size (as much as feasible) to display the entire cell contents within the cell's current width and height. If you click Merge Cells, Excel combines adjacent cells into a single wide cell.

Special Cell Borders

When you select Format, Cells and click the Border tab, the Border page (shown in Figure 10.7) is displayed. You can use options on this page to apply an outline, or *border*, around selected cells.

Slanted text alignment

FIGURE 10.6

You can change the vertical alignment of selected text.

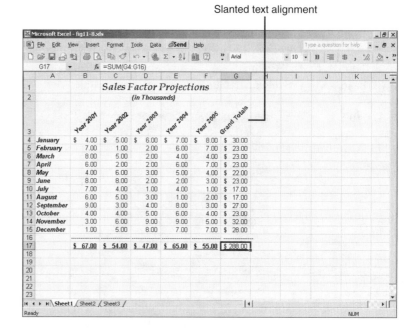

FIGURE 10.7

Add borders around cells to highlight key data.

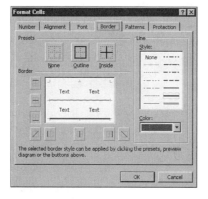

The Border dialog box enables you to add a border to any side of the selected cells as well as diagonal lines inside the cells so that you can show a cell x'd out or otherwise cross off a cell's contents for a printed report. As you select among the Outline and Inside options, the preview area shows what the resulting border looks like.

The Draw Borders toolbar button is quicker to use than the Border dialog box, but you cannot control as many border details.

Select Style options on the Border page to change the pattern of the border that you choose. If you want to remove any selected cell's border, click None on the Style list. Of course, the border's color, although black by default, can be changed easily from the Color drop-down list box.

Special Cell Shades

When you select Format, Cells and click the Patterns tab, the Patterns page appears and enables you to add color or a shading pattern to selected cells. The Fill Color button colors cell backgrounds more quickly than using the Patterns page options. However, the Patterns page enables you to add a shading pattern to the background in addition to a colored background.

Figure 10.8 shows the Patterns page's extended Patterns palette that is displayed when you click the Pattern drop-down list.

10

FIGURE **10.8**
Choose a pattern for the selected cell.

Available patterns

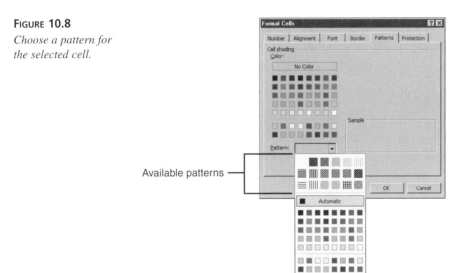

Protecting Cells

When you create worksheets for others, you want to lock titles and formulas so that users can enter and change the data areas without harming the worksheet's format. A hidden cell is useful when you want to block a cell's value from showing temporarily.

The Protection page controls locked and hidden status of selected cells. You enable and disable locking as well as control the hidden status by clicking the appropriate Protection options. Excel does not ensure that your users won't deactivate the protection and modify the worksheet. The protection helps protect the worksheet from accidental damage, but anyone can modify the protection status and change locked cells.

The locked and hidden cell settings activate only after you activate worksheet protection by selecting Tools, Protection and selecting one of the protection options. In other words, you must first select the cells to lock or
protect. After you've set the Tools, Protection options, those locked and protected cells activate.

Cell locking is great when you want to keep accidental worksheet changes from occur-
ring. If the protection needs to go further than simple safety, add a password when you
protect the selection. Only someone with the worksheet's (or workbook's) password can
unlock locked cells or show hidden cells. To add a password, select Tools, Protection.
You can add a password to the worksheet or to the entire workbook.

Conditional Formatting

Excel supports *conditional formatting*, whereby you apply a format based on data values
and not based on data type or position on the worksheet. Suppose, for example, you were
the manager of a company and needed to be alerted when sales fell below a fixed level of
$500,000. You could set a conditional format on your sales report worksheets to boldface
and color the sales values red if any of them fell below 500,000.

Figure 10.9 shows the Conditional Formatting dialog box that appears when you select
Format, Conditional Formatting. The Conditional Formatting dialog box uses these parameters:

- The cell value or the formula result of the selected cell (or cells) determines the
  format.
- The value or formula falls between or somehow relates the two values.
- The starting value and the ending value of the condition's range. Click the icons
  (named the collapse dialog box arrows) to point to cells that form the range if
  desired.
- The format that Excel is to apply if and only if the condition is met.
- You can set multiple conditions for the same selected range by clicking Add and
  setting up additional conditions.

Collapse dialog box arrows

FIGURE 10.9

*Format based on the
data value.*

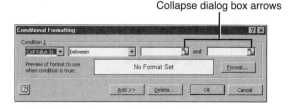

Tab Colors Help Separate Worksheets

If you do need to store multiple worksheets within the same Excel workbook file, you can apply a unique color to each worksheet tab. The colors enable you to more easily distinguish the worksheet tabs at the bottom of the screen.

To apply a color to a worksheet tab, right-click any worksheet tab and select Tab Color. Excel displays a color palette from which you can select.

> The tab colors affect only the tab and not the worksheet. After you click a tab to bring that worksheet into focus, the tab color, just as the worksheet (unless you've modified the worksheet's background) becomes white.

10

Summary

Having completed this hour, you can format your worksheets to look any way you want. If you want to let Excel give formatting a try, select your worksheet data and start Excel's AutoFormat feature. Add color, patterns, shading, and borders to your worksheets.

You have learned how to create great looking worksheets, but you have yet to see other ways that Excel can present data to users. In the next hour's lesson, you learn how Excel can display graphs and charts of the data you enter.

Q&A

Q When would I want to create a style?

A If you find yourself applying the same kinds of format commands to cells quite often, consider giving that set of format commands a style name by using the Format, Style dialog box. After you create a style, you can apply it by selecting it from the Style dialog box's list.

Q How can I change a locked cell?

A If you lock a cell, your intent is to prevent changes. Locked cells are especially useful when you create worksheets for others to use. By locking the titles and formulas, you ensure that the user can only change data areas. If you need to edit a locked cell, deactivate the worksheet's protected status. After you edit the cell, activate the protection (by choosing Tools, Protection, Protect Sheet) so that the worksheet is safe from inadvertent changes.

Hour **11**

Charting with Excel 2002

Your worksheet data can contain a ton of numbers, but many times you can present data better with a chart. The actual raw data supplied by a worksheet is accurate and vital information for analysis, but for trends and overall patterns, charts demonstrate the data's nature quickly and effectively. After you create and format your worksheets, use Excel's Chart Wizard to produce colorful charts (also known as graphs). The graphs that the Chart Wizard generates look great, and Excel does all the drawing work for you. After the Chart Wizard creates your charts, you then can customize them to look exactly the way you want.

The highlights of this hour include the following:

- How to use the Chart Wizard to produce graphs that show data trends and comparisons
- When to choose one chart type over another
- How to modify your charts so that they look the way you want them to
- Why an instant chart can come in handy
- How to add graphics to your chart's background area to improve the chart's presentation

Creating Custom Graphs

A picture is worth a thousand words—and worth even more numbers. Luckily, Excel can produce professional-looking graphs from your worksheet data. You don't need to know a lot about graphing and charting unless you want to create extremely sophisticated Excel graphs. Instead you can use Excel's *Chart Wizard* to produce great-looking graphs quickly and easily. When you click the Chart Wizard toolbar button, Excel displays the first Chart Wizard dialog box, as shown in Figure 11.1.

FIGURE 11.1

Excel's Chart Wizard creates graphs for you.

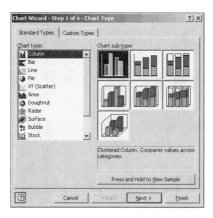

Choosing the Chart Type

Table 11.1 describes each of the chart types that Excel's Chart Wizard can generate. You select an appropriate chart type from the list on the Chart Wizard's first page. To preview the chart, click the Press and Hold to View Sample button. Excel then analyzes your worksheet data and displays a small sketch of the chart in the Sample box. The chart is only a preview of your final worksheet's chart, but a preview is all you need in most cases to know whether the chart is appropriate.

TABLE 11.1   Excel Chart Options

Chart Type	Description
Column	Shows changes over time and compares values.
Bar	Compares data items.
Line	Shows trends and projections.
Pie	Compares the proportional size of items against the parts of the whole.
XY (Scatter)	Shows relationships of several values in a series.
Area	Emphasizes the magnitude of changes over time.
Doughnut	Illustrates the proportional size of items in multiple series.

TABLE 11.1   continued

Chart Type	Description
Radar	Each category contains an *axis* that radiates from the center of the graph (useful for finding the data series with the most penetration, as needed in market research statistical studies).
Surface	Locates optimum combinations between two data series.
Bubble	Shows relationships between several series values, but also (with circles or bubbles of varying sizes) shows the magnitude of data intersections.
Stock	Illustrates a stock's (or other investment's) high, low, and closing prices.
Cylinder, Cone, Pyramid	Indicates trends and comparisons with special 3D cylinder, cone, and pyramid symbols.

If you are new to charting, you might not know which chart works best for a particular worksheet. If so, you only need to try a chart! If you see that a bar chart does not show a trend that you want to demonstrate, convert the bar chart to a line chart. Excel makes it easy to select from among several charts to find the best chart for your needs. Simply right-click the chart and select Chart Type from the shortcut menu that appears.

11

Selecting Data for Your Graph

A *data series* is a single group of data that you might select from a column or row to chart. Unlike a range, a data series must be contiguous in the row or column with no cells in between. Often, a series is composed of a time period, such as a week, month, or year. One person's weekly sales totals (from a group of several salespeople's weekly totals) could also form a series. Some graphs, such as pie charts, graph only a single series, whereas other graphs show comparisons between two or more data series.

As you look over your chart, if one of the series looks extremely large in comparison to the others, Excel is probably including a total column or row in the graph results. Generally, you want to graph a single series (such as monthly costs) or several series, but not the totals—the totals throw off the data comparisons. Therefore, if you see extreme ranges at the beginning or end of your graph, select only the data areas (not the total cells) from the Chart Wizard's second screen, shown in Figure 11.2.

Options on the Chart Wizard's second screen provide a way for you to determine exactly what data is to be charted. In a worksheet with lots of data, Excel cannot be expected to select data automatically. Not only must you inform the Chart Wizard of the data range (or series), but you also need to tell the Chart Wizard which direction the data series flows by clicking either Rows or Columns from the Chart Wizard's second screen.

FIGURE 11.2
*Be sure to select only
data areas for your
graph.*

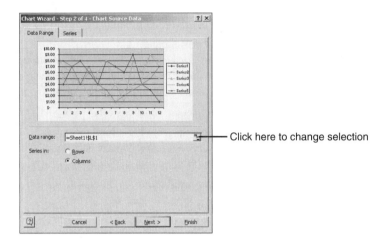

Click here to change selection

To change the range that the Chart Wizard is to use, click the Collapse Dialog button located to the right of the default Data range, select a different range, and then click the Expand Dialog button.

When you click the Next button to see the third Chart Wizard screen, shown in Figure 11.3, Excel enables you to enter a chart title that appears at the top of the resulting chart as well as axis titles that appear on each edge of your chart.

FIGURE 11.3
*Enter titles that you
want to see on the
chart.*

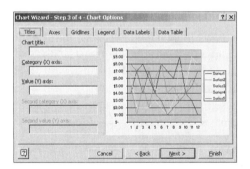

You find other tabs in the Chart Wizard's third screen that enable you to control the placement of the *legend* and a *data table*. The legend tells the chart's reader what series each chart color represents. A chart's bars and lines appear in different colors to represent the different series being plotted. You can also control the placement of the legend. As you select from the various legend placement options, the thumbnail picture of your chart updates to reflect your selection.

When you click on the Data Labels tab, you can determine how the Chart Wizard selects and places labels on your chart. For example, in addition to a legend, you might want to display the labels next to each piece of a pie chart, as Figure 11.4 illustrates. The Chart Wizard's charting options on the third step's tabbed pages change depending on the type of chart you selected. You might want to try different combinations of legends and labels until you find one that you prefer.

FIGURE 11.4

The Chart Wizard can place legends and labels where you want them to appear.

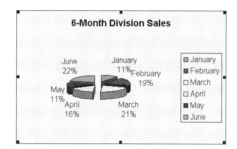

Click Next to see the final Chart Wizard screen, in which you determine exactly where and how to place the generated graph. Excel can create a new worksheet for the graph or embed the graph inside the current worksheet as an embedded object. Advantages exist for each placement; you might want the chart's data to appear next to the chart, or you might want to use the chart by itself. You can, in turn, embed the chart object in the other Office products, as you will learn in Part VII, "Combining the Office XP Products and the Internet."

Modifying the Graph

Click the Finish button to see your resulting graph. If you have chosen to embed the graph inside your current worksheet, you might have to drag the graph's *sizing handles* to expand or shrink the graph. In addition, you can drag the graph anywhere you want it to appear on your worksheet. Excel displays the Chart toolbar right below the graph in case you want to change it. Figure 11.5 shows a chart embedded as an object in the worksheet, along with the toolbar with which you can modify the graph.

If your graph does not display data the way you prefer, you can click the Chart toolbar buttons to change the graph's properties. You can even use the Chart toolbar to change the chart type (from a line chart to a bar graph, for instance) without rerunning the Chart Wizard. If you need to make more extensive graph changes, rerun the Chart Wizard.

In addition to using the Chart toolbar, you can often change specific parts of your graph by right-clicking the graph and choosing options on the pop-up menu. If you point to your chart's title and right-click your mouse, for example, Excel displays a pop-up menu from which you can choose Format Chart Title to display the Format Chart Title dialog box.

11

FIGURE **11.5**

The worksheet, graph, and Chart toolbar all appear together so that you can make necessary changes.

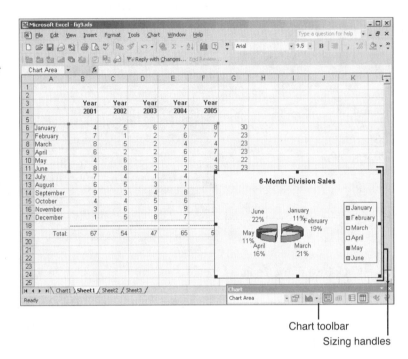

Chart toolbar

Sizing handles

When you single-click a graph's element, such as the legend or a charted data series, Excel displays sizing handles so that you can resize the element. If you double-click an element, Excel displays the Format dialog box for that element, allowing you to select the formatting options you want.

The mouse makes quick work of the chart's placement as well. You can click and drag within the chart area to move the chart to another location in your worksheet (assuming that you chose to embed the chart in the worksheet at the Chart Wizard's final step). You can also move the chart inside its own enclosing box to make more or less room for the legend.

A Quick Chart

If you want to create a chart in a hurry, you only need to do the following to generate a default column chart:

1. Select a range of values from your worksheet.

2. Press the F11 key or the Alt+F1 key. Excel immediately analyzes the data and instantly presents a generic graph on your screen such as the one in Figure 11.6.

FIGURE 11.6
Excel can generate an instant graph from a range.

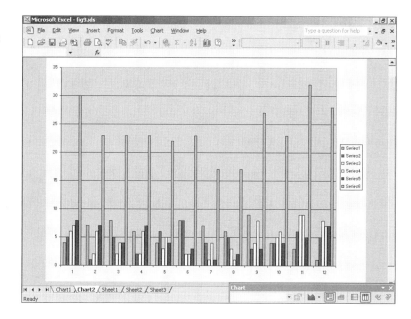

This quick graph won't have proper labels, Excel won't place the graph exactly where you want it (as a matter of fact, the chart will be placed on a newly-created, separate chart sheet), and it's possible that Excel will choose a chart type that does not suit your data. That's okay. The instant graphing feature exists to give you a quick glimpse at your selected data.

11

If the instant chart that Excel produces is somewhat like the chart you were hoping for, don't run the Chart Wizard to create a similar graph. Instead, right-click the chart's elements that you want to modify, such as the legend, and make your change. Excel already created the chart, so you don't need to go through the Chart Wizard once again to generate another chart.

Making Your Chart Fancy

In spite of the huge assortment of charts, you don't have to limit yourself to the chart types that Excel provides. You can customize virtually any part of the chart, including adding a background image.

Consider the rather simple-looking chart in Figure 11.7. When the user created this chart, she added a chart title and titles for the x- and y-axis descriptions as well. Nevertheless, the chart is lacking in style. It has no personality. It might be fully functional, but if the user wants to use it for a presentation, she might want to pretty it up somewhat.

FIGURE **11.7**

*Your chart can contain
chart titles that you
specify.*

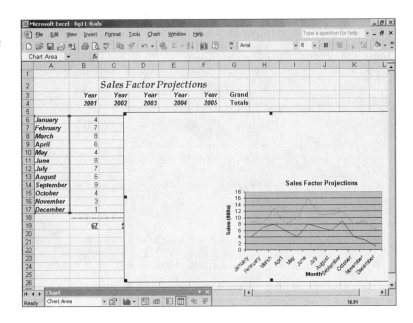

To add a background picture, you only need to follow these simple steps:

1. Click the chart to display the chart's resizing handles. Increase the size of the chart area by dragging the resizing handles outward.

2. Click the plot area to display its resizing handles and return the plot area to its original size. Move any titles and legend labels back to their place around the graph. You have now added some whitespace inside the graph's area where you can place a picture.

3. Click the Formatting toolbar's (not the Chart toolbar's) Fill Color down arrow to open the Fill Color palette. Make sure that you have the chart area selected and not a label or a title.

4. You could simply select a color and that color would fill the area around your graph. If you'd rather not use a simple color, you can fill your chart's background with a picture by clicking the Fill Color palette's Fill Effects to open the dialog box shown in Figure 11.8. Using the Fill Effects dialog box, you can select many different interesting fills for your chart such as the Variants area, which gradually changes one color to another.

5. Click the Fill Effects dialog box's Picture tab.

6. Click the Select Picture button and locate a picture on your disk to use as the background of your chart. Depending on how the picture mingles with your legend and graph titles, you might need to reformat the color and font size of those so they appear on top of the picture. Figure 11.9 shows the dramatic difference that a background picture can make as opposed to a chart by itself.

FIGURE 11.8

You can create a customized chart using the Fill Effects dialog box.

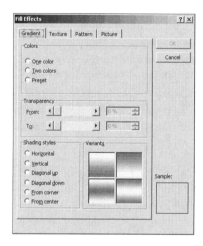

FIGURE 11.9

A background picture makes a dramatic difference in your chart's presentation.

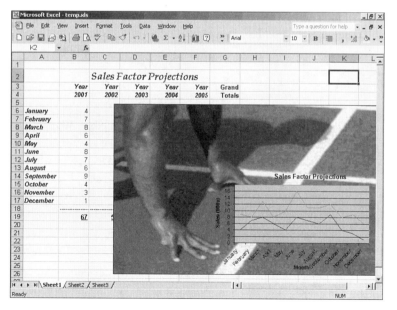

11

Use the Chart Toolbar

When you work with charts, the Chart toolbar comes in handy. If you don't
see the Chart toolbar, select View, Toolbars, Chart. From the Chart toolbar,
you can select any element in your chart from the Chart Objects drop-down
list box. You can then change any property about that chart object. Here's
how: Click the Properties button to display a Properties dialog box with
options that control the look of the object.

The remaining toolbar buttons come in handy when you need to modify
the chart. Perhaps the most commonly used are the Chart Type and the
Legend buttons that allow you to change the chart's type and show or hide
the legend.

Summary

This hour augmented your Excel tutorial by showing you how to turn your numeric
information into a graph. The numerous chart types that Excel supplies provide you with
a wealth of charting options. When you select the data you want to chart, the Chart
Wizard takes over and walks you through the rest of the chart's creation. After the Chart
Wizard does its job, you still are able to modify virtually every element of the chart.

In the next hour, you learn about PowerPoint. PowerPoint provides a way for you to present your data to the world by enabling you to create effective presentations.

Q&A

Q Can I add a picture as a background inside the chart's data area itself?

**A You can easily add a background to your chart. Whereas Figure 11.9 shows a pic-
ture that appears behind the chart's normal gray charting area (called the *fill area*),
you can override this background and place a picture behind the actual data lines,
bars, and points themselves. To do so, right-click over the fill area's background
and select Format Plot Area. Next, select Fill Effects and place the picture just as
you did in the final section of this hour.**

**Q Why would I want an instant graph from the F11 keypress if none of the
labels are accurate and if I cannot determine the graph type ahead of time?**

**A Excel's instant charting feature certainly does not produce final, presentation-ready
charts, but that's not the point. When you have data to analyze and you need a quick
look at the data, select the data in a range and press F11 (or Alt+F1) to see whether
Excel's default Column chart fits the nature of the data. If you want a fancier graph,
use the Chart Wizard and specify all the details of the chart. The instant charting
feature is available, however, for an initial look at a picture of your data.**

Part IV

Presenting with Flair

Hour

HOUR 12

PowerPoint 2002 Presentations

This hour introduces you to PowerPoint and shows you how to prepare for effective presentations. PowerPoint is a program that produces presentation graphics. By using the predefined presentation tools of PowerPoint, you generate good-looking presentations without needing to worry about design, format, and color specifics. After PowerPoint generates a sample presentation, you need only follow a few simple procedures to turn the sample presentation into your own.

The highlights of this hour include the following:

- What a presentation is
- How PowerPoint creates new presentations for you
- What kinds of data you can display in a presentation
- When to use the AutoContent Wizard

Presenting PowerPoint

Figure 12.1 shows the opening PowerPoint screen. (Your screen might differ slightly depending on the options that you chose during installation.) As you can see, PowerPoint is ready to begin. You can begin working on the first screen of your presentation right away by clicking and entering a title and subtitle for the presentation. The Task Pane shows a list of options for creating a new presentation (such as creating a blank presentation or opening a template on which you want to base a presentation).

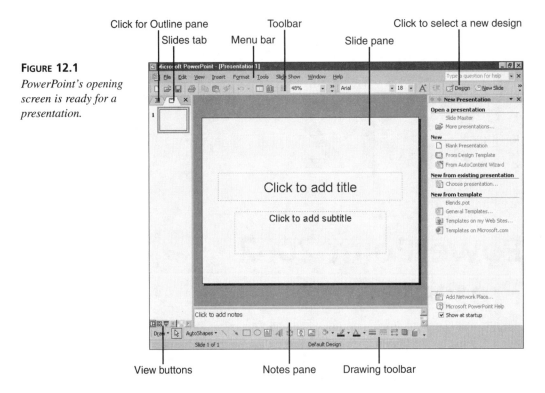

FIGURE 12.1
PowerPoint's opening screen is ready for a presentation.

The next section explains the importance of slides, or individual screens, within your PowerPoint presentation.

Understanding Presentations and Slides

The primary purpose of PowerPoint is to help you design, create, and edit presentations and printed handouts. A *presentation* is a set of screens (called slides) that you present to people in a group. Because PowerPoint provides a wide variety of predefined templates, you don't have to be a graphics design specialist to create good-looking presentations.

Throughout this book, the term *presentation* refers to the entire PowerPoint collection of slides whereas the term *slide* refers to an individual screen within a presentation.

PowerPoint slides can hold many kinds of information. Here are a few of the things you can add to a PowerPoint presentation:

- Data you insert into PowerPoint, including text, charts, graphs, and graphics
- Word documents
- Live data from the Internet including complete Web pages
- Excel worksheets
- Excel graphs and charts
- Access databases
- Multimedia content such as movies and sound
- Graphics programs that you use to create and edit graphics
- Other software programs whose data you import into PowerPoint

Creating a New Presentation

Figure 12.1 shows the opening window that you see when you start PowerPoint and begin a new presentation. If you close the Slide and Outline tabs window on the left side of the screen, you gain more room to work on the individual presentation slides that appear in the center of the screen.

The New Presentation Task Pane includes an option under the New section labeled From Design Template. Instead of starting to work right away on a blank (and generic) presentation, you can click the option to choose from one of many predefined presentation templates. Click the option now to see your New Presentation Task Pane change to the Slide Design Task Pane as shown in Figure 12.2. The Task Pane displays a list of many presentation style choices, all defined by templates. The idea is that you'll find the style you like, click that style, and your presentation's elements such as headings, background artwork, and fonts will all have a uniform appearance and tone.

The figure shows several design templates that contain layouts you can use. (Templates are stored in files that contain the .pot extension.) For now, don't select a template style, but scroll through the styles to see what is available. Design templates work well for creating PowerPoint presentations one slide at a time, but the design template might not be the best place to begin most presentations.

12

FIGURE **12.2**

*Templates help you
generate uniform pre-
sentations.*

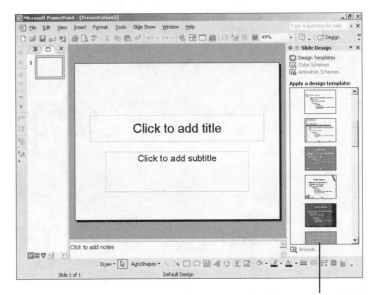

Available template-defined styles

Now that you've seen some of the ways presentations can look from the styles, you
should begin your first PowerPoint presentation by letting PowerPoint help you. The
AutoContent Wizard, covered in the next section, is often the best place to begin a new
presentation. Once you create a presentation, you can apply a different template if you
want to give your generated presentation a different style. If the Slide Design Task Pane
is still showing, click the back arrow at the top of the Task Pane window to return to the
previously displayed Task Pane. There, you will see the AutoContent Wizard option, and
you'll be set for the next section.

Planning is best done...in advance!

Plan your presentations! Think about your target audience. Presenting identical information to two different audiences might require two completely
different approaches. A company's annual meeting for shareholders would
require a different format, perhaps, from the board of director's meeting.

After you determine your target audience, think about the content of the
presentation. Create an outline before you begin. In the next hour, "Editing
and Arranging Your Presentations," you learn about PowerPoint's outlining
feature, which you can use to outline a presentation as you create the presentation slides.

The AutoContent Wizard and Presentation Design

Perhaps the best place to begin creating a new presentation, particularly if you are new to PowerPoint, is the AutoContent Wizard. This wizard contains a sample presentation with sample text and a selected design. To use the AutoContent Wizard, you follow a series of screens or pages to select a design and sample content that best suits your needs. After you create the sample presentation, you will enter and edit text that replaces the sample's text.

To use the AutoContent Wizard to create your presentation, follow these steps:

1. Start PowerPoint.

2. Click the New Presentation Task Pane's From AutoContent Wizard option to start the AutoContent Wizard's question-and-answer session. Figure 12.3 shows the first of four Wizard screens.

3. Answer the AutoContent Wizard's questions to design a presentation that best fits your needs.

FIGURE **12.3**

The AutoContent Wizard creates an initial presentation.

The AutoContent Wizard helps you to create a presentation with content in place. This presentation's design is intended to match the goals of your presentation. As you follow the AutoContent Wizard, you have to determine the answers to these questions: Who is your audience? What message do you want to convey? Are you selling or offering something? Do you want to display your presentation on a computer screen (as you might do via an overhead projection system), over the Internet (your PowerPoint presentations become Web pages if you want), as overheads that you print first (black-and-white or color), or as 35mm slides?

The best approach now might be to run through the wizard once to see the kinds of questions you are asked.

As you will recall from the previous section, PowerPoint comes with several predefined style templates. The AutoContent Wizard uses those templates by selecting the one that

12

best suits the goals you indicated by answering the AutoContent Wizard's questions. After the wizard generates the sample presentation, you can change the sample to include the details of your specific presentation.

Here are some of the template styles and presentation types the AutoContent Wizard chooses from:

- Bad News Communications
- Business Plan
- Corporate Financial Overview
- Corporate Handbook
- Corporate Home Page
- Employee Orientation
- Financial Plan

- Marketing Plan
- Project Status
- Reward Certificates
- Sales Flyers
- Team Motivation
- Technical Reporting
- Training

All these AutoContent Wizard presentations are available to you even if you don't want the help of the wizard. Instead, you can choose to create a blank presentation directly from a template. PowerPoint supplies two styles for each template: one for an Internet (or company intranet) presentation and one for a standalone PowerPoint presentation.

After you complete the AutoContent Wizard's steps, the wizard generates a sample presentation that matches the style you requested. The wizard generates several slides from that presentation and you can then rearrange, copy, edit, and delete them as needed. Figure 12.4 shows the screen after the AutoContent Wizard was used to generate a sample sales presentation. The left side of the screen shows a list of slide images or a descriptive outline of your presentation, depending on the tab you click. PowerPoint devotes the rest of the screen to whatever slide you select by clicking on a small slide thumbnail to the left.

Although your primary editing area for individual slides resides in the center of the screen, you can rearrange the presentation's slide order, delete slides, copy and paste slides to and from the clipboard, and see a high-level view of your presentation by clicking the Outline or Slides tabs. When you click on any thumbnail slide image on the Slide tab, that slide appears in the Slide Pane, where you can make specific edits.

After the AutoContent Wizard creates the presentation outline, you have to fill in the details. The AutoContent fills the slides with sample text and images, but you'll want to change that content to match the presentation you want to give. The remaining lessons on PowerPoint in this part of the book describe how to modify individual slides.

FIGURE 12.4

The AutoContent Wizard presents you with sample slides that you can edit.

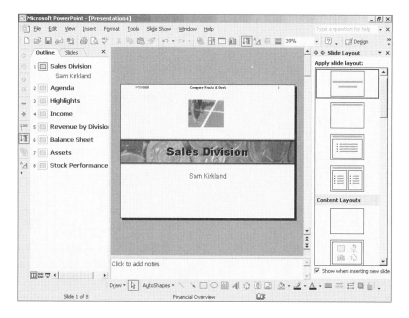

Creating Presentations Using Design Templates

As you learned in this lesson's first section, you can begin working on your presentation's first slide the moment you start PowerPoint. Instead of letting the AutoContent Wizard generate a sample presentation, you can select from one of the templates to get your presentation started with a design, and then add slides as you create your presentation using the same template so that your presentation maintains a uniform appearance.

If you click the toolbar's New button, PowerPoint does not open the New Presentation Task Pane but begins a new presentation with a blank slide and the Slide Layout Task Pane as Figure 12.5 shows. The presentation often includes placeholders that you can use to enter your presentation's content. You can choose from among the layouts to generate each slide's look. You won't have the uniformity throughout your presentation that a template would give you, but at the same time you have more flexibility to create exactly the look you require.

When you finish with a slide and are ready to add the next one, click the New Slide toolbar button and PowerPoint adds a blank slide to your presentation and presents you with the Slide Layout Task Pane once more. A presentation contains one or more slides, so you need to click the New Slide button every time you are ready to add the next slide to your presentation.

12

Slide layout task pane

FIGURE 12.5

You can forgo the AutoContent Wizard and templates and add slides that fit any layout.

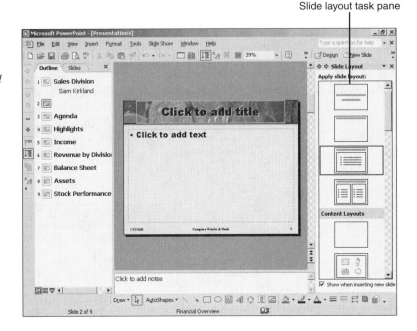

You can change the template design at any point while you're developing your presentation. To do so, just click the toolbar's Design button and the templates appear in the Slide Design Task Pane. When you select a template, PowerPoint converts your entire presentation to that template's format. Each slide's background image and standard text such as headings and footers will then take on a uniform appearance. If you then click another template, PowerPoint converts the entire presentation once again to that new template. You'll want to experiment with different templates to see which, if any, match the tone of presentation you want to achieve.

The instructions on the template's generated slide, as shown in Figure 12.6, indicate what to do next. These preset areas on each slide (placeholders) are designed to accept various kinds of data and make entering information on slides a snap. For example, you can click in a text placeholder and then type your text. In most cases, you edit the text, possibly change colors, and perhaps add a graphic image to the slide. Placeholders help you more easily do this.

After you have added the presentation's final slide, you can save your presentation. You can save the presentation in PowerPoint format or in HTML for embedding into Web pages. Even if your presentation has video and other multimedia content, you can save the presentation as a Web page for viewing from a browser.

FIGURE 12.6

The template's place-holders provide instructions you follow to create a unique slide.

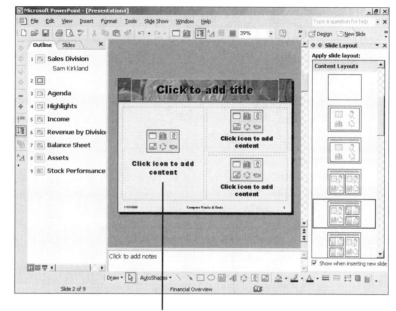

Placeholders with
editing instructions

You can save a presentation in much the same way as you save a file in Word or Excel. Choose File, Save As and then specify a name for your presentation. PowerPoint automatically adds the filename extension .ppt to your presentation's file.

12

As you can see, if you start out designing your own slides without the use of a template, you can, at any time later, apply one of the template styles to the slide. Therefore, if you don't like what you generate from scratch, PowerPoint enables you to redesign the slide or entire presentation without requiring that you re-enter the slide's text. If you save a presentation as a template file, you can use that presentation's format for subsequent presentations.

Without a template to get you started, presentations require that you manually create every slide element, including the text, titles, and body. Most slides have a title and text, and many have a graphic image. Why not let the AutoContent Wizard or the templates start things off right? The predefined slides work for so many purposes. Resist the temptation to create your slides from scratch until you acquaint yourself with the predefined slides. In most cases, the AutoContent Wizard and templates provide exactly what your presentation needs.

Presenting Your Work

As mentioned earlier this hour, after you create your presentation, you will be giving it to an audience using transparency overheads, computer screens, Web pages, or some other means of presentation.

Not only does PowerPoint help you create your presentations, but also it provides a way to present them. PowerPoint enables you to move from screen to screen, as a slide projector does, at whatever pace you request.

If you do not have access to a high-quality color printer or a 35mm slide printer, many of today's retail office product stores and retail copy centers let you take your PowerPoint presentations, on disk, to their stores where you can request color transparencies and copies of your presentations. In addition, major photography development businesses can turn your disk-based PowerPoint presentations into 35mm slides.

Summary

This hour introduced you to PowerPoint by showing you how to start PowerPoint and how to prepare for your initial slide presentation. PowerPoint prepares all kinds of presentations, all of which have one or more slides (screens). Use PowerPoint to create, edit, and even show your presentations in a slide-projector format.

The AutoContent Wizard is perhaps the best way to start using PowerPoint. Based on your answers to a few simple questions, the AutoContent Wizard creates a presentation with sample text and formatting. To turn the generated presentation into your own, just change the text and, optionally, change the slides' design elements.

The design templates also provide help when you want to add a new slide to a presentation. When you need to create a new slide, select the closest match from the list of design templates. After the design template creates a sample slide, just edit and modify the text.

The next hour shows you how easy it is to turn the AutoContent Wizard– or template-designed slides into your own.

Q&A

Q Do I begin with a PowerPoint template, the AutoContent Wizard, or a blank presentation when I want to create a presentation?

A Unlike the other Office products, you almost always create a presentation using the AutoContent Wizard or a template. A blank presentation requires you to lay out all your slide titles and text, which is too much work for most presentations. Unless your presentation requires unusual features, the AutoContent Wizard and templates produce presentations that will be close to your desired presentation.

Basically, all PowerPoint presentation-generation techniques end up producing a new slide on which you must add text, modify colors, change formatting, and add optional graphics. You learn how to apply these slide edits and make specific presentation improvements in the next hour.

Q **I'm still confused. What is the difference between the AutoContent Wizard and the design templates?**

A The AutoContent Wizard uses the design templates for its slides. The biggest difference between the two presentation-design tools is that the AutoContent Wizard creates a multiple-slide presentation with the sample content *and* designs in place, whereas the design templates develop a one-slide presentation with design elements present (but no content). You can use either the AutoContent Wizard or a template as a springboard to start your presentation and then customize it to fit your needs.

If you want to add a new slide to a presentation, you might want to use a design template for that individual slide. If you want PowerPoint to generate an entire set of general slides for a specific presentation, such as a corporate business meeting, you can let the AutoContent Wizard generate the entire presentation and then you can fill in the details that your presentation requires.

12

HOUR 13

Editing and Arranging Your Presentations

This hour shows you what to do after you generate a sample slide or presentation. PowerPoint's AutoContent Wizard and template samples generate good-looking presentations, but it is up to you to add the specific details that you need.

First, you need to change the sample's text. In the process, you might change or add slide titles and formatting, or maybe a graphic image for more impact. This hour teaches you a few shortcuts to turn the sample presentations into the presentation you need.

The highlights of this hour include the following:

- When to use the various views that help streamline your PowerPoint work
- Why you work most often using the Normal view
- What editing tools PowerPoint supplies
- How you can use the Slide Sorter view to arrange your slide show
- How to select the presentation printing option you need

Getting Acquainted with PowerPoint's Views

As do all the Office XP products, PowerPoint allows you to change the screen's view to make certain tasks more manageable. Therefore, you will produce presentations more quickly if you master PowerPoint's views now and learn the advantages and disadvantages of each view.

When you first start PowerPoint and work on a specific presentation, PowerPoint displays a three-pane view (called the *Normal view*) with the presentation's Slides tab and Outline tab in the left pane, a specific slide's content in the top center (called the Slide pane), and the Notes pane at the bottom of the screen. The Notes pane is where you can type notes for the speaker (later in this section, you will read about this Notes pane). The Task Pane is technically not considered to be part of a view because a different Task Pane appears depending on what you do within the same view.

The following list not only describes PowerPoint's views, but also explains how to use them to convert the template and AutoContent Wizard text to a specific presentation. As you read this section, pay attention to the information that teaches how and when to edit text from the AutoContent Wizard and design templates.

You display PowerPoint's various views from the View buttons in the lower-left of the screen as well as from the View menu. PowerPoint supports the following views:

- *Normal view*—The default, three-pane view from which you can manage your presentation's slide order as well as edit specific slides. In the previous hour's lesson, you worked only from the Normal view. To the left of the large presentation area reside two tabs, the Slides tab that displays thumbnail images of your presentation and the Outline tab that documents your slides' content.

  The Outline tab area enables you to edit and display all your presentation text in one location rather than one slide at a time. Figure 13.1 shows the Normal view that contains a presentation's Outline view in the left pane of a presentation. The large titles (by the slide icons) start new slides, and the details below the titles provide bulleted text for each slide. You can click and drag the dividing line between the presentation area and the outline to see more or less of either side.

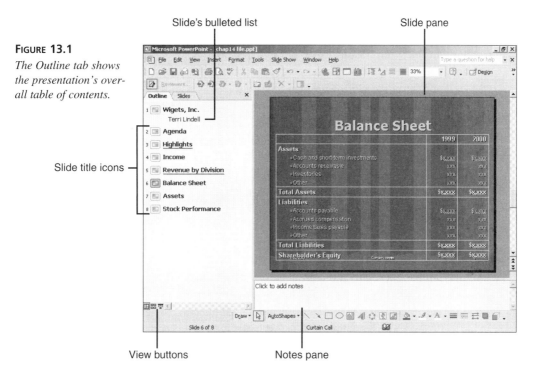

Slide's bulleted list

Slide pane

FIGURE 13.1

The Outline tab shows the presentation's over-all table of contents.

Slide title icons

View buttons

Notes pane

- *Slide Sorter view*—Displays your entire presentation so that you can easily add, delete, and move slides. The Slide Sorter view acts like a preview tool. You can review your presentation and use the Slide Sorter to present your slides in various ways. For example, you can use the Slide Sorter toolbar to set timings between slides and create special transitional effects when one slide changes to another.

- *Slide Show view*—Displays your presentation one slide at a time without the typical PowerPoint toolbars and menus showing.

- *Notes Page view*—Enables you to create and edit notes for the presentation's speaker. You don't normally have to select the Notes Page view to see the Notes pane because a small portion of the Notes pane always appears beneath the slide's detail in the Normal view. Click in the Notes pane and then add your text.

Change views by selecting the one you want from the View menu. You can also click the Normal View, the Slide Show or the Slide Sorter View buttons to the left of the horizontal scrollbar. You work in the Slide Sorter view most often when working with your presentation's layout and slide order, and you work in the Normal view most often when formatting individual slides. Slide Show view is used to display your presentation as a series of electronic slides.

13

Using the Outline

An outline helps you organize your presentation and sequence the slides properly. Although PowerPoint makes it easy for you to create the presentation slides themselves, the outline is easier to work with than the full slides, especially when you are still in the process of gathering your thoughts on the presentation's content. If you get in the habit of first working on the presentation's outline (after the AutoContent Wizard generates the presentation), you have less editing and slide rearranging to do later in the development of your presentation.

After you generate a sample presentation by using the AutoContent Wizard or by creating slides from the design templates, use the outline to work on your presentation's details. You can reorganize your slides and edit text in this mode. Click the topic or detail you want to change and edit the text. As you enter and change outline text, PowerPoint updates that individual slide in the Slide pane so that you also see the results of your edit to the outline.

All the familiar copy, cut, and paste features work in the outline. If you drag a title's icon or a bulleted list's item down or up the outline area, for example, PowerPoint moves that item to its new location. When you drag a title, all the points under the title move with it. This is a good way to reorganize slides. When you drag an individual bulleted item, PowerPoint moves only that item.

> Unlike previous versions of PowerPoint, PowerPoint now makes a copy of any outline item that you drag to another location if you hold the Ctrl key before you begin the operation.

Adding and Importing New Items

To add items to the text in the Slide tab's outline, click at the end or beginning of a bulleted item and press Enter to insert a new entry. If you want to insert a completely new slide, click the New Slide toolbar button, and PowerPoint displays the Slide Layout Task Pane from which you can select a design and then enter the text. You can also click at the end of an item and press Enter to enter a new slide.

One of PowerPoint's most beneficial text features is its capability to read documents from other Office products. If you create a Word document that you want to include on a slide (or series of slides), select Insert, Slides from Outline and select the Office file that you want to import to your presentation. The file does not have to be in an outline format. For example, you can insert a Word file that is either a Word document or a Word outline file.

As with all Office XP products, PowerPoint also recognizes HTML documents so that you can import or save Web page content directly within a presentation.

Promoting and Demoting Elements

From the Normal view, click the Outline tab to display the outline. When you select View, Toolbars, Outlining, the Outlining toolbar appears to the left of the Outline tab area as Figure 13.2 shows. The Outlining toolbar's most important buttons might be its *promotion arrows*. If you type a detail item that you want to become a new slide's title, click the left arrow of the Outline toolbar (the *Promote button*). To convert a title to a bulleted item, click the right arrow of the Outline toolbar (the *Demote button*).

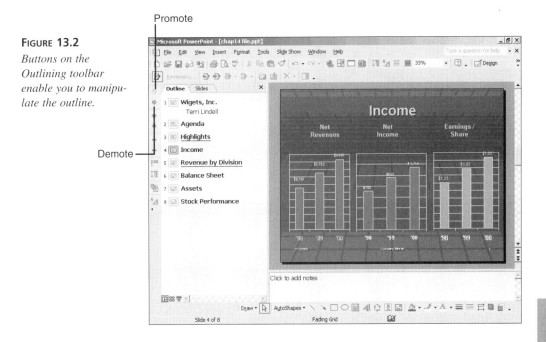

FIGURE **13.2**

Buttons on the Outlining toolbar enable you to manipulate the outline.

Working on the Slide

While in Normal view, you can look at and edit the selected slide in the Slide pane. As Figure 13.3 shows, the slide's viewing area appears in a full-screen view when you close both the left pane and the Task Pane. You can make edits directly on the slide and see the results of those edits as you make them. Use the Slide pane for viewing changes to your slide's design or for inserting graphical elements into the slide.

FIGURE **13.3**

By closing the surrounding panes, you devote more screen area to editing individual slides.

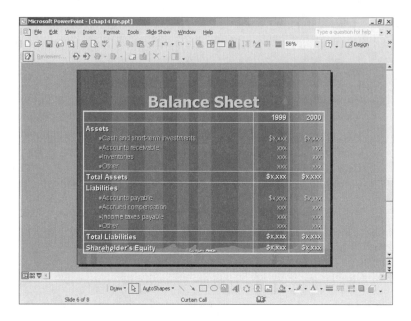

To move from slide to slide while viewing a single slide at a time, perform any of the following:

- Click within the vertical scrollbar area.
- Press the PageUp or PageDown keys.
- Click either the Next Slide or Previous Slide button on the vertical scrollbar.

When you want to edit a text (or graphic) object on an individual slide, click that object. PowerPoint displays the object surrounded by sizing handles. PowerPoint treats a slide's title as a single object and the slide's bulleted set of items as another object. If you've inserted other elements onto the slide, such as a sound or video clip, you can click on that object and move, edit, or delete the object as well. Figure 13.4 shows a busy slide with multiple selections. By holding Ctrl when you click over objects on the slide, you select each of those objects at the same time so that you can apply the same formatting task to the selected items. When you want to change the font or screen size of multiple objects at one time, select them all at once and perform the change only once.

To edit a slide's text, perform these steps:

1. Click the text you want to edit to display the text's sizing handles.
2. To move the text, drag one edge of the text's placeholder in the direction you want to move the text.
3. To shrink or enlarge the selected text object, drag one of the sizing handles in or out to adjust the object's size. (PowerPoint does not shrink or enlarge the actual text inside the placeholder as you resize the sizing box.)

4. After you display the placeholder, click inside the box at the point in which you want to edit text. PowerPoint inserts the text cursor (also called the *insertion point*) at the location of your desired edit. Move the mouse pointer out of the way so you can see the insertion point.

At the insertion point, you can insert and delete text. You can also change the font, color, size, and style of any text that you select using the Formatting toolbar or the Format, Font menu option. For example, to increase or decrease the font size, use the Font dialog box and select a different size. Displaying the Formatting toolbar will make the most common text formatting tools available, including font, size, bold, and underline.

FIGURE 13.4

Select multiple objects to apply a uniform edit to them at once.

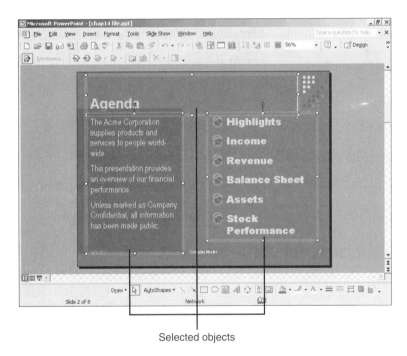

Selected objects

13

Select any text, and then click the Increase Font Size toolbar button to quickly increase the font size of the selected text. The Increase Font Size button works faster than opening the Font dialog box. (A Decrease Font Size button is also available.) Depending on your screen size and resolution, you might have to click the toolbar's Toolbar Options button to see the Increase Font Size and Decrease Font Size buttons.

If graphic images appear on the slide, double-click them to edit the images with the graphic-editing tools.

> If you right-click an object (such as a graphic image) while editing a slide and select the Action Settings option, PowerPoint displays the Action Settings dialog box, as shown in Figure 13.5. By assigning an Internet hyperlink address, a Windows program, or a sound wave file to a mouse click or movement, PowerPoint connects to that hyperlink location, runs the program, or plays the sound during the presentation. You can provide pushbutton access to programs and Internet Web pages while presenting your presentation!

FIGURE 13.5

Assign events to mouse clicks and movements.

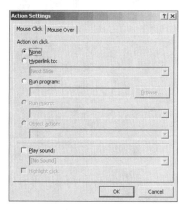

Using the Slide Sorter View

Use the *Slide Sorter view* to rearrange slides, not to edit text or graphics on individual slides. When you display the Slide Sorter view, PowerPoint presents several of your presentation slides, as shown in Figure 13.6. The Slide Sorter view enables you to quickly and easily drag and drop slides to reorder your presentation. Although you can rearrange slides from the outline, the Slide Sorter view lets you see the overall visual results of your slide movements.

Use your mouse to drag slides from one location to another in the presentation. Remember that the Undo command (Ctrl+Z) reverses any action that you accidentally make. You also can use the Windows Clipboard to copy, cut, and paste, although dragging with your mouse is easier. The Clipboard holds up to 24 entries that you can copy, cut, and paste as with Word and Excel. To delete a slide, click the slide once and press the Delete key.

Click to change slide transition   Slide sorter toolbar

FIGURE 13.6

Rearrange slides in the Slide Sorter view.

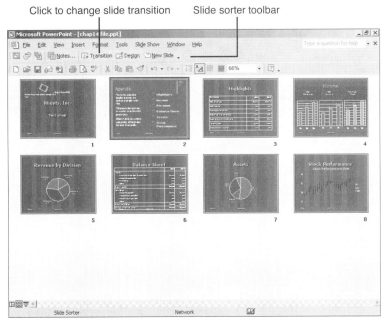

One of the more advanced (but useful) Slide Sorter features involves the Slide Sorter toolbar, which appears at the top of the Slide Sorter view (refer to Figure 13.6). When you click the Transition button, the Slide Transition Task Pane appears. These transition effects determine how the Slide Show feature *transitions* (dissolves) from one slide to the next when you display your presentation. The next two lessons discuss PowerPoint's Slide Show in more detail. For now, click a Transition button inside the Transition Task Pane to see the various ways that PowerPoint can move from one slide to the next.

Using the Notes Page View

When you select View, Notes Page, PowerPoint displays your slide, as shown in Figure 13.7, with a blank area at the bottom of the screen for speaker notes. This Notes Page view contains a slide image and, below it, a Notes box for the slide. Therefore, the speaker's notes contain the slides that the audience sees as well as notes the speaker wrote to tell the audience about each slide. Your audience does not see the speaker's notes. You click inside the Notes box to type or edit slide notes.

The Notes Page view is designed to allow printing of the notes for the speaker. However, the speaker can also display the Notes Page view during a presentation to eliminate paper shuffling. If the speaker's computer has two video cards and two monitors, PowerPoint can send the slides to one monitor and the speaker's slides and note pages to the other. When the speaker moves to the next slide, the speaker's notes change as well. When you're ready to return to the Normal view, simply double-click the slide image.

13

FIGURE 13.7

*Prepare speaker's
notes using the Notes
Page view.*

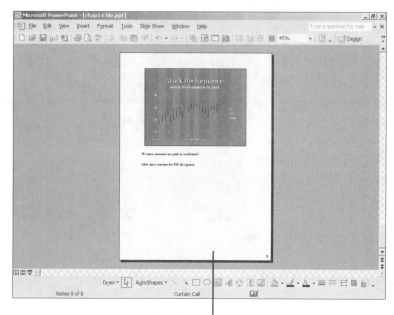

Type speaker's notes here

When the presentation is displayed in Notes Page view, you can use the
PageUp and PageDown keys to scroll through the slides and see the
speaker's notes at the bottom of each slide. If the text area is not large
enough to read the notes, expand the viewing area by using the Zoom command in the View menu.

Saving and Printing Your Work

Be sure to save your presentation after creating and finalizing it. PowerPoint automatically saves your presentation with the .ppt document filename extension unless you
override the default file type and save your presentation in another format, such as the
Web-based HTML format.

Of course, you also need to print your presentation, either to a color printer, or to a
printer that supports transparencies. The File, Print dialog box works somewhat differently in PowerPoint than in Word and Excel to take advantage of the special nature of
presentations. You can print your entire presentation one slide at a time or elect to print
multiple slides on one page for handouts. In addition, you can print only speaker notes,
and enclose printed slides in framed borders.

When you display the Print dialog box, shown in Figure 13.8, open the Print What drop-down list to view the selection list.

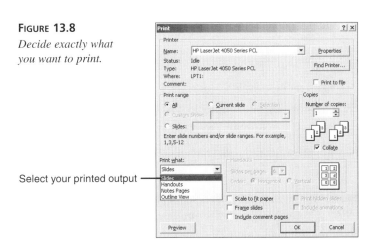

FIGURE 13.8
Decide exactly what you want to print.

Select your printed output

The Print Preview feature is new in PowerPoint. You can get an idea of how your presentation will look on paper by selecting File, Preview. If you have a black-and-white printer or one that is capable of printing multiple shades of gray (called *grayscale*), the print preview will display in black-and-white or grayscale. If you have a color printer, the print preview will display the presentation's slides in color.

PowerPoint can print your color presentation in grayscale if you don't have a color printer. Select Grayscale from the Print dialog box. In addition, the Print What drop-down list box enables you to print your presentation in any of these styles:

- Slides only for the presentation
- Handouts (which can hold from two to nine slides per page) so that you can give comprehensive notes to the audience
- Notes for the speaker
- The outline for proofreading purposes

If you want to print the entire presentation, you have to select File, Print and select All in the Print range section.

Summary

This hour furthered your PowerPoint knowledge by showing you how to turn a sample presentation into the presentation you want. The views are more critical in PowerPoint

13

presentation development than in Word or Excel. The different views give you a completely new perspective of the presentation. In addition, you use the different views for different functions, such as editing, rearranging slides, and previewing your presentation. Whereas one view is for the audience, another view exists for the speaker.

As you might expect, you can change PowerPoint slide text easily by using the basic text editing skills you have already mastered. The views enable you to view your slides, outline, and speaker's notes in their most usable form.

The next hour demonstrates how to format your slides with more detail, how to test and start the PowerPoint Slide Show, and how to spruce up your slides with graphics.

Q&A

Q I want to use PowerPoint to present my slides, but I don't want it controlling the transition and timing of the Slide Show. Can I use PowerPoint to display my slides manually?

A You learn about the details of the PowerPoint Slide Show in the next hour, but rest assured that it supports manual slide shows in which you control the appearance of the next slide. Actually, most presenters want complete control over the timing of the slide presentations, and PowerPoint supports such manual transitions. If you want to use PowerPoint to produce Web-based presentations, you can use the Slide Show feature as well.

Q Can I print everything (all views) with a single File, Print command?

A No, you can only print individual slide-show components, such as the speaker's notes, audience handouts, or slides from the File, Print menu. If you want to print all presentation elements, select File, Print Multiple Times and print a different component each time.

Q I'm using a bureau service to turn my presentation into individual color slides. Do I need the PowerPoint Slide Show?

A You learn about the Slide Show in the next hour's session. PowerPoint creates individual slides that you can print or display inside PowerPoint, over a Web page, or from any other source that displays PowerPoint presentations. The Slide Show does not have anything to do with the medium on which you present your final presentation, however, so you can turn your presentation into slides without using the Slide Show.

HOUR 14

PowerPoint 2002 Advanced Features

This hour explains how to format your presentations to add pizzazz and flair. With PowerPoint, your presentations won't be boring. You can format your entire presentation at one time or apply design templates one slide at a time. In addition to applying global presentation and templates, you can edit text and other objects on specific slides. Generally, the AutoContent Wizard and the design templates create presentations that require little editing; if you want to touch up specific parts of your slides, however, PowerPoint provides the tools you need.

The highlights of this hour include the following:

- How to modify your entire presentation's design template
- Why you sometimes need to make minor edits to individual slides
- How to insert art and text from other programs into a slide
- How to insert art and other clip files from the Media Gallery
- What PowerPoint tools you can use to work with text objects

Changing Your Entire Presentation's Design

PowerPoint enables you to apply a design template to your entire presentation. No matter whether you develop a presentation with the AutoContent Wizard, with individual design templates, or from scratch, you can easily change the format and look of your entire presentation. You might change your presentation's overall design because you want to give your presentation to a different audience, perhaps one that is more or less formal than the original audience. If you're publishing your presentation on the Internet, you might want to apply a template you've created that incorporates various design elements of your Web site.

> An audience change always warrants a review of your overall design. Suppose that you give a seminar to your employees on ethics and morals in the workplace, and then learn that your local Chamber of Commerce wants to see your presentation. You would formalize the style when you give your presentation to strangers. You would use a more serious tone provided by another template's design.

Use the following process to change the entire presentation's design template:

1. With your presentation open, click the Slide Design button on the Formatting toolbar to display the Slide Design Task Pane as shown in Figure 14.1.

2. Search through the templates for a design you prefer.

3. When you point (not click) your mouse on a template's thumbnail image, an arrow appears to the right of the image that you can then click to provide a menu of choices. You can choose to apply the new template's design to all your slides, to selected slides, and you can even display a larger image of the template to determine if it's one you want to use.

> You can enlarge the thumbnail views of the template's designs by selecting Show Large Previews from any of the template drop-down menus.

4. Instead of selecting from the template menu, simply click any template style once and PowerPoint will change the slides in your presentation to match the style you clicked.

5. After PowerPoint finishes changing the template design for your presentation, page through the slides to see whether you chose a good design. You can always go back through the process to change the design again, or undo the change.

FIGURE 14.1

You can apply a completely new design template to your presentation.

Use this task pane

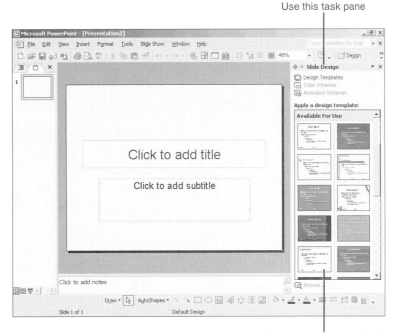

Click a template to select it

Changing a Single Slide's Design

In the previous section, you saw that you could change an entire presentation's design. Also, by simply selecting Apply to Selected Slide from the Slide Design Task Pane's drop-down menu, you can change only the current slide.

In either the Normal view or the Slide Sorter view, you can change the design of an individual slide by selecting the Apply to Selected Slides option from the template's drop-down list box of options.

You might be happy with the template but want to change the color set for a slide (or even the entire presentation). When you click on the Color Schemes at the top of the Slide Design Task Pane, PowerPoint presents you with a list of color schemes for your chosen template, as shown in Figure 14.2. Again, you can apply a color scheme to an individual slide to make that slide stand apart from the crowd, or you can apply the color scheme to the entire presentation by choosing the appropriate option on the drop-down menu.

The preceding section explained how to change the layout of your overall presentation. If you change an individual slide's color or template-based style and then apply a different template or color scheme to the entire presentation, the overall template design takes

14

precedence and changes any individual slide that you might have customized. Therefore, attempt to complete your presentation's overall design and color scheme before you modify individual slides.

Click here to display color schemes

Figure 14.2
Select a color scheme that you want for your presentation.

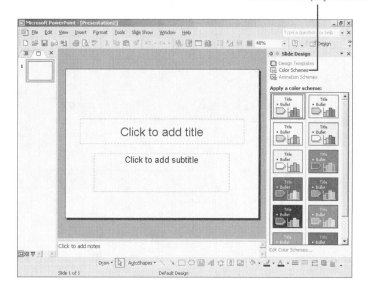

Editing Individual Slides

In most instances, the templates and individual slide layouts and color schemes provide ample variability and style. Rarely do you have to make substantial design edits to your presentation slides; usually you'll change only the text. Unlike most PowerPoint tutorials, this book does not go into great detail about slide editing. You don't need to edit the design of individual slides in most cases because of the detailed layouts that PowerPoint provides.

The major change you must make to the slides for a presentation created with the AutoContent Wizard is to add and edit text on the slides. All the spell checking and AutoCorrect features that are so important in Word and Excel also work for text you place in a presentation; a red wavy line beneath a word indicates that Office XP's spelling checker does not recognize the word. Correct the word, or add it to PowerPoint's dictionary by right-clicking the word.

You can create your presentation's slide text in Word and take advantage of Word's advanced word processing capabilities. For example, you can import a Word document into PowerPoint. You must, while creating the Word document, use the standard Word styles (such as Heading 1 and Heading 2) and not create your own because PowerPoint

uses these standard styles to determine what text converts to slide headings and to bulleted items beneath the headings on the slides. Use Word's File, Send To, Microsoft
PowerPoint option to send the Word document to PowerPoint and convert the document
to a presentation. You can then select styles that you want to change to add flair to the
presentation. Therefore, if you are planning to turn a report into a presentation, save
yourself some trouble and use some of the built-in styles in Word, such as the Heading
styles, for any headings in your presentation.

Word documents aren't the only documents you can import into a presentation. You can import an Excel worksheet, HTML-based Web page, chart, or
just about any other kind of file (including multimedia files) into a presentation. Select Insert, Object to display the dialog box shown in Figure 14.3,
click the Create from file option, and click Browse to locate the document
that you want to import.

FIGURE 14.3

*You can insert almost
anything into a presen-
tation.*

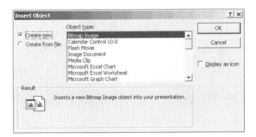

Given that PowerPoint 2002 makes quick work of modifying your overall presentation's
design and colors, you will need to spend some time concentrating on how to edit individual slides. The individual slides take a generic presentation that the AutoContent
Wizard generated and turns that presentation into your unique presentation that performs
the work you need done.

The Contents of the Master Style

The *Master style* is a collection of headings, colors, and fonts that give a presentation its personality. By selecting View, Master, Slide Master, you can see,
and edit, every element defined in your current Master style. Figure 14.4
shows the screen that appears when you display your Slide Master.

You can edit a Slide Master's title style, text styles, and level styles. In addition,
you can give your presentation a uniform header and footer appearance from
the Master style window. When you change something within the Master
style, that element of your presentation changes everywhere it appears.

14

FIGURE **14.4**

*View the Slide Master
to customize the way
key elements of your
presentation appear.*

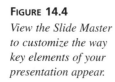

FIGURE **14.4**

*View the Slide Master
to customize the way
key elements of your
presentation appear.*

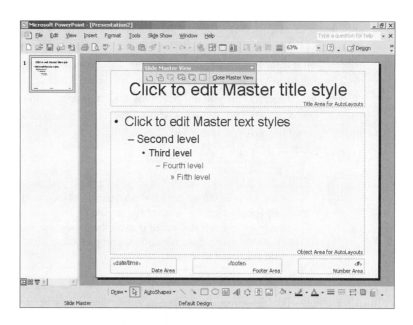

The following section describes the kinds of edits that you might want to make on individual slides when you need to hone a presentation.

Putting Comments in Your Presentations

The Insert, Comment menu option enables you to insert comments on a slide. The comments appear like small yellow post-it notes and automatically display your name and the date when you insert the note. After you enter a comment, close the note by clicking outside of it. When you do, it becomes a small box with your initials in it. Later, to read the note, you point to the small comment's icon box to read or edit the comment.

You can add as many comments to a slide or to a presentation as you want. After you add a comment, you can drag the comment to any place on the slide. The comment will not display in the final presentation's slide show.

Comments provide you with a simple annotation tool. You can add to-do notes to yourself for later modifications to the presentation. If you work in a group that is presenting this presentation, each member of the group can add comments for the rest of the group to read as the presentation is passed from worker to worker. This group annotation is perhaps the primary reason why PowerPoint automatically adds the user's name and date to the top of each new comment.

If you have used previous versions of Office, you were able to use the Drawing toolbar to customize the shape of your comments. You can no longer change the comments but must accept the default rectangular shape. Perhaps Microsoft took away this feature to make PowerPoint 2002 comments look and behave exactly like Word and the other Office products' inserted comments.

Adding Text and Text Boxes

To add text to a slide, such as text that describes artwork you've placed, you can use a text (or bulleted list) placeholder on a slide. Text placeholders are automatically included as part of some slide layouts. In addition, you can add a text box. A *text box* holds text that you can format. To add a text box, follow these steps:

1. Click the Text Box button on the Drawing toolbar. (The Drawing toolbar is located toward the bottom of your screen. If the Drawing toolbar is not there, select View, Toolbars, Drawing. The ScreenTips that pop up tell you what each tool on the Drawing toolbar does.)

2. Drag your mouse from the text box location's upper-left corner to the text box's lower-right corner. When you release the mouse, PowerPoint draws the text box, as shown in Figure 14.5.

FIGURE 14.5
You can type and format text inside a text box.

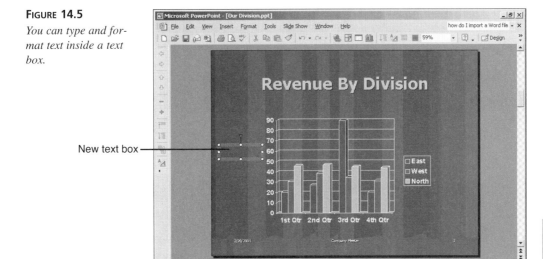

New text box ——

Text box button

14

3. Type your text. As you type the text, if your text box is not wide enough to hold the text, the text box will grow to accommodate your text by adding new lines when your typing reaches the right side of the box.

4. Use the Formatting toolbar and the Format, Font command to modify the text style and format.

5. Click anywhere outside the text box to deselect the text box and return to the rest of your editing chores.

As Figure 14.6 shows, when you click the toolbar's Font drop-down list box, PowerPoint displays each font name in its own font style so that you will see how each font looks before you apply one of them.

Click here

FIGURE 14.6

See a preview of the fonts before you select one.

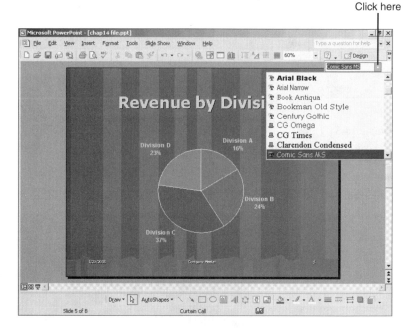

Modifying, Moving and Rotating Text

You can resize the text box, change the justification and font formatting, move the text box, add a border, and change the font and background colors by right-clicking the text box or by selecting the appropriate toolbar buttons.

If you want to format a copyright message at the bottom of every slide, for example, click the slide master's footer area (to turn the footer area into a text box) and edit the text there (or delete the text to get rid of the footer throughout your presentation).

One of the most impressive text-editing features is the *Free Rotate tool*. The Free Rotate tool enables you to rotate text to any angle. You might want to slant a title toward or away from text that falls below the title to add a special effect or to call out a cautionary note on a slide, for example.

To rotate text, click the text to display the text box. Remember that a placeholder or text box can appear around any text, including bulleted lists and titles, when you click those objects. After you display the text box, click the toolbar's Free Rotate button. The mouse pointer changes to a spiral-shaped pointer when you point to one of the text box's corners. Drag any of the four corners of the text box to rotate the text along an axis. (Figure 14.7 shows a rotated text box.) When you press Escape or click anywhere on the slide, the text box outline disappears and you see the rotated text.

The Free Rotate tool rotates selected bulleted lists and graphics, as well as text boxes.

FIGURE 14.7
Use the Free Rotate tool to rotate any slide's object.

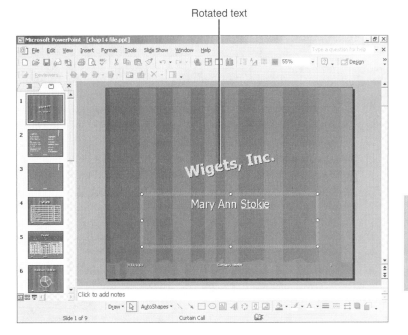

Rotated text

14

Adding Art

Suppose that you select a slide layout that contains a placeholder for art. Presumably, you have an art image to place on the slide or you would have chosen a different slide layout. When you select a slide layout that includes a placeholder for art, PowerPoint indicates exactly where the art is to go. Figure 14.8 shows an applied slide layout that includes a placeholder for artwork, for example. PowerPoint makes it easy to add the art. Follow the slide's instructions, and double-click within the placeholder to add the art.

FIGURE 14.8

PowerPoint indicates exactly where the art is to go on the slide.

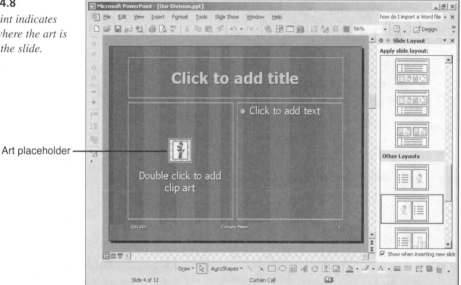

Art placeholder

When you double-click the clip art placeholder, PowerPoint displays art from your Office Media Gallery (you learned about the Media Gallery in Hour 6, "Advanced Word 2002." Your images appear in a dialog box such as the one shown in Figure 14.9. The art can be any graphic image, in addition to other kinds of objects such as video or sound. Scroll down through the clips to see what is available. If you have not yet set up the Media Gallery in another Office product, PowerPoint will first have to locate available clips on your computer. (To add and manage your clips, click the Task Pane's Media Gallery option.)

You can locate clips available online while in the Media Gallery. You are not limited to inserted clips from your own computer.

Click to insert

FIGURE **14.9**

PowerPoint indicates
exactly where the art is
to go on the slide.

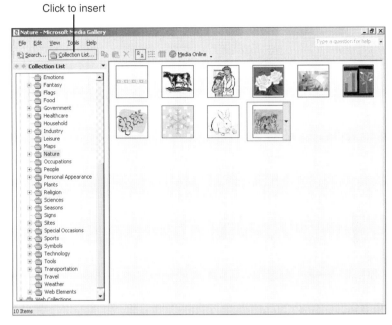

If you want to change the slide's clip art, click the image, press Delete, and insert
another one.

Your slide does not need to contain a placeholder for you to insert art. The placeholder
enables you to more easily manage the artwork, however, and to keep the art separated
from the rest of the slide's text and art. If you work with a slide layout that contains a
placeholder, you can move and resize the placeholder while you add the rest of the
slide's elements. When you are ready for the art, double-click the placeholder to insert
the art inside the placeholder's border. Without a placeholder, your artwork overwrites
existing text and graphics that already appear on the slide. You have to move and resize
the inserted art manually to make it fit with the rest of the slide.

Your art does not have to reside in the Media Gallery for you to insert it. You
can insert your own art files, such as logos and pictures, by choosing Insert,
Picture, From File and then selecting your file from its directory location.

14

If you want to import a scanned or digital camera image into a slide, you don't have to exit PowerPoint to scan the image. Select Insert, Picture, From Scanner or Camera. PowerPoint starts your scanner or camera image-loading software. Wait while you scan the image or connect your digital camera to your PC, and then insert the image into your slide.

Summary

You learned in this hour how to make presentations look professional, and how to modify individual slides when needed. When you work on a presentation with others on a team, the annotated comments provide you a means for distributing notes about the presentation to each other.

Get fancy with your presentation slides by adding graphics and rotating text. As long as your presentation does not get too busy, such distinguishing elements make your presentation more appealing and interesting.

One other technique that can really allow you to show off your presentations is animation. In the next hour's lesson, you will learn some of the ways that you can automate your presentation by controlling automatic presentations and determining the way that slides transition from one to the next.

Q&A

Q Why would I add a text box instead of using Outline view to add the text?

A The text on the Outline view is either a title or a bulleted item. If you want to place text outside these areas, you must draw a text box. You can draw a text box anywhere on a slide, and can even overwrite parts of a clip art image with a text box. Text boxes are useful for describing figures and for placing extraneous notes on your slides.

Q What if I don't have extensive clip art to embed in my presentations?

A PowerPoint comes armed with many images, so you might not need external graphics-art packages. In addition, PowerPoint includes links to the online world so you can search the Internet for clip art (as well as picture, video, and sound) files.

HOUR 15

Animating Your Presentations

This hour wraps up your PowerPoint tutorial by explaining how to accent and automate your presentation. PowerPoint's Slide Show feature enables you to watch an automated, pre-timed presentation one slide at a time. PowerPoint follows your slide show instructions and moves the slides forward at the pace and in the style you request. In addition to setting up an automatic presentation, you can control how PowerPoint transitions between slides and spruce up presentations with animation.

The highlights of this hour include the following:

- How a Slide Show automates your presentations
- How to set up a timed Slide Show
- How to add voice narration to your Slide Show
- How to add animated effects to your slides
- How to create custom animated effects that you design

Using PowerPoint's Slide Show

One of the best ways to see the overall effect of your presentation is to run a simple Slide Show; that is, walk through your presentation displaying your slides in sequence, moving from one slide to another, transitioning (changing) from one slide to the next without any special effects, but automating the moving at a preset timing that you can control.

An automated Slide Show is useful for creating self-running demonstrations, product presentations, and conference information distribution. PowerPoint screens use the term *kiosk* to describe the idea of a self-running presentation. Although you can control each and every detail of a self-running Slide Show, start with the basics and then expand your skills: add a timer to the presentation to control the amount of time each slide is displayed.

Timed Transitions

The Slide Transition Task Pane is the easiest place to specify slide transition details such as the timing required before the next slide in a presentation appears. Select Slide Show, Slide Transition to display the Slide Transition Task Pane. Figure 15.1 shows the Slide Transition Task Pane that appears.

Slide Transition task pane

FIGURE 15.1
Select the transition effect and timing.

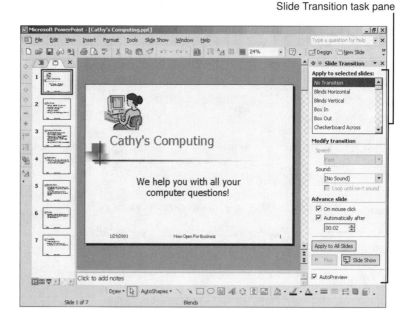

Follow these steps to automate the presentation:

1. Towards the bottom of the Task Pane, you will find an Advance Slide section. Uncheck the option labeled On Mouse Click. Doing so ensures that the presentation

speed will not be affected by mouse clicks; the presentation will be fully automated to change slides at a preset time interval.

2. Check the option labeled Automatically After (if it is not already checked).

3. Adjust the value of the minutes and seconds box to 3 seconds (displayed as 00:03).

4. Click the Apply to All Slides button so PowerPoint does not apply the timed transition just to the current slide. Leave all other values in the Task Pane alone for now. You have just informed PowerPoint that you want your Slide Show to run in a kiosk-style with each slide transitioning to the next every three seconds.

5. Start the Slide Show by clicking the Slide Transition Task Pane's Slide Show button or by pressing F5. The presentation begins. Each slide displays for three seconds before the next slide appears. When the final slide displays, PowerPoint displays a blank screen that you can click to exit and return to PowerPoint. During the presentation, click the mouse button and notice that the click has no effect on the presentation's speed. Ordinarily, a mouse click sends the presentation to the next slide.

6. Press Esc to stop the presentation and redisplay your presentation.

Just as Hollywood sometimes fades from one scene to the next, PowerPoint provides some interesting transitional effects that can make your slide transitions more interesting as you'll learn next.

Transition Effects

If you want more control over the transition, display the first slide in the presentation and select Slide Show, Slide Transition to display the Slide Transition Task Pane (if it is not still showing from the previous section). The top portion of the Task Pane determines how your slides can transition from one to the next.

You can control the way an individual slide transitions or the way all slides in your presentation transition. For example, to make the first slide transition to the second by dissolving from the first to the second, click the Dissolve option under the Task Pane's section labeled Apply to selected slides. PowerPoint shows you what the dissolve will look like by dissolving the current slide (as long as the box labeled AutoPreview is checked at the bottom of the Task Pane). Figure 15.2 shows the dissolve in progress.

 To adjust the speed of the transition, click the Speed drop-down list. As soon as you select a speed, PowerPoint dissolves the current slide once more at the new speed so that you can review the speed and adjust again if necessary.

FIGURE 15.2

You can dissolve from one slide to the next.

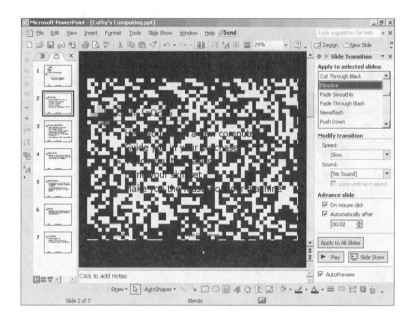

For an even more interesting effect, select a sound as well as a transition. PowerPoint will play the sound, such as applause, when that slide transitions. Some sounds are shorter than the dissolve effect. To repeat the sound until the next sound begins (so that the sound plays during the entire slide's appearance), click the option labeled Loop Until Next Sound.

For both sounds as well as transitions, if you don't click the Apply to All Slides button at the bottom of the Task Pane, PowerPoint applies the transition and sound only to the current slide.

If you want to use a uniform transition for all slides, click the Apply to All button. If you want the transition to affect only the current slide, click the Apply button to close the Slide Transition Task Pane.

Run through your presentation, using all transitions, before you make your presentation to your audience. Too many transitions can be distracting and can often slow down a presentation and reduce its effectiveness.

Setting Up Shows

PowerPoint provides a Set Up Show dialog box, shown in Figure 15.3, that you display from the Slide Show, Set Up Show menu option. The Set Up Show dialog box lets you control several features of your presentation and is useful whether or not you want to present an automated slide show.

FIGURE 15.3

The Set Up Show dialog box helps you manage your slide show.

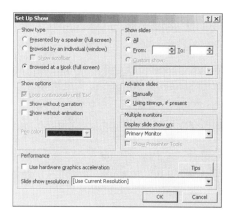

Table 15.1 explains the various options of the Set Up Show dialog box.

TABLE 15.1 The Set Up Show Dialog Box Options

Option	Description
Show type	Determines whether the presentation is fully automated, controlled by a speaker, or seen by an individual at the keyboard. The latter option displays the Slide Show inside a window, and the other two options display the Slide Show in full-screen mode.
Show slides	Determines if all the presentation slides appear or only a range of slides during the presentation.
Show options	Enables you to run the Slide Show presentation without narration or animation. In addition, you can select a pen color for marking during the Slide Show and set the Slide Show to loop continuously until you press Esc.
Advance slides	Determines if the speaker or PowerPoint transitions one slide to another.
Multiple monitors	If your computer has multiple monitors, as might be the case if you use a laptop and connect a projection screen to a second monitor card, you can request that the Slide Show appears on the second monitor while you control the presentation from the first monitor.
Performance	On slower computers, checking the Use hardware graphics acceleration can speed up a Slide Show assuming the computer has no system problems with the acceleration (errors will appear the first time you try this if the PC will not work). In addition, you can specify the resolution of the Slide Show no matter what the screen resolution was before the Slide Show began.

Rehearsing Your Slide Show

If you want your slides to transition at various speeds, you can manually adjust the speed one slide at a time. Some slides might require more time to read than others and you'll want such slides to remain on the screen longer than others. One of the easiest ways to adjust the timing between slides is to select Slide Show, Rehearse Timings.

As soon as you select the Rehearse Timings option, PowerPoint begins the Slide Show. As each slide appears (with whatever transition you've applied to that slide's appearance), keep the slide on the screen as long as you think it should remain and then click Next to move to the next slide. Keep clicking through the presentation at the speed you want PowerPoint to move. As you click, PowerPoint records the timing of each slide. At the end of the presentation rehearsal, PowerPoint displays a message box with the total amount of time that the presentation requires. You can save the timings or re-run the rehearsal to specify different timings.

If only one or two slides need their time adjusted, after you walk through the entire rehearsal, you can adjust those slides' transition time individually from the Slide Show Task Pane.

Voice Narration

If you have a microphone, speakers, and a sound card on your PowerPoint machine, you can add narration to your presentation. Doing so enables you to completely automate all the details of the presentation and not just the slides themselves. Voice animations are great for training sessions, employee orientations, and product demonstrations. They are also helpful for presentations that you distribute via the Web or a company intranet. You can record your voice as you narrate through the Slide Show, or you can use a sound file you've saved to your disk.

When you select Slide Show, Record Narration, the Record Narration dialog box appears (shown in Figure 15.4). Before you add narration for the first time, click the Set Microphone Level button to let PowerPoint adjust its recording volume as you speak into the microphone. You can also select a higher or lower quality of sound by clicking the Change Quality button. The higher the quality, the more disk space your presentation will require.

After setting up the sound levels and quality, click OK so that PowerPoint will begin the Slide Show. Even if you've already applied timing to the slides, PowerPoint waits for you to click your mouse button before moving to the next slide. Therefore, when the first slide appears, record the narration that you want your audience to hear on that slide.

Then click the mouse when you are ready to see the next slide and record narration for it as well. If you've set up transition effects, PowerPoint retains those effects as the Slide Show continues. At the end of the narration recording, PowerPoint gives you a chance either to save the presentation with the narration or not saving it so that you can have a go at it once again.

FIGURE 15.4

The Record Narration dialog box enables you to add your voice to presentations.

Using Action Buttons

An *action button* is a button you place on a presentation's slide that, when clicked during the presentation, performs a preset action. To add an action button, follow these steps:

1. Select the Slide Show, Action Buttons menu option. PowerPoint displays a sub-menu of Action buttons—many of which look somewhat similar to the buttons on a cassette deck. (If you wish, you can drag these Action buttons off the toolbar to create a floating toolbar.)

2. Select a button by clicking it.

3. Point to the location on the slide where you want the button to appear and drag your mouse to place the button on the slide. Resizing handles appear around the button (these resizing handles reappear if you select something else on the slide and return to the button) so that you can change the side of the button. You can also move the button by clicking on the button and dragging the button elsewhere on the slide.

4. The button by itself, no matter what the button's icon shows, does nothing. For example, if you placed an action button that looks similar to the Rewind button on a cassette deck, the button will not rewind your presentation. The button does nothing until you specify an *action setting* by selecting Slide Show, Action Settingsto display the Action Settings palette shown in Figure 15.5.

Table 15.2 describes the actions you can apply to the button. For example, if, during your presentation, you want to jump to the Internet and show your audience data from a Web site, you can place an Internet *hyperlink* (also known as a Web address) for the button's action so that when clicked, a Web browser opens and the Web page appears during the presentation. (If you are not connected to the Internet already, the presentation will log you onto the Internet and then display the Web page.)

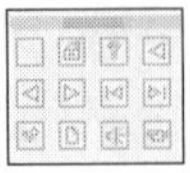

FIGURE 15.5

Specify exactly what you want the action button to accomplish.

The Mouse Over tab describes the action that occurs when the user points to the button on the screen. In other words, you can apply actions to the user's mouse movement so that certain things happen when the presentation's speaker moves the mouse pointer over the item on the screen without clicking the mouse.

TABLE 15.2   Actions You Can Apply to Slide Elements

Action	Description
None	Removes or keeps any action from occurring.
Hyperlink to	Jumps to the Web site specified by the hyperlink address when you click the button (the Web address must follow a standard format such as http://www.samspublishing.com/).
Run program	Executes the program you select (use the Browse button to locate the program if you don't know its exact location or name).
Run macro	Executes a set of keystrokes you've saved as a macro from the Tools, Macro menu.
Object action	Opens a special object, such as a video file, you've placed on the slide using the Insert, Object menu option.
Play sound	Plays a sound clip when the action occurs.

By the way, if you place action buttons on a slide, you should always specify actions for those buttons. Nevertheless, other elements of your presentation can also take on actions as well as the buttons. Any item you can select, such as a heading, title, or graphic image, as well as a bulleted item on a slide's list, can take on an action that you specify. Therefore, you can simply type the name of a Web site in a slide, select the Web site name, and apply a specific hyperlink to that text from the Action Settings window. You can click the link todisplay that Web page when you present the Slide Show.

Introducing Animation Schemes

One of the more interesting features of PowerPoint is its ability to animate the various elements of your slides as the slide appears during the presentation. Consider how captivating your presentation could be when any of the following occurs:

- The title flies onto the slide from the side before the rest of the slide's contents appears.

- The top half of the slide falls down from the top while the bottom half of the slide rises up from the bottom of the slide.

- The slide's graphics appear and the text slowly fades into view.

- Each bulleted item in the list comes onto the slide by each letter cart-wheeling into view.

- Paragraphs of text fade in at different moments.

- The title of your slide bounces into view and when it finally comes to rest at its anchored location, the rest of the slide appears.

The biggest problem with animation is not getting it to work but getting it to work far too well. Don't overdo animation. The animated effects are so fun to work with that it's tempting to add all sorts of fades, cartwheels, wipes, and bounces to the slides. After so many, your presentation will become so top-heavy with animation that the effect will be lost on your audience and the presentation will take on an over-done appearance.

To get started with animation effects, select Slide Show, Animation Schemes to display the Slide Design Task Pane shown in Figure 15.6 with the Animation Schemes option displayed. Read through the different animation options, and you'll see the plethora of effects that PowerPoint provides.

To apply an animation, first display the slide to which you want to apply the animation. Locate the slide by clicking on the slide's thumbnail at the left of the screen or by pressing PageUp or PageDown to display the slide. With the slide showing, click on one of the animation effects.

PowerPoint groups the animation effects by three primary categories: Subtle, Moderate, and Exciting. Each refers to the impact of the effect you choose. Any of the Exciting animation schemes will have far more action than any of the Subtle schemes. At the top of the Slide Design Task Pane, a list of Recently Used schemes will appear (assuming that you or someone else using your computer has ever applied a scheme in the past). Often, you'll want to reuse your favorite animation scheme, and PowerPoint keeps track of your most recent five animation schemes so you can quickly select that scheme once again.

FIGURE **15.6**

Specify animation by selecting from the Slide Design Task Pane.

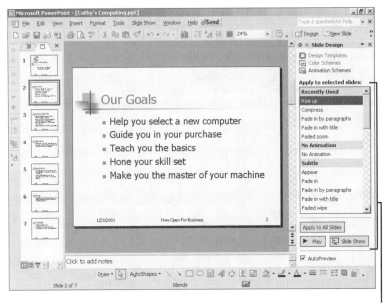

Animation Schemes task bar

If, after applying a scheme, you decide that you don't want the animated effect, click the No Animation option to remove the animation. If a slide is showing, display the Slide Design Task Pane and click on different schemes. PowerPoint will show you what the animation looks like.

All animation schemes—as well as transitions, sounds, and other actions you've learned about in this lesson—work whether you manually present your presentation or set up the presentation as a self-running, automated Slide Show.

Keep in mind that the animation schemes apply to specific elements of your presentation's slides. For example, the Rise Up animation first shows your slide's background image, then the title rises up from the bottom of the screen, then the rest of the slide appears. Unless you've created a slide from a blank slide—keeping all text in the same format and on the same outline promotion level with no animation added—the animation schemes can consistently apply themselves across your presentation if you reuse the same animation on different slides. If you ever change the presentation's Design Template (by clicking on the Slide Design Task Pane's Design Templates option and choosing a new design), the animations will still work but will be applied to the new design's elements.

Customizing Your Own Animation

In the previous section, you saw that PowerPoint comes equipped with numerous animations that apply themselves to various slide elements. For example, you can select animations that wipe the title onto the screen from the left, bring the details from the bottom, and fade the background graphics into view.

You don't have to use these pre-designed animations. You can specify your own with PowerPoint's Custom Animation feature. In other words, if you want the bulleted details of your slide to each appear individually, fading in from a diamond shape, you can instruct PowerPoint to produce that effect.

As with the non-customized animated effects that you learned about in the previous section, the Custom Animation effects will apply to presentations that automatically display in a kiosk-style Slide Show as well as animations that you present. You can set up the animation effects to appear due to one of several *triggers* including the following:

- When the slide loads
- When you click your mouse button
- As the slide exits and makes way for the next slide

You also control the speed of the animated effect as well as the *motion path*—the path that the animation follows if the animation moves around, onto, or off your slide.

Here is the general approach you will take when you want to create a custom animation:

1. Display the slide you want to customize.
2. Select any element on the slide by clicking on an image, on a title, on a chart, or on one of the details of the slide.
3. Select Slide Show, Custom Animation to display the Custom Animation Task Pane. You'll use this Task Pane to apply custom animations to your slide.
4. Suppose that you selected the title and you want to make the title spin 360 degrees, in a circle, when you click the slide during the presentation. Open the Custom Animation Task Pane's Add Effect menu and select Emphasis, Spin. The Emphasis effects are designed to help add emphasis to specific elements of your slide, such as an important point that you want to fly in from the side of the slide when you click your mouse button during the presentation. As soon as you select the emphasis, PowerPoint demonstrates how the spin will look, as Figure 15.7 shows. After the animation's preview stops, you'll notice that PowerPoint places a number 1 to the left of the title. This number is called an *animation tag*. As you keep adding your customized animation, PowerPoint will add more animation tags to the animated elements.

FIGURE 15.7

Preview how your Custom Animation's effect will appear.

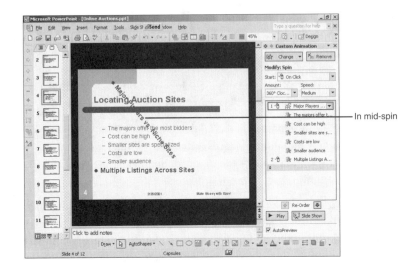

The reason the animation occurs when the speaker clicks the mouse is only because the default trigger for the effect, On Click, is selected in the Task Pane's Start list box. If you want your slide's animations to occur all at once, make the first one occur on a mouse click and then select With Previous from the list box for all subsequent effects.

When you click on a bulleted list of items on a slide, PowerPoint selects the entire list. Therefore, you can specify animation for the entire list. When you do specify customized animation for a list, PowerPoint puts the same animation tag number next to each item in the list. Figure 15.8 shows that the title has one customized animation and the bulleted list has another defined for it. All the items in the bulleted list appear together when the animation occurs because the animation tag number 2 appears next to each item.

Notice that Figure 15.8's Custom Animation Task Pane includes a Custom Animation list. PowerPoint adds to this list as you add more Custom Animation effects to the slide. Several slides within the current presentation might appear at any one time inside the Custom Animation Task Pane, depending on the amount of animation defined and your screen's resolution.

The Custom Animation list provides the details of your animation. Not only can you use this list to review the slide's animation, but also you can click on any item in the list to modify that animated effect. For example, if a slide's title fades into view too slowly, you can click on that animation effect with the Custom Animation list and change the effect to a faster speed. To review all the slide's animation, click the Play button at the bottom of the Custom Animation Task Pane.

One animation effect   Custom Animation list

FIGURE 15.8
Animation tags show which elements take on the same animated effect.

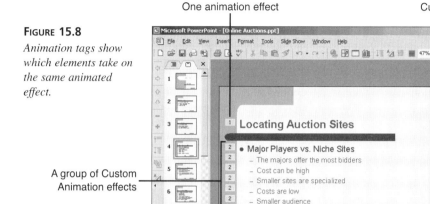

A group of Custom Animation effects

 If you apply multiple animated effects to the same item on a slide, PowerPoint places several animation tags next to that item to show that multiple animations exist for that slide's element. You can click on the individual tag numbers to modify the way the animation behaves.

Look through the Custom Animation Task Pane's options and review the many effects that you can create.

Summary

This hour concludes the tutorial on PowerPoint. You can now add animated effects to your presentations to add pizzazz to them and to create attention-grabbing kiosk Slide Shows. You can select from a wide range of animation effects that automatically and uniformly add animated effects to the elements throughout your Slide Show. In addition, PowerPoint gives you control over your specific animations by providing you with Custom Animation tools to create your own special effects.

Hour 16, "Communicating with Outlook 2002," shows you how to manage your contact, calendar, and e-mail with another Office product, Outlook.

Q&A

Q **Should I create an entire, narrated presentation when I give my presentation or control the presentation myself and narrate live?**

A PowerPoint makes it extremely easy to create a 100%, ready-to-go presentation that automatically moves from one slide to the next, in synch with a narrated sound clip that you store. The problem with this is, why would you want to do that if you were there and could give the presentation yourself live? Your audience will surely prefer to hear you give the presentation. You can still use the many slide tools available to give a powerful punch to your presentation, such as animation and transition effects between slides. By giving the presentation live, you can interact with your audience and go at the pace you sense is best for thcm.

People who give the same presentations, however, often have an entire kiosk-style presentation set up, with narration and timed transitions. If that speaker arrives on the scene of a presentation and has a cold or otherwise does not feel up to a live presentation, the audience still gets to hear the show. In addition, Web-based presentations require the automation that the kiosk-style presentations provide. Also, product demonstrations make excellent kiosk-style presentations.

PART V

Organizing with Outlook 2002

Hour

HOUR 16

Communicating with Outlook 2002

This hour introduces Outlook 2002, a program that can change the way you organize your life. Outlook is many things including an e-mail center, contact manager, electronic calendar, meeting scheduler, journal, and daily planner for to-do lists and other tasks. Outlook integrates with the other Office products so you can access name and address information from Excel or Word if you need to. Outlook can help handle the details of your life. Not only is Outlook a truly interactive planning and scheduling program, but it is also fun to use.

The highlights of this hour include the following:

- What Outlook is all about
- How Outlook differs from Outlook Express
- How to read and reply to e-mail messages
- What a contact is
- How to maximize your use of the Outlook 2002 Contacts database

An Outlook Overview

Here is a list that includes just a few of the tasks you can do using Outlook:

- Send and receive all your e-mail.
- Record business and personal contacts.
- Organize your Calendar.
- Schedule meetings.
- Manage appointments.
- Track prioritized to-do task lists.
- Keep a journal.
- Write notes to yourself that act as yellow sticky notes when you view them (similar to the comment feature of Word and Excel).

Outlook and Outlook Express

Do not confuse Outlook with Outlook Express. Outlook Express is an add-on program that comes with Internet Explorer and Windows. Outlook Express is a slimmed-down version of Outlook. Outlook Express supports only e-mail, a limited contact database, and a handful of other Internet-related features. Outlook Express does not replace Outlook, so feel free to use Outlook rather than Outlook Express for your contact information.

The Outlook Screen

The opening screen of Outlook can vary considerably depending on the current configuration. The default screen that shows after installing Outlook is the Outlook Today screen, shown in Figure 16.1. This Outlook Today view is defined by a folder inside Outlook called the Outlook Today folder and it shows an overview of messages, to-do tasks, and appointments for the current time period.

Figure 16.2 shows the Outlook Calendar folders that you see when you click the Calendar option at the left of Outlook's screen. The figure includes the Folder List, an optional pane that you can display or hide by selecting View, Folder List. The Folder List displays a list of all folders available to Outlook. As you use Outlook to organize your data, the amount of information you track with Outlook will grow considerably. To organize your data, you can create folders to store various messages and notes in. The problem with the Folder List is that it consumes screen space. However, most of the time, you can opt not to show it.

Today's appointments   To-do list   E-mail summary

FIGURE 16.1

Outlook's Outlook Today opening screen summarizes your current activities and messages.

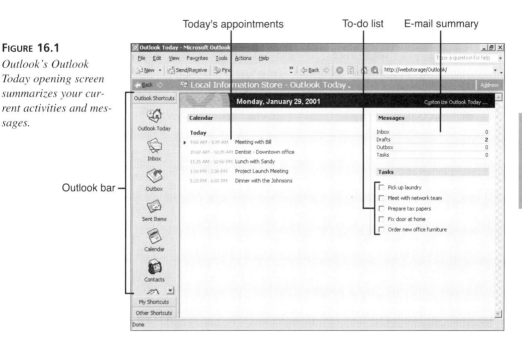

Outlook bar

Folder list   Select time frame

FIGURE 16.2

The Calendar folder's view shows appointments you've set up.

Click to change folder

The Folders List comes in handy because it shows all Outlook folders, whereas the Outlook Bar shows only icons for the default folders and any folders you've specifically chosen to place there. Folders not shown in the Outlook Bar appear when you click the My Shortcuts button at the bottom of the Outlook Bar.

The different Outlook folders produce screens that are quite different from each other, more so than the different views of the other Office programs. Here are common Outlook Bar folders you will find:

- *Outlook Today*—The at-a-glance overview of your current activities that you saw in Figure 16.1.
- *Inbox*—A collection of your e-mail messages, organized in topic folders that you set up, or contained in the default Inbox folder.
- *Calendar*—The scheduling screen where you can track appointments, as Figure 16.2 shows.
- *Contacts*—A card catalog of contact name and address information.
- *Tasks*—Items you have to prioritize and complete.
- *Journal*—A log of activities you perform on the computer.
- *Notes*—Notes on any topic that you want to organize.

Click the My Shortcuts button to see additional folders. The Outlook Bar is separated into groups, such as the Outlook Shortcuts group, the My Shortcuts group, and the Other Shortcuts group. If you need to further divide your Outlook data, you can create additional groups for related folders by right-clicking over the Outlook Bar and selecting Add New Group from the shortcut menu that appears.

> You can change the first folder that appears by selecting Tools, Options, clicking the Other tab, and then clicking the Advanced Options button. The drop-down list box, labeled Startup in this folder, determines the folder that appears when you first start Outlook.

The Outlook screen's format differs quite a bit from that of other Office products. You won't see the typical Formatting toolbar, for example. The Inbox folder (see Figure 16.3) is one of the most common folders you will display. Using Figure 16.3 as a reference, read through these descriptions to familiarize yourself with the Inbox screen elements:

- *Outlook Bar*—Displays the Outlook folders. You can rearrange the Outlook Bar contents and resize its icons. The Outlook Bar enables you to access all of Outlook's most frequently used data. You will use Outlook's default folders and create your own.

- *Inbox Folder contents*—Lists the e-mail that resides in your Inbox folder. When you want to read a specific message, double-click the message and Outlook opens a message window so that you can read the message.

- *Preview pane*—Shows the selected e-mail message's contents. You can display or hide the Preview pane from the View, Preview pane menu option. The Preview pane shows as much of the selected message as will fit; drag the separating window edge between the message list and the Preview pane to change the size of the Preview pane so that you can read more or less of the selected message.

16

Figure 16.3
The Inbox folder displays your e-mail messages.

Toolbar

Outlook bar

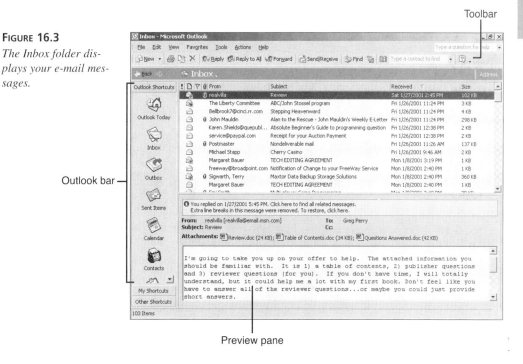

Preview pane

View Non-Outlook Data

Outlook is a versatile program as you are beginning to see. Word's primary purpose is to manage documents. Excel's is to manage worksheets. Access's is to manage databases. PowerPoint's is to manage presentations. On the other hand, Outlook manages many different kinds of information. The Outlook screen changes considerably as you work with the various kinds of folders. While in Outlook, you can even view non-Outlook data including Web sites.

When you click the Other Shortcuts button at the bottom of the Outlook Bar, you can display the contents of your My Computer folder, your My Documents folder to view files compatible with the Office products, and your Favorites folder to view Web sites that you have bookmarked. When you select a file or Web site from the Outlook Bar, Outlook starts your Web browser and displays the page or an Office program so that you can view and edit the file.

While working in Outlook, youcan view Web pages from within Outlook itself. Outlook provides a Web toolbar with which you can enter a Web page address and view the page from within Outlook, as done in Figure 16.4. When you click the Back button, Outlook returns you to whatever folder you were working in before displaying the page.

Web toolbar

FIGURE 16.4

Display Web pages from within Outlook.

Mastering Outlook Mail

The Outlook Bar displays the following labeled icons:

- *Inbox*—Holds incoming e-mail messages.
- *Sent Items*—Displays mail messages you have sent to others.
- *Outbox*—Holds messages that are queued to be sent.
- *Deleted Items*— items, including e-mail messages, that you have deleted but not removed from Outlook. Select Tools, Empty Deleted Items Folder to empty the Deleted Items folder.

When you remove an item from the Deleted Items folder, Outlook does not send the item to the Windows Recycle Bin; Outlook deletes the item completely from your system.

Organizing Messages

You can leave all incoming messages that you don't delete inside your Inbox. However, you can organize your e-mail by creating folders for different purposes and then moving e-mail messages (related to those folders) there. For example, you might want to store business-related messages in one folder named Business and e-mail for your family in one folder named Family.

Outlook manages e-mail from multiple e-mail accounts. The ability to separate messages into various folders comes in handy when you have two or more e-mail accounts. As messages come into the Inbox, you can move those messages to a folder for that e-mail account if you want to save them. Outlook supports a *rules wizard* that will even analyze your e-mail and automatically place e-mail messages in appropriate folders.

Outlook's Hotmail Connection

Beginning with Outlook 2002, Outlook integrates with Microsoft's free, online e-mail account named *Hotmail*, located at www.Hotmail.com.

You can send and retrieve Hotmail account e-mail messages from any Web browser in the world. Therefore, you don't need your Outlook to get your messages while traveling.

Outlook supports Hotmail accounts so that, when on your own computer, you can use Outlook to send and receive Hotmail e-mail. Therefore, you get the benefits of working in Outlook when in town, but you still get e-mail when you're away.

When you sign up for Hotmail, you can register for a Microsoft Passport account which is a service that enables you to log into different Web sites automatically but safely and securely. With a Passport account, you can take advantage of Hotmail's Messenger chat service to talk with other Messenger users around the world. Messenger supports both typed and even voice messages (as long as you have a microphone and speakers on your PC, although a headset works best), so you can talk free to anyone in the world. To activate Messenger once you've registered as a Messenger user, select Tools, Options, Other, and check the Instant Messaging option.

If the target folder appears in your Outlook Bar, you can drag any message to that folder. In addition, you can drag a message to a group name on the Outlook Bar and wait, while still holding your mouse button, until Outlook displays the folders in that group where you can place the file. You can right-click any message, select Move to Folder, and select any folder to which to move that message even if that folder is not listed on the Outlook Bar's currently-selected group.

To remove a message, just move the message to your Deleted Items folder. You can also click to select a message and press Delete or click the Delete button on the toolbar. If you change your mind about getting rid of a message stored in your Deleted Items folder, you can move that message from the Deleted Items folder to a different folder. Only when you delete a message from within the Deleted Items folder is that message completely deleted.

Setting Up an E-mail Account

When you first install Outlook on a computer that hasn't had a previous version used for e-mail, you will need to set up an e-mail account so that Outlook can send and retrieve messages. Setting up an e-mail account can, in some situations, be difficult to describe and perform because of the differences among the way that e-mail services function.

Fortunately, most current e-mail providers are following e-mail account standards, and e-mail accounts are more uniform that ever before. In addition, many *ISPs (Internet Service Providers)* automatically set up your Outlook e-mail account when you set up your computer for Internet access. Nevertheless, if you must install your own e-mail account, you can expect to follow these general guidelines:

1. Select Tools, E-Mail Accounts.

2. Click the option labeled, Add a new e-mail account and click Next. Outlook displays the E-mail Accounts dialog box that requests your e-mail account's server type.

3. Select the type of e-mail system your ISP uses. Unless you use a Web-based e-mail system such as Hotmail.com, most of today's e-mail systems follow the POP3 standard but you *must* get the server type from your ISP to be sure.

4. On the next dialog box, shown in Figure 16.5, assuming that you selected a POP3 e-mail account in the previous step as is most common today, you specify the most important parameters of your e-mail account. Specify the name that you want to appear as the recipient in messages that you send. Enter your e-mail address as well. You will need to obtain the POP3 and SMTP information from your ISP. Finally, if your e-mail account requires that you specify a name and password, you will have to enter that information as well. The information in this dialog box is generally supplied by your ISP, so contact your ISP for the details.

FIGURE **16.5**

Set up the specifics of your e-mail system.

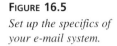

5. Click Next and Finish to finalize your account.

Creating and Sending Messages

A task you will perform often will be sending a message to a recipient across the Internet. To create an Outlook e-mail message, perform these steps:

1. From the Inbox folder, click the New button (or select File, New, Mail Message) to display the Message dialog box (shown in Figure 16.6).

Recipient's e-mail address

Click to change importance   Formatting toolbar

FIGURE **16.6**

Enter the message you want to send.

Enter subject here

Type message here

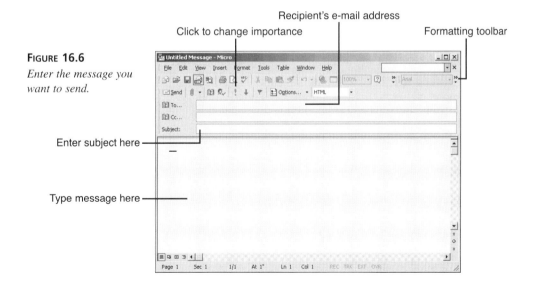

2. Enter the recipient's name in the To (your primary recipient) field. If you enter a name in the Cc (carbon copy) field, Outlook sends a copy of the message to that recipient. After you've set up contacts in the Contacts folder (described in a later section entitled, "Keeping Contacts"), you only need to click the To (and Cc)

buttons to display a list of contacts from which you can select. Your Contacts folder keeps track of names, phone numbers, addresses, and e-mail addresses so that when you've built a large collection of e-mail contacts, you'll rarely have to type an e-mail address in the To field again.

If you want to send the same message to multiple recipients, enter the e-mail addresses directly in the To field, separating each with a semicolon (;) or select multiple recipients from the Select Names dialog box that appears when you click the To button.

3. Enter the subject of the message. Your recipient sees the subject in the list of messages that he receives. The subject line is important for organizing e-mail messages in programs such as Outlook, so be sure to include a subject.

> Always enter a subject for your e-mail messages so that your recipient knows at a glance what your message is about. This also makes it easier for you to track sent messages.

4. Type your message in the large message area at the bottom of the Message dialog box. If you've got automatic spell checking turned on (available from the Tools, Spelling & Grammar dialog box just as in Word), Outlook locates spelling problems by flagging them with a red wavy underline.

5. Click the Options tab to select certain message options (such as the message importance level and a delivery date). The recipient, like you, can order received mail by importance level when reading through the messages. The toolbar's Importance button also determines an e-mail's importance.

6. Click the Send button. Outlook sends the message to your folder named Outbox.

7. Select Tools, Send/Receive to send your Outbox messages. Outlook finishes sending your mail and also collects any incoming messages waiting for you. If you are not logged on to the Internet, Outlook displays the Logon dialog box. Always check your Inbox for mail after sending mail from the Outbox using Tools, Send/Receive in case new mail was delivered to you.

Not all messages are text-only, and Outlook works with all file types. To attach another file to your message, such as a Word or Excel document, click the Insert File toolbar button and select a document file from the Insert File dialog box that appears.

You'll notice that the Message window sports a Formatting toolbar just as Word and Excel does. If your recipient can receive formatted e-mail (as most can today, with the exception of some older free e-mail services still in use), feel free to format your message's text.

Checking Mail

Regularly, you need to check your Inbox folder to see what items await you. As mentioned in step 7 of the preceding section, you must select Tools, Send/Receive to send Outbox items and receive Inbox folder items. Outlook logs you on to your Internet provider if needed. Your Inbox folder on the Outlook Bar displays a number indicating how many unread messages require your attention. When you select the Inbox folder, the unread messages appear in bold.

If you use multiple e-mail accounts, select Tools, Send/Receive and select the e-mail account that you want to check. You might use Microsoft Network at home and a local Internet provider at work, for example. You can set up both accounts on your home and office computer and select which account's e-mail to retrieve when you select the Tools, Send/Receive option.

Outlook uses icons to let you know what is happening. As you read each message, the message icon changes to show that the message has been read. Revert the read message flag back to an unread state by right-clicking the message and selecting Mark as Unread from the pop-up menu. A paper clip icon appears next to each message that contains an attached file. When you open a message with an attached file, Outlook shows the attachment as an icon that you can right-click to save or open it.

To read a message, just double-click it. To reply to the sender (in effect, sending a new message to your Outbox folder), click the Standard toolbar'sReply button and enter a reply. You can reply to the sender and all Cc recipients of the sender's message by clicking the Reply All toolbar button.

Outlook's e-mail management system is quite advanced with far too many options to cover in one hour. Generally, however, to send and receive e-mail, two of the most common uses of Outlook, you already have enough Outlook skills to do the job.

Keeping Contacts

The Outlook Contacts folder tracks your contacts so that you have a central, uniform repository of information to use when you send e-mail, hold meetings, and record calls. You can add new contacts, delete old ones you no longer need, and change information of a contact from the Contacts folder. The Contacts folder maintains name, title, address, phone, and e-mail information on your contacts, and it offers fields that you can use for additional information such as notes, family information, and more. In addition to the recording of contact information, Outlook uses an intelligent name and address checker to help ensure that your names and addresses are uniform for more accurate searching.

Recording Contacts

When you first use Outlook, you have no contacts entered in the Contacts folder (except for a sample contact that you can click to highlight and press Delete to remove). To record a new contact, perform these steps:

1. Click Contacts on the Outlook Bar.

2. Click the New Contact toolbar button on the Contacts screen to open the Contact dialog box (shown in Figure 16.7).

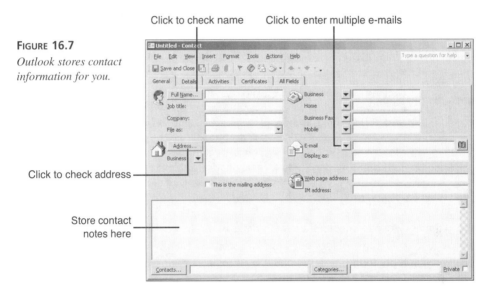

FIGURE **16.7**

Outlook stores contact information for you.

3. Type the contact's full name. If you click the Full Name button, Outlook displays the Check Full Name dialog box, shown in Figure 16.8, to maintain separate fields for each part of the name (such as title, first name, and last name). The time you take to separate the parts of a name pays off if you use your contact information in form letters and database work.

4. Enter the rest of the contact's information. Click the Address button to track separate parts of the contact's address using a Check Address dialog box similar to the Check Full Name dialog box. Click the drop-down Address list to record multiple addresses for the same contact. You can record a business, a home, or another address, for example, by clicking the appropriate drop-down address type before entering the address. Open the phone number drop-down lists as well to store different kinds of phone numbers for your contacts.

FIGURE 16.8

The Check Full Name dialog box ensures that your names are entered properly.

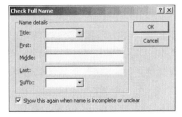

16

Click an arrow to the left of one of the phone number fields to see how many types of phone numbers Outlook tracks per contact. In addition to the four you see on the form, phone numbers for Business, Home, Business Fax, and Mobile, you can click the down arrow inside each of these fields to display a list box full of additional numbers such as Business 2, TTY/TDD, and Pager. Today's communication needs often require multiple phone numbers for the same contact, and Outlook provides all the phone fields that you might need. Any of the list boxes on the Contact form drops down to provide additional choices. You can enter multiple addresses and e-mail accounts for each contact, for example, although only one physical address and one e-mail address shows at any one time.

5. After you enter the phone numbers and e-mail addresses, you can enter a Web page site address in case you want to record the contact's Web page or the contact's company Web page.

6. The large text box toward the bottom of the New Contact window holds any notes you want to keep for this contact.

7. Click the Details tab to record other information, such as a spouse name, with the contact. The other tabs are for advanced purposes such as keeping digitally signed security IDs, and the All Fields tab enables advanced users to rearrange the fields on a contact's form. For most Outlook users, the General and Details tabbed pages are more than adequate to hold the information a contact requires.

8. Click the Save and Close button to save the contact information and view your contact in your Contacts folder.

When you close the Contact dialog box, your first contact appears in the Address Book. As you add more entries, your Contacts list grows, as shown in Figure 16.9. After you build a collection of contacts, you will click the alphabetic tabs to the right of the Address Book to locate specific contacts.

Index for contacts

FIGURE 16.9

Your contacts appear in Outlook's Address Book.

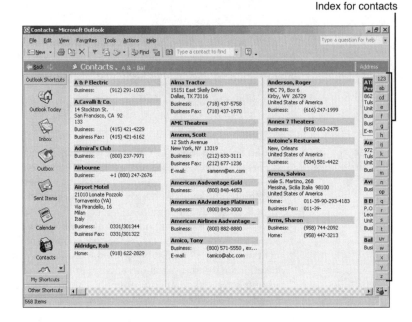

Selecting Contacts

To select a contact, display your Contacts folder and double-click the contact's entry. After you display a contact, you can do the following things:

- Directly edit the addresses, phone numbers, and e-mail addresses displayed on the page by clicking the appropriate fields.

- Right-click the contact name, select Call Contact, and dial the contact's phone number from the New Call dialog box (shown in Figure 16.10). If you click the Journal option, Outlook adds the call to this contact's Journal; the Journal records the call details. You can use the Journal to track calls such as payment requests so that you have a record of who you called and when you placed the call. The next hour's lesson explains more about the Journal feature.

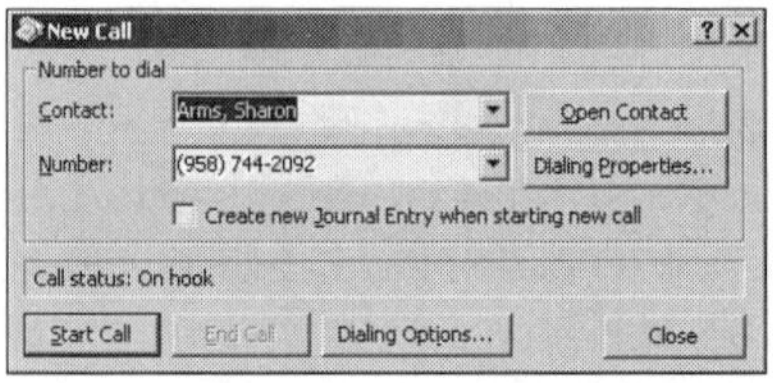

FIGURE 16.10

Outlook automatically dials your selected contact.

- Drag the column separators right or left to see more or less of each column. If you prefer to view narrow columns in the Contact folder, you see more contacts but not the full Phone Number and Address field. If you widen the columns, you see more detail for the contacts (but fewer of them at a time).

- Right-click the contact name and select New Message to Contact to write and send an e-mail message to the contact's first e-mail address.

- After you double-click on a contact to open that contact's information window, you can click the toolbar's Display Map of Address button (also available from the Actions menu) to see a graphic map of the contact's general address. Outlook goes to the Web (assuming that you have Internet access), locates the contact's address on a Microsoft Expedia Web map, and shows that location such as the one shown in Figure 16.11. Not only does the map pinpoint the address, but it also includes links to Web sites related to that area of the country.

FIGURE 16.11

View a map of where your contact resides.

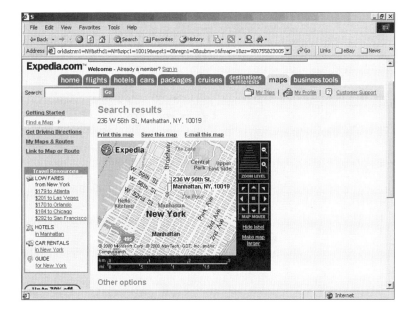

Summary

This hour introduced Outlook and explained Outlook's folders as well as how you can use Outlook to manage all your e-mail accounts. By adding to your contacts, you can place your e-mail recipients just a few mouse clicks away when you want to send them e-mail. When you master the next hour's lesson, you will know enough to manage appointments, schedule meetings, track to-do tasks, and keep notes for reminders you must remember. Additionally, the journal tracks events as they happen, including incoming mail that you receive inside the Inbox. All the features of Outlook work together to help organize your time tasks.

Q&A

Q How does a message reply differ from a forwarded message?

A When you reply to a message, you create a brand new message that contains new information about the recipient's original message. If you forward a recipient's message, you send the message exactly as you first read it to another recipient (or to a list of recipients).

Q Why doesn't Outlook send my messages immediately after I complete them?

A Outlook does not send messages until you select Tools, Send/Receive (F5 is the shortcut key for sending and receiving from all your e-mail accounts). If you use the Internet in an office setting with a T1 or other connection, you are probably logged on to the Internet most of the time. If you use a modem to access the Internet, however, you have to initiate the logon sequence when you want to check for e-mail.

Dialing and logging on takes time. Instead of logging on to your Internet provider every time you create an Outbox folder message, Outlook waits until you request the check for new mail to get your waiting mail and to send your outgoing mail. By waiting, Outlook only has to log on to the Internet one time to send all your messages.

HOUR 17

Planning and Scheduling with Outlook 2002

Outlook 2002 can handle the details of your life. Not only is Outlook an e-mail and contacts manager (as you learned in Hour 16, "Communicating with Outlook 2002"), but Outlook also manages your calendar, to-do tasks, and other items that help you perform your routine duties. In this hour, you'll learn how to use Outlook's calendar for keeping track of appointments and scheduling reminders for those appointments. In addition, you will learn how to use Outlook's secondary features such as journaling and notes management.

The highlights of this hour include the following:

- How to navigate through the Calendar views
- How to schedule meetings and events
- Which tools help you manage tasks
- How to use Outlook to keep notes
- When the Journal tracks items automatically
- How to incorporate smart tags to make it easier to locate and create new Outlook contacts and appointments

Using the Calendar in Outlook

Outlook includes a Calendar that not only enables you to organize and record dates, but also enables you to keep track of birthdays and anniversaries (and gives you automatic time-for-a-gift reminders), find open dates, keep a task list, and schedule meetings. It can also remind you of appointments. The following sections show you how to use the Outlook Calendar to organize your life.

> Not only does Outlook remind you of specific appointments with an audible and visible reminder, but Outlook also easily sets up recurring appointments, such as weekly sales meetings or annual birthday reminders.

When you are ready to work with Outlook's Calendar, display the Calendar by clicking the Calendar folder on the Outlook Bar at the left of the screen. You can also select Calendar from the Folder list. To display more of your Calendar, you can decrease the amount of screen space devoted to the Outlook Bar and Folder list by dragging their edges toward the left side of the screen.

> You can adjust the screen columns to show more of Outlook's features. Most Outlook users prefer to hide the Folder list, displaying it only when needed by selecting View, Folder List. Figure 17.1 shows the Outlook screen with the Calendar activated. In the figure, the Folder list is hidden to give more room to the appointments in the Calendar.

Navigating Times and Dates

Notice that the Calendar appears with these major sections:

- *The Date Navigator* (shown as a monthly calendar pane with two months displayed by default)—Enables you to move quickly through the calendar year
- *Daily Scheduler*—Enables you to enter and edit appointments for specific days
- *TaskPad pane*—Enables you to enter and edit a to-do list

When you first open Calendar, the Date Navigator always highlights the current date (getting its information from the computer's internal clock and calendar) by placing a square outline around the day. The current date's daily scheduler appears in the center of the screen showing the current day's appointments if any exist. The Date Navigator might show two months or just one, depending on your Outlook configuration. You can navigate the Calendar through days and months by following these simple guidelines:

- Change days by clicking the left- or right-arrow keys in the Date Navigator or by clicking a specific date with your mouse.
- Change months by clicking to the left or right of the Date Navigator's month name or by clicking the Calendar's month name and selecting from the pop-up month list that appears.

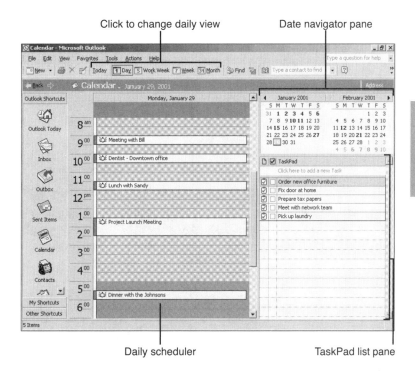

FIGURE 17.1
Working with the Calendar.

Click to change daily view   Date navigator pane

Daily scheduler   TaskPad list pane

Click through the Calendar's days and notice that the daily time planner changes days as you do so. Although you might not have any appointments set yet, you quickly see how you can look at any day's appointments by clicking that day's date in the Date Navigator.

The weekend's daily appointment pages are darkened to remind you that you are looking at Saturday or Sunday. In addition, Outlook darkens all weekday times before 8:00 a.m. and after 5:00 p.m. The darkened areas are typical nonbusiness hours. Of course, you can enter appointments into the darkened areas. The darkened highlight is just Outlook's way of letting you know the times are not typical business hours.

You can change the hours that Outlook designates as business hours by selecting Tools, Options and clicking the Calendar Options button on the

Preferences page. The Start time and End time list boxes hold the business hours that Outlook maintains. In addition, you can select other days to appear as workweek days in case you normally work on Saturday or Sunday. If you want Outlook to use a color that differs from the default yellow highlight, you can also select another color.

The Calendar also provides a month-at-a-glance format when you click the Month button on the toolbar. (Figure 17.2 shows the month-at-a-glance calendar that appears when you click Month.) When you click any of the month's weekday abbreviations in the Date Navigator area, Outlook displays the schedule for the entire month. If you click either the Work Week or Week toolbar buttons, Outlook shows the week's daily appointments but also still shows the Date Navigator in the upper-right corner. To return to the daily appointment view for today, click Day on the toolbar.

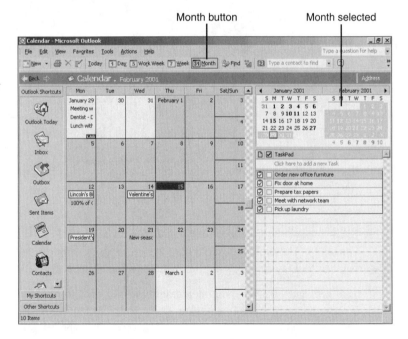

FIGURE 17.2

The month-at-a-glance calendar provides a long-range overview of your scheduled appointments.

Use the Date Navigator to show the daily appointments you need to see. As Figure 17.3 shows, if you select two days in the Date Navigator, both those days' appointments show in the center of the Calendar screen. The multiple days that you select in the Date Navigator do not have to be contiguous; hold Ctrl and click the days you want to see, and Outlook displays the daily appointments for those days.

Two days of appointments   Two days selected

FIGURE 17.3

You can view appointments for two non-contiguous days.

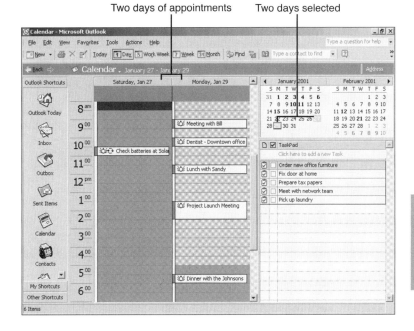

As you acquaint yourself with Outlook's Calendar, select from the View menu to customize the screen for your particular needs. In addition, you can drag any bar separating the window panes to provide more or less room to any portion of the Outlook screen that you need.

Setting Appointments

To schedule an *appointment*, perform these steps:

1. Click the Day button to display a single Day view.

2. Select the day on which you want to schedule the appointment by clicking it in the Date Navigator.

3. Locate the appointment time. You might have to click the daily appointment area's scroll bar or use your up- and down-arrow keys to get to the time you want to use.

4. Double-click the appointment time to display the Appointment dialog box, shown in Figure 17.4.

5. Enter the appointment's subject and location. Outlook keeps track of your locations as you add them, so you don't have to retype them for subsequent appointments. (You need only to select them from the drop-down list.)

6. Set the start and end times or click the All day event option if you want to schedule an all-day appointment.

FIGURE 17.4

*Scheduling an appoint-
ment is easy.*

Click to set a reminder ——

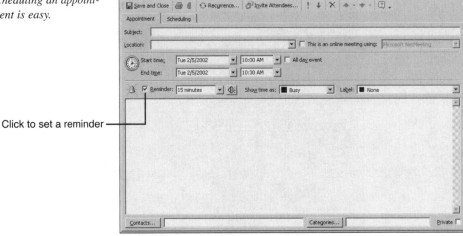

7. Click Reminder and enter the reminder lead time if you want a reminder. Outlook
   audibly and visibly reminds you of the appointment at the time you request.

8. Click the Recurrence toolbar button if the appointment occurs regularly. Outlook
   displays the Appointment Recurrence dialog box, shown in Figure 17.5. Set the
   recurrence options to enable Outlook to schedule your recurring appointment.

You could select Actions, Recurrence to go directly to the Appointment
Recurrence dialog box when you set up recurring appointments.

FIGURE 17.5

*Calendar easily
accommodates
appointments that
occur regularly.*

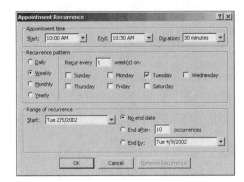

9. Click OK to close the Appointment Recurrence dialog box.

10. Click the Save and Close button. Outlook displays your appointment in the time planner by showing the subject in the daily appointment planner at the time of the appointment.

If you don't run Outlook all the time, Outlook cannot remind you of pending appointments. Therefore, add Outlook to your Windows Startup folder so that Outlook starts automatically every time you start up your computer.

If you need to change a set appointment, double-click the appointment to display the Appointment dialog box, in which you can change the appointment details. Drag the appointment's top or bottom edges from the time planner to increase or decrease the appointment's duration. Drag the appointment's side edges to change the appointment's start time.

17

If you select View, Preview Pane, Outlook displays a new pane below the daily appointments. When you click on an appointment, the Preview pane shows that appointment's details, but you can still see the daily appointments as Figure 17.6 shows. Many Outlook users think the screen gets too busy when this Preview pane is active. Instead of viewing appointments in the Preview pane, they double-click an appointment to open the Appointment window.

FIGURE 17.6

Use the Preview pane to see both the day's appointments as well as the selected appointment's details.

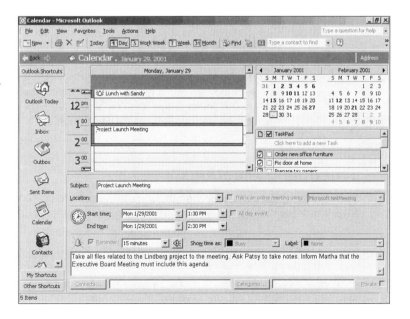

You can remove an appointment at any time by right-clicking over the appointment to display a shortcut menu and then selecting Delete. You can also click on an appointment and then click the toolbar's Delete button.

Instead of using the Appointment dialog box to schedule an appointment, you can enter an appointment quickly by clicking the appointment time once to highlight it and entering the text for the appointment directly on the daily appointment pane. When you press Enter, Outlook adds the appointment to the daily planner.

Outlook reminds you of the appointment with an audible alarm 15 minutes before the appointment. In addition, Outlook displays a Reminders window, such as the one in Figure 17.7. From the Reminders window, you can dismiss a reminder or click Open Item to modify the appointment's details. Click the Snooze button to be re-reminded of the appointment and select how much time you want to pass before being reminded once again.

FIGURE 17.7

Outlook reminds you
of any appointments.

You might not want an audible alarm on all appointments. If you use your laptop in meetings and do not want audible alarms interrupting conversations, for example, you can remove any appointment's audible alarm by double-clicking the appointment and clicking the speaker icon to uncheck the Play This Sound option. (You can also change the sound; play "Happy Birthday" on your spouse's special day!)

Scheduling Meetings

In Outlook terminology, a *meeting* differs somewhat from an appointment. An appointment is for you; it does not involve other resources (such as people and equipment). A meeting, however, requires that you schedule more people than yourself, and perhaps requires that you reserve other resources (such as audio-visual equipment and a room in which to hold the meeting). If you work in a networked environment and others on the network use Outlook, Outlook can scan other people's computer schedules to help you plan meetings that others can attend.

Follow these steps to schedule a meeting:

1. Create an appointment for the meeting's day and time.

2. Click the Scheduling tab in the Appointment window. (Figure 17.8 shows the page that appears.)

3. Click the All Attendees box to type the names of those whom you want to invite.

4. Click the Invite Attendees button and type the names of those attending. If you begin typing a name from your Contacts list and then press Ctrl+K after typing enough of the name for Outlook to locate the contact, Outlook retrieves the name from your Contacts folder and completes it. If two or more names exist that begin with the letters you've entered before pressing Ctrl+K, Outlook lets you select the correct name. Outlook displays the attendee's busy and free time in the grid to the right of the names.

5. Use the scrollbars to view the free and busy times for the people you invite. You must also select the meeting time. Outlook shows you the attendees' available free time when you click AutoPick Next, or you can use your mouse to schedule the attendees even if their free times conflict. (Outlook adjusts for time zones if you invite someone from another time zone.)

17

FIGURE **17.8**

You can schedule meet-ings, invite people, and reserve resources.

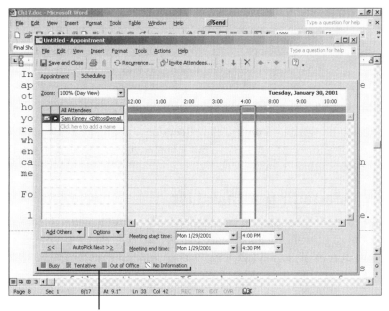

Legend shows grid's meaning

Obviously, you must be organized and know the attendees quite well to have access to their schedules. Outlook will search your network for the contacts and their free times. If you are not on a network, you do not have access to the free times of the people you invite.

When you click Send, all recipients (if networked or available by e-mail) get invited to your meeting by being sent the appointment's request.

Scheduling Events

An *event* is an activity not specifically tied to a time frame, such as a holiday or birthday. When you want to record an event, such as your boss's birthday, perform these steps:

1. Select Actions, New All Day Event. The Event dialog box appears (looking very much like the Appointment dialog box) with the tabbed Appointment page displayed.

2. Schedule the event as you would schedule an appointment, but click the All Day Event check box to show that the event lasts the entire day (otherwise, the event automatically turns into an appointment).

3. Select the Show Time As option if you want your calendar to show the time as Free, Tentative, Busy, or Out of Office. Outlook uses this value to send to others on your network who might invite you for an appointment during this time.

4. Select an appropriate reminder time from the Reminder list, such as 2 days, to receive an audible alarm and reminder window entry that informs you of the event so that you can purchase gifts or prepare for the event in some other way.

5. Click the Save and Close button to return to Calendar.

If the event is recurring, click Recurrence to initiate a new recurring event. When you view the event, Outlook shows it in a *banner* (a highlighted heading) for that day in the day planner's views.

Managing a Task List

A *task* is any job that you need to track, perform, and monitor to completion. Outlook tasks (such as appointments and meetings) might be recurring, or they might happen only once. You can manage your Outlook task list either from the Tasks folder in the Folder list or from the Calendar folder.

Unlike appointments, meetings, and events, tasks don't belong to any specific date or time. Tasks are jobs you need to finish but are not linked to a date or time.

To create a one-time task, perform these steps:

1. Click the New Task toolbar button or select File, New, Task. You can create a task even faster by double-clicking the Calendar screen's TaskPad's entry labeled Click Here to Add a New Task.

2. Enter a task description.

3. Type the due date (the date you must complete the task, but not necessarily the day you perform the task). If you click the Due Date drop-down list, you can select from a calendar that Outlook displays. You can enter virtually any date in virtually any format, including Next Wednesday. Outlook converts your format to a supported date format.

4. Click Save and Close to finalize the task.

After you complete a task, click the task's check box to cross the task from the list. Delete a task by selecting it and clicking the toolbar's Delete button.

> If you want to remind yourself of a task's deadline, make an appointment for the deadline on the task's due date. Set the alarm for 24 hours or 2 days. When the deadline draws near, you then are reminded that the task is wrapping up fast.

The Task window's Details page (see Figure 17.9) displays fields you fill out as you complete the task. The Details page even tracks such task-related information as mileage, time involved, companies utilized, and billing information.

FIGURE 17.9

You can track a task's completion details.

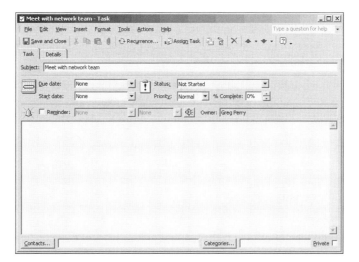

Writing Yourself Notes

Outlook notes are equivalent to sticky yellow-paper notes. You can post a note inside Outlook and retrieve, edit, or delete the note later. To see your notes, click the Notes icon on the Outlook Bar or display the Notes item from the Folder list. Double-click any note to see its contents.

To create a new note, click the New Note toolbar button to display a yellow-note window. Type your note and click the note's Close button to close the note. Resize the note by dragging its lower-right corner. Outlook records the note's date and time at the bottom of each note. Change the note's font by selecting a new font from the Tools, Options dialog box and clicking the Note Options button. You can quickly select a different note color by right-clicking the note's icon.

Turn notes into appointments and tasks easily if you need to. Drag a note from the Notes folder to the Calendar or Tasks Outlook Bar folder. Outlook will open an appropriate window with the note's contents, filling in the task or appointment's description. If you drag a note to your Outbox, Outlook creates an e-mail message with your note's contents.

Keeping a Journal

The Outlook *Journal* keeps track of all your interactions with contacts, Outlook items, and activities. Although you can make manual entries, the real power of the Journal appears when you automate Outlook to record the following types of Journal entries:

- Track and record all items (such as e-mail) that you send to and receive from contacts. Depending on the option you selected when you set up a contact, the Journal can automatically record all interactions with that contact, or you can record interactions selectively.

- Keep track of all Office documents that you create or edit. Browse the Journal to find a summary of the documents you created and the order in which you created (and edited) them.

- Track all meetings automatically.

- Track all appointments and tasks manually. (Outlook does not track appointments and tasks automatically; you must enter them yourself every time you add an appointment or task.)

- Manually record *any* activity in your Outlook Journal, including conversations around the water cooler.

Setting Automatic Journal Entry

Have you ever wished that you had recorded a complaint call you made when you got a bad product or service? Let Outlook track all your calls automatically. The Journal records times, dates, and people you called. As you use Outlook to make calls, record notes about the calls and track those notes in your Outlook Journal. After you open the Journal by clicking the Journal folder on the Outlook Bar or selecting Journal from the Folder list, you'll see the Journal Options dialog box shown in Figure 17.10 where you can inform Outlook exactly what to track. Request that Outlook record activities in selected Outlook activities, Office programs that you use, or contacts with whom you send or receive e-mail.

FIGURE 17.10

Select what you want Outlook to track.

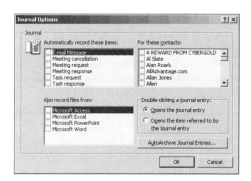

17

Adding Journal Entries Manually

The Journal cannot automatically record all activity in your life; however, you can add manual entries for any activities you want recorded. If you want to record an appointment, open that appointment (from within the Calendar). If you want to record an item not related to Outlook, such as a conversation, create a note for that item and transport the information from the note to the Journal folder.

To record a manual Journal entry from an existing item (such as a new contact you just entered), perform these steps:

1. Double-click the item you want to record to display the Edit dialog box for the item.

2. Select the item's Actions, New Journal Entry option. The Journal now contains an icon that represents the item, such as a phone call to the contact. Double-click the Journal's icon to display the item's details.

Suppose that you wrote a letter to your phone company, for example, and you want to record the complete document in your Journal. If you have set up your Journal to track all Word documents automatically, the document appears in your Journal. If you have not set up the Journal to track Word documents automatically, however, just display the document's icon in the My Computer window on the Outlook Bar and drag the document to the Journal icon on the Outlook Bar.

Periodically, delete older entries from your Journal that you no longer need. The Journal entries add up quickly. When you delete a Journal entry, the files the Journal entry describes are not deleted, only their entries in the Journal are.

The Journal consumes resources quickly. With the Journal recording activities, your use of Office can slow down because your computer will constantly be checking and updating your requested journal entries. Many advanced Office users simply don't use the Journal. They uncheck all activities from the Journal Options window and just use appointments to keep track of activities.

Smart Tags

If you've been working with Office as you've worked through this and the earlier lessons of the book, you have probably seen *smart tags* as you followed along and learned the software. When you enter data in an Office program such as Word or PowerPoint, that Office program underlines the data with a purple dotted line indicating the smart tag. A smart tag is data that an Office product recognizes as data that fits within a category, such as one of these:

- A person's name
- A time (dates, times, even relative dates such as Last Friday)
- Places
- Recent Outlook recipients

The primary purpose of smart tags is to keep you from having to leave your current program to perform a common task related to that smart tag. Outlook is the primary program in question. To clarify, suppose that you were writing a letter to a new client. When you type the client's name, Word displays or changes the name to include a smart tag underline. If you point to the name with your mouse, a smart tag action button appears as an icon above the name. Click the icon to display the menu shown in Figure 17.11.

Action button's icon

FIGURE **17.11**

Perform common
Outlook-related tasks
from a Word document.

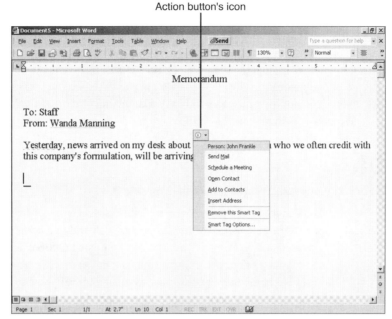

The actions on the shortcut menu enableyou to add the contact to your Outlook Contacts folder. If the name already resides in your Contacts folder, you can select Open Contact and the contact's window opens so that you can copy and paste information from the contact to your Word document. If the smart tag appeared on a date, you could schedule a meeting or show your appointments for that date while still working inside your Word document.

Without smart tags, you would normally have to leave your document to open Outlook, locate the contact, and then copy and paste the contact's information to your document. The smart tags save you some steps in this process. Although you still must work in Outlook's Contact windows, you are still closer to your Word document than you would otherwise be without smart tags.

You can modify the behavior of smart tags by selecting Tools, AutoCorrect and clicking the Smart Tags tab from your Word document. From the dialog box, you can turn off smart tagging, modify the smart tags that are currently active, and download additional smart tags from the Internet.

17

Summary

This hour explained some of the ways you can use Outlook to check your Calendar; manage appointments, meetings, and events; track tasks; keep notes; and explore your computer. Additionally, the journal tracks events as they happen, including incoming mail that you receive inside the Inbox. If you have used any other personal-information management program, you will really like the integration of Outlook into the Office and Windows environment.

Q&A

Q How can I assign a task to a specific day?

A You cannot assign tasks to days. Tasks transcend days because tasks are one-time or recurring items that you must accomplish within a certain time frame, but not on a particular day. Perhaps you are only confusing Outlook terminology. If you want to assign a particular event to a time and day, assign an appointment or meeting. Tasks are items that you must accomplish and that you can track and assign to other people, but tasks are not tied to a specific time and date.

Q After I set a reminder, how does Outlook inform me of the appointment, meeting, or event?

A You must continually run Outlook during your computing sessions for Outlook to monitor and remind you of things you have to do. Outlook is one program that you probably want to add to your Windows Startup folder so that Outlook always starts when you start Windows. Outlook cannot remind you of pending appointments if you are not running it.

Outlook tracks incoming and outgoing events. Also, as you learned in the previous hour, Outlook monitors your electronic mail, faxes, and network transfers, and keeps an eye on your reminders to let you know when something is due. The only way Outlook can perform these tasks is if you keep it running during your work sessions.

PART VI

Tracking with Access 2002

Hour

HOUR 18

Access 2002 Basics

Everyone trudges through data at work and at home. With the proliferation of computers, information overload seems to be the norm. A database manager, such as Microsoft Access 2002, enables you to organize your data and turn raw facts and figures into meaningful information. Access processes data details, so you can spend your valuable time analyzing results. Suppose that your company keeps thousands of parts in an Access inventory database, and you need to know exactly which part sold the most in Division 7 last April. Access can find the answer for you.

This hour introduces you to the world of databases with Access. The nature of databases makes Access one of the more involved programs in the Office suite. Generally, people find that they can master Word, Excel, PowerPoint, and Outlook more quickly than they can Access. Access is not difficult to learn and use, but you must understand the structure of database design before you can fully master Access.

The highlights of this hour include the following:

- What a database is
- Which database-related objects Access manages

- Why databases contain tables
- What fields and records are
- How to create and modify tables

Database Basics

Whereas previous hours of this book began by introducing you to the program right away, this hour begins by explaining database concepts. You need to learn how a database management system organizes data before you jump into Access.

A *database* is an organized collection of data. Access is called a *database management system* because it enables you to create, organize, manage, and report from the data stored in databases.

> Database experts have written complete books on database theory. This hour won't give you an extremely in-depth appreciation for databases, but you will learn enough to get started with Access.

A database typically contains related data. In other words, you might create a home office database with your household budget, but keep another database to record your rare-book collection titles and their worth. In your household budget, you might track expenses, income, bills paid, and so forth, but that information does not overlap the book collection database. Of course, if you buy a book, both databases might show the transaction, but the two databases would not overlap.

Technically, a database does not have to reside on a computer. Any place you store data in some organized format, such as a name and address directory, could be considered a database. In most cases, however, the term database is reserved for organized, computerized data.

When you design a database, consider its scope before you begin. Does your home business need an inventory system? Does your home business need a sales contact? If so, an Access database works well. Only you can decide whether the inventory and the sales contacts should be part of the same system or separate, unlinked systems. The database integration of inventory with the sales contacts requires much more work to design, but your business requirements might necessitate the integration. For example, you might need to track which customers bought certain products in the past.

Not all database values directly relate to one another. Your company's loan records do not relate to your company's payroll, for example, but both probably reside in your company's accounting database. Again, you have to decide on the scope when you design your database. Fortunately, Microsoft made Access extremely flexible, so you can change any database structure when you begin using your database. The better you analyze the design up front, however, the easier your database is to create.

Database Tables

If you threw your family's financial records into a filing cabinet without organizing them, you would have a mess. That is why most people organize their filing cabinets by putting related records into file folders. Your insurance papers go in one folder; your banking records go in another.

Likewise, you cannot throw your data into a database without separating the data into related groups. These groups are called *tables*; a table is analogous to a file folder in a filing cabinet. Figure 18.1 illustrates a set of tables that hold financial information inside a business's database.

18

FIGURE 18.1

A database will contain data separated into groups called tables.

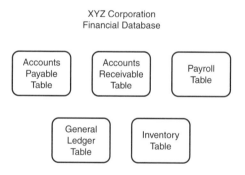

A database might contain many tables, each being a further refinement of related data. Your financial database might contain tables for accounts payable, customer records, accounts receivable, vendor records, employee records, and payroll details (such as hours worked during a given time period). The separate tables help you eliminate redundant data; when you produce a payroll report, Access might retrieve some information from your employee table (such as name and pay rate) and some information from your time tables (such as hours worked).

Access is a *relational database* as opposed to a *flat file database*. That means Access uses data from multiple tables instead of requiring you to duplicate data in two or more places. Therefore, if you increase a customer's discount, you need to change the discount in only one customer table rather than in the customer table, the pricing table, and the sales table.

Access stores all tables for a single database in one file that ends with the .mdb extension. By storing the complete database in one file, Access makes it easier for you to copy and back up your database. You never have to specify the .mdb extension when you create a database.

 You can import data from an Access database table into a Word document or Excel worksheet. The interaction between Access and the other Office products makes the creating and reporting of data simple. Hour 22, "Sharing Information Between Programs," explains more about sharing Office data between the Office products.

Records and Fields

To keep track of table data, Access breaks down each table into *records* and *fields*. In some ways, a table's structure looks similar to an Excel worksheet because of the rows and columns in a worksheet. As Figure 18.2 shows, a table's records are the rows, and a table's fields are the columns. Figure 18.2 shows a checkbook register table; you usually organize your checkbook register just as you would organize a computerized version of a checkbook, so you will have little problem mastering Access's concepts of records and fields.

FIGURE 18.2

Tables have records (rows) and fields (columns).

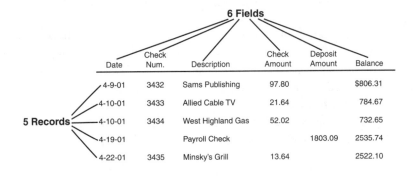

Date	Check Num.	Description	Check Amount	Deposit Amount	Balance
4-9-01	3432	Sams Publishing	97.80		$806.31
4-10-01	3433	Allied Cable TV	21.64		784.67
4-10-01	3434	West Highland Gas	52.02		732.65
4-19-01		Payroll Check		1803.09	2535.74
4-22-01	3435	Minsky's Grill	13.64		2522.10

Your table fields contain different data types. As Figure 18.2 shows, one field might hold a text description, whereas another might hold a dollar amount. Every item within the same field must be the same data type, but a table might contain several fields that differ in type. When you design your database, you are responsible for indicating to Access which data type you want for each field in your database tables.

The types of data that you can store in an Access database table are

- *Text*—Text data consists of letters, numbers, and special characters. You only report text data; you cannot calculate with it. A balance-due field would never be a text data type, but addresses, names, and Social Security numbers are examples of text fields. Generally, you store short text items (names, addresses, cities, product names, and part codes) in text fields.

- *Memo*—The memo field can hold an extremely large amount of text, including paragraphs. Memo fields consume a lot of space, and not all tables require them. Memos are great for documenting table entries, and adding textual data that is free-form. For example, an Evaluation field for an employee database would be a good Memo candidate because one could then make entries that describe the employee's performance.

- *Number*—A number field holds numbers. Use this field to calculate values.

- *Date/Time*—These fields hold date and time values (similar to the date and time format in Excel). Access enables you to enter data into date and time fields using many formats. Additionally, Access respects your Windows international settings, so you are able to enter a date in your country's format.

- *Currency*—This field holds dollar amounts. Access keeps the dollar amounts rounded to the correct decimal alignment needed to match your currency designation. Access recognizes your Windows international settings, and uses international currency amounts when needed.

- *AutoNumber*—This field holds sequential numbers, a different number for each record in the table.

- *Yes/No*—These fields hold Yes and No (or True and False) two-pronged values to indicate the existence or absence of an item or to indicate the answer to an implied question. For example, some items in an inventory database might be tagged for a special discount whereas others are not tagged.

- *OLE object*—This is an embedded object, such as a graph you create in Excel. Your Access databases can hold any kind of OLE-compatible embedded object.

- *Hyperlink*—This is an Internet Web site address. Such a field can hold an Internet address for a file as well as a network or an intranet address within your system network. When the database user clicks the hyperlink, Access shows the hyperlink's Web page or network file.

18

The Internet integration of the other Office products extends to Access. When you click a table's hyperlink to an Internet Web page address, Access sends you to the Web page, logging you on to your Internet provider if necessary.

Using a Key Field

Every Access table requires a *primary key field*. The primary key field (often just called a key) is a field that contains a unique value and no duplicate entries. Whereas a table's city field might contain multiple occurrences of the same city name, a key field must be unique for each record. You can designate an existing data field as the table's key field, or you can use the AutoNumber field that Access adds to all tables as the key field.

If you access a particular field very often, even if that field is not a key field, designate it as an *index field* in the Design view property settings. Access creates an index for every database and locates the index fields in that index. Just as an index in the back of the book speeds your searches for particular subjects, the index field speeds searches for that field.

If you were creating a table to hold employee records, a good key-field candidate would be the employee's Social Security number because each one is unique. If you are not sure that your data contains unique information in any field, specify the AutoNumber field that Access creates as the key. In the AutoNumber field, Access stores a unique number for each table record.

Access uses the key field to find records quickly. When you want to locate an employee's record, for example, search by the employee's key field (the Social Security number). If you search based on the employee's name, you might not find the proper record; two or more employees might be named *John Smith*, for example.

So many companies assign you a customer number because the customer number uniquely identifies you in their database. Although today's computerized society sometimes makes one feel like "just another number," such a customer number enables the company to keep your records more accurate and keep costs down.

Looking at Access

When you start Access, you'll see a screen that looks similar to Word as Figure 18.3 shows. The New File Task Pane provides you with links you can use to create a new database or load an existing database. As with Word and Excel, Access supports the use of template files on which you can base new database files that conform to a predetermined pattern.

New File task pane

FIGURE **18.3**

The Access screen is empty when you launch Access from the Start menu.

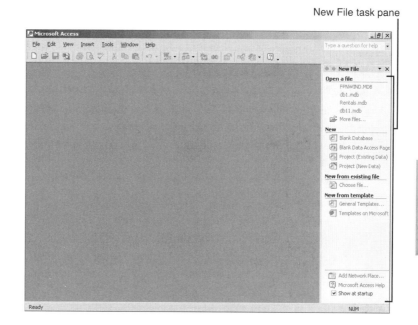

18

Here are the fundamental steps you follow most of the time when you want to work with Access:

- Open an existing database so that you can modify the database structure or work with the database information. Select a database from the list or click the More Files option to browse a list of existing database files. The section of the New File Task Pane where you open an existing database is labeled Open a file.

- Create a new database, which requires that you manually set up the entire database structure including tables, fields, and other pertinent database-structure information. You can also create a more advanced database *project*, which creates a database system that runs in a networked client-server workspace where the Access database might transfer data to multiple workstations attached to the server. The section of the New File Task Pane where you create a blank database is labeled New.

- Create a new database that is a copy of an existing database. The section of the New File Task Pane where you create a database from an existing one is labeled New From Existing File. This New File Task Pane option in effect makes a copy of an existing database file.

- Create a database file based on a template. Access provides templates that create sample, blank databases that track data such as asset management, expenses, and inventories. Microsoft provides additional templates on the Web as well. The section of the New File Task Pane where you create a database from a template is labeled New From Template.

Creating a Database

Generally, when you need to create a new database, you'll start Access and select Blank Database from the New File Task Pane. Enter the name of your database in the File New Database dialog box and click Create to generate the blank database file. Access offers the default database filename db1.mdb, but you should give your database a more meaningful name. For example, if you wanted to track rental property information, you might name the database Rentals. (Access adds the .mdb extension, so your database will be stored as Rentals.mdb.)

When you enter a name and click the Create button, Access displays the *Database window*, shown in Figure 18.4. The Database window title bar includes the name of your database (Rentals in Figure 18.4). As you add to your database, the Database window will show the various components of the database, such as tables.

FIGURE 18.4

The Database window displays a list of your database objects as you create them.

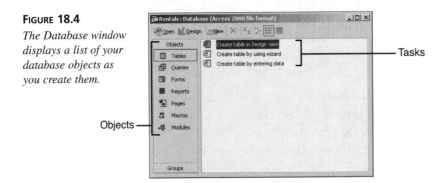

Tables are not the only items that appear in databases. You will generate database reports and other elements, called *objects*, as you work on your database file. The Database window lists the names of all database objects at the left of the window. In the right side, you will see a list of tasks that Access is ready to perform on whatever object you click.

A database object is a piece of an Access database. A table is an object, for example. A database report that prints database data is an object. Your data values, however, are not objects.

In most cases, when you create a database, the first task you will want to perform is to create the database's first table. The first Database window task, Create Table in Design View, will help you create a new table to hold data.

Understanding Database Objects

As you create your database, you add objects to the Database window's seven object categories. Any database can contain many objects from each category. The following are brief descriptions of seven kinds of Access objects:

- *Tables*—Related data within a database
- *Queries*—Stored instructions that select data from one or more tables for reporting, analysis, and data-management purposes
- *Forms*—Onscreen representations of paper forms that you and others use to enter data into tables
- *Reports*—Printed listings of database data
- *Pages (also called Data Access Pages)*—Internet-ready data table pages that you can view with Internet Explorer 5 from Web pages
- *Macros*—Stored task lists for Access commands
- *Modules*—Programs written in Visual Basic, a powerful (but advanced for nonprogrammers) programming language with which you can automate any database task

As you create your database, you create one or more instances of the database objects. You might create 25 tables and 50 reports, for example. When you want to create, edit, or work with one of the database objects, return to the Database window to do so. The toolbar always contains a Database Window toolbar button that quickly returns you to the Database window. To create a new instance of one of the objects, click on the object and select the appropriate task that works with the object.

Access provides an Outlook-style grouping mechanism at the bottom-left of the Database window. If you find yourself creating many objects within the same database, you might want to group some objects into new groups that you create. To create a new group, right-click a blank area under the Groups label and select New Group, enter a group name, and click OK to add the new group to the existing group list. For simple databases, you'll probably just keep all the objects ungrouped within the Database window.

Creating a Table

You must create tables before you can enter data in a database. The tables hold the data on which the other objects operate.

When you create a table, you will follow these general steps:

1. After creating a new database, select the Database window's option called Create Table in Design View and then click Open to create a new table. The *Design view window* appears (shown in Figure 18.5). You must now describe your table's fields in the Design view dialog box.

FIGURE 18.5

Define your table's fields in the Design view window.

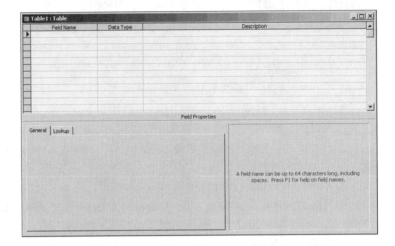

2. Type a field name, such as First Name or Quantity, for the first field in your database. The names have nothing to do with the data type that you will eventually store in the table's field. The field name enables you to refer to the field as you design your table. Only after you completely design the table do you enter data in the table. The order in which you add fields does not affect the order in which you will ultimately enter the table data. Nevertheless, try to add the fields in the general order in which you want to enter the table data.

3. Press Tab and click the drop-down list that appears in the Data Type field to select the field's data type.

4. Press Tab and type a description for the field. Some field names are optional and don't require a description, but the more you document and describe your data, the easier it is to modify your database later.

5. After you enter the first field's name, data type, and optional description, describe the field properties in the lower half of the Design view dialog box. Some fields do not require property settings, but most require some type of setting.

The next section describes in more detail how you will set field property values.

Setting Field Properties

The lower half of the Design view contains settings for your field property values. Each field has a data type, as you already know. In addition to describing the field's data type in the Design view's top half, you can further refine the field's description and limitations in the Field Properties section.

You can configure a different set of field property values for each data type. Text fields contain properties related to text data (such as an address or a name), for example, whereas numeric fields contain properties related to numbers (such as decimal positions).

The field properties appear in the lower half of the screen. A few common field property values that you might want to set as you create your table are as follows:

- *Field Size*—Limits the number of characters the field can hold, thereby limiting subsequent data entry of field data.

- *Format*—Displays a drop-down list with several formats that the field's data type can take.

- *Caption*—Holds a text prompt that Access displays when you enter data into this table's field. If you don't specify a caption, Access uses the field name. Access displays the caption in its status bar when you enter data into the table.

- *Default Value*—Contains the field's default value, which appears when you enter data into this table. The user can enter a value that differs from the default if desired. A common default field value would be your company's state. Many of your vendors will be located in your own state so, if this is the case, your vendor database's State field would include your company's state as the default value.

- *Required*—Holds either Yes or No to determine whether Access requires a value in this field before you can save a table's data record. If you don't want the user leaving a field blank, enter Yes for the Required property.

- *Decimal Places*—Holds the number of default decimal places shown for numbers entered into this field.

Figure 18.6 shows a completed table's Design view. The selected field's (the field with the arrow, or *field selector* in the left column) property values appear at the bottom of the dialog box. As you enter your own table fields, edit any information that you type incorrectly by clicking the field name, data type, description, or property value, and move the insertion point to the mistake to correct the problem.

18

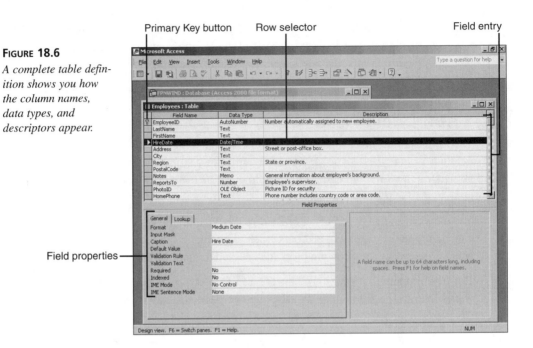

FIGURE **18.6**

A complete table defin-
ition shows you how
the column names,
data types, and
descriptors appear.

Setting the Key and Saving the Table

After you complete your table's fields, you cannot close the table's Design view without
designating a field as the table's primary key field. If you do not designate a key and
attempt to close the table, Access warns you that no key exists. Access adds a key field
using the AutoNumber format if your data does not contain a key field.

Consider adding your own key field for tables that you access often. The key field enables
you to search the table more quickly. The key might be a Social Security number, a phone
number, or some other code (such as a unique inventory code or customer number) that is
unique for each record in the table. The Key field also prevents duplicate entries.

To specify a key field, select the field by clicking the row selector at the left of the field
name and then clicking the Primary Key toolbar button (the button with the icon of the
key). Access adds a small key icon to the left of the record, indicating the table's key
field.

After you add the key field, save the table by clicking the Save button on the toolbar. (If
you attempt to close the table before saving it, Access prompts you for a name.) If you
don't specify a new name, Access uses Table1 (and Table2, Table3, and so on as you
create additional tables); however, you should use a more meaningful table name, such as
Tenants, so that you can easily identify the table. When you close the table, Access
returns you to the Database window where you will see the table in the right pane.

Modifying Table Structures

The beauty of Access is that, unlike some other database programs, you can easily change the structure of your tables even after you have added data. Access makes it easy to add and delete fields, as well as change field properties.

> Some table-structure changes affect table data. After you add data to a table, for example, you lose columns of data if you delete fields, and you lose some data through truncation if you limit a field's Size property after you've entered data. If you add fields to an existing table, you have to add the data for the new fields in every existing record in the table.

To modify a table, switch to the table's Design view. If you have closed the table and returned to the Database window, select the table name (which now appears in the Database window) and click the Database window toolbar's Design button.

Adding Fields

When you've returned to the Table Design view, you can add a field to the end of your table just by clicking the first empty Field Name box and entering the field information as you did when adding the table's initial fields.

To insert a new field between two other fields, right-click the row to display the shortcut menu and select Insert Rows. Access opens a new field row and enables you to enter the new field information. Figure 18.7 shows a new field being inserted into a table.

Deleting Fields

To delete a field, right-click over the field name and select Delete Rows from the shortcut menu that appears. To delete multiple fields, first select them by holding Ctrl and clicking in the gray area to the left of several rows; then select Delete Rows from the shortcut menu.

> Use Undo (Ctrl+Z) to reverse an accidental field deletion. Access supports multiple levels of Undo so that you can reverse several recent row deletions by issuing Undo multiple times. Once you save your new table design, however, you will not be able to reverse the row deletions.

18

Room for new field

FIGURE 18.7
*The new field will go
in the empty space.*

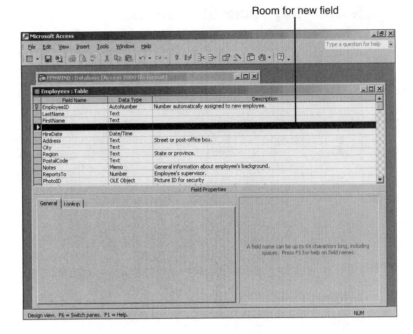

Resizing and Rearranging Fields

Drag your mouse pointer to make minor size adjustments to your table (such as the height of each row and the width of columns). Although the Field Size property determines the exact data storage width of each field in your table, the column widths determine how much of a field you can read while entering and editing table data and the table's structure.

At any time during your table design or subsequent data entry, you can drag a column divider left or right to increase or decrease the width of a column displayed. For example, if your field names are short, you might want to shorten the width of the Field Name column by dragging the right edge to the left to make more room for the field's Description. You can also drag a record divider up or down to increase or decrease a record height.

To rearrange the location of a field, drag the field name by dragging its selector (the gray area to the left of the field) to its new location in the table and release the mouse. Access moves the field to the location you select.

After you make changes to a table's design, Access will prompt you to save your changes when you leave the Table Design view. Always save any changes you want Access to keep.

The order in which you structure a table's fields has little bearing on the table's use. You can report a table's data in any field order that you want regardless of the physical field order you entered the fields. Order your fields in whatever way makes the most sense to you.

Viewing Table Design and Entering Simple Data

Until now, you have worked exclusively in the Design view of the table, which describes the table's fields, properties, and key. From the Database window, if you double-click a table name (or select the table and click the Open button), Access displays your table with the Datasheet view, such as the view shown in Figure 18.8. Unlike the Design view, the Datasheet view enables you to enter and edit data in the table. For a new table, only one table row appears and it's blank because the table has no data. If the table contained data, you would see rows from the table with data. Unlike the Design view, you cannot change the table's structure from the Datasheet view.

FIGURE 18.8

Use the Datasheet view to enter data into your table.

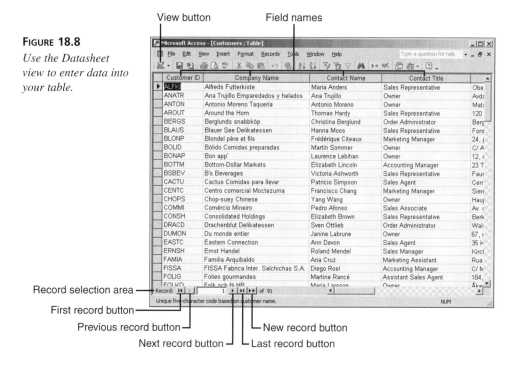

18

You can easily switch from Datasheet view and Design view by clicking the Access toolbar's View button. As you design a table and add the table's initial data, the two views help you pinpoint design and data problems.

The Datasheet view enables you to work with your table in row and column format, similar to an Excel worksheet. Until you enter data in the table, the Datasheet view shows only one empty record, but as you add to the table, the Datasheet view grows to resemble an Excel worksheet with cells that represent each table's field.

Although Access offers several ways to enter data into a table, the Datasheet view is the fastest and simplest if you understand records and fields. The Datasheet view is not fancy, however, and some users need more help when entering data. If you build a database application for a video store's inventory, for example, the clerk should not be adjusting the inventory table directly within the Datasheet view when a customer rents a tape. You learn in Hour 19, "Entering and Displaying Access 2002 Data," how to design data-entry forms that walk the user through the data-entry process for specific scenarios so that the user does not inadvertently change information in the wrong record.

Although the Datasheet view is not fancy, it enables you to quickly see your table's design results and to enter data. If you cannot read a full field name, drag the field separator left or right to increase or decrease the field width shown on the screen.

Most of the Database window objects offer two views: a Design view and another view that displays the final object, such as the table's Datasheet view and the form's Form view.

You can design a table from the Datasheet view, but you make more work for yourself if you do. The default Datasheet view field names are Field1, Field2, and so on until you right-click the names and change them. You cannot set specific field properties from the Datasheet view because Access assumes that all fields are text. In addition, you cannot specify a primary key field in the Datasheet view. Use the Datasheet view for simple data entry and for testing your table's design. Skip the Design view phase only if you want to create an extremely simple, all-text table.

Using Wizards to Create Databases

While you are learning Access, practice designing your early databases without the help of the Access wizards. In most cases, the wizards do not create exactly the kind of database you require, and you have to change the database structure as soon as the wizard completes the database design and creation. Changing an existing database is difficult to do if you have never worked with Access. The best way to gain Access mastery is to design and create your own database from scratch so that you better understand the inner workings of data.

After you master Access, however, a wizard saves you a lot of time if you find one that creates a sample database close to what you need. After the wizard creates the database, you can modify the database to suit your needs.

Some of the Access Database Wizards that you can use after you master Access's fundamentals are as follows:

- *Address Book*—This wizard keeps track of names and addresses.
- *Asset Tracking*—This wizard manages your company's assets.
- *Contact Management*—This wizard keeps track of client information.
- *Order Entry*—This wizard is a complete order-entry and transaction system.
- *Service Call Management*—This wizard enables you to track service calls that your company makes.
- *Time and Billing*—This wizard helps track expenses related to billable labor.

In addition to the wizards, Access comes with a comprehensive database called the *Northwind Traders, Inc., Database*, which you can study to learn about advanced database operations.

18

Always quit Access and shut down Windows before turning off your computer; otherwise, you might lose data that didn't get saved in your database tables.

Summary

Much of this hour's lesson was theory-based because Access requires more preparation than the other Office products. After you learn about the elements that make up a database—tables, records, and fields—the Access mechanics are easy to understand.

To create an Access database, add tables that describe the database data. Each table contains fields and records. When you design a table, you must describe the field names and data types that the table requires.

Now that you know how to create and edit tables, you are ready to enter data and master forms in Hour 19. By using forms for data entry and editing, you make Access tables easier to manage for you and others who use databases that you create.

Q&A

Q Would I ever want to configure a field with the AutoNumber format?

A Your data might require a unique sequential number for each record, such as an invoice number. Most often, however, Access uses the AutoNumber format for the key field that is added when you don't specify a key field.

Q Can I enter data in the Datasheet view?

A Certainly. As explained in this and the next hour, the Datasheet view is a handy view for entering simple data and for viewing multiple records of data from a table. The Datasheet view offers a worksheet-like view of your data in a row and column format. The Datasheet view gives you quick access to a table's data.

Remember that a Datasheet view shows only a single table's data. It does *not* show the entire database because a database often contains multiple tables of data.

Q Can a key field contain duplicates?

A No. If you have to locate records by field and that field is not unique, you cannot make the field a key. You must decide on another key or let Access add the key field.

Hour **19**

Entering and Displaying Access 2002 Data

This hour explains how to use the Access 2002 tables you learned to create in the Hour 18, "Access 2002 Basics." After you master this lesson, you will be able to enter and edit database table data. After you enter the data, you need to print the data to proofread for accuracy and to keep a hard copy as a backup. Although Access provides advanced and fancy reporting tools, you don't have to master those tools to print your Access data as you learn in this hour. When you gather a large amount of data, being able to print the data in a meaningful format is important and Access gives you the tools to do just that.

Finally, this lesson explains how to use the Form Wizard to generate forms that match your data. Forms offer a different perspective from datasheets. The Access forms you create resemble printed forms onscreen.

The highlights of this hour include the following:

- How to enter data into tables
- Which table-editing commands Access supports
- How to print tables

- When to use the Form Wizard to generate forms from tables
- How to use forms for data entry and editing
- How to print forms

Entering Table Data

Access gives you two primary means for adding data to tables that you create:

- Datasheet view
- Forms

The Datasheet view that you saw in Hour 18 enables you to enter and view several records at one time as well as edit any record that you view. When you use a form, on the other hand, you typically work with only one record at a time. The record takes on the format of a printed form, giving you a better focus on individual records. You learn more about forms in a later section, "Using Forms to Enter and Edit Data." The next section focuses on the Datasheet view.

Using the Datasheet View

In the previous hour, you learned how to display the Datasheet view. The Datasheet view offers one of the simplest ways to enter and edit data in an Access database. The rest of this section shows you how Access makes entering data easy.

Entering Data

To enter data in the Datasheet view after you have displayed the Datasheet view, just click the Datasheet view's first field and enter the field information. When you enter data into the first field, Access opens an additional blank record below the one you are entering. Access always leaves room for additional records. As you enter data, press Tab, Shift+Tab, or the arrow keys to move from field to field. You can also click any field into which you want to enter data. As you enter data, watch the status bar at the bottom of your screen. If you entered a description for a field, Access displays that description in the status bar when you enter data in that field.

If, while entering data, you see a number automatically appear in a field, don't panic. Access is automatically entering an AutoNumber into a field defined as an AutoNumber field (such as the key).

Figure 19.1 shows a Datasheet view that contains several records. The record selector always moves as you enter and edit data to show the current record. When you edit one row and then move to another, Access automatically saves that row to the table. As you make an edit, the Editing icon appears to the left of the row to indicate the row being edited. A second kind of record selector, an asterisk, always appears to the left of the next empty record and indicates a new record into which you can enter data.

Supplier ID	Company Name	Contact Name	Contact Title	
1	Exotic Liquids	Charlotte Cooper	Purchasing Manager	49 C
2	New Orleans Cajun Delights	Shelley Burke	Order Administrator	P.O
3	Grandma Kelly's Homestead	Regina Murphy	Sales Representative	707
4	Tokyo Traders	Yoshi Nagase	Marketing Manager	9-8
5	Cooperativa de Quesos 'Las Cabras'	Antonio del Valle Saavedra	Export Administrator	Call
6	Mayumi's	Mayumi Ohno	Marketing Representative	92 S
7	Pavlova, Ltd.	Ian Devling	Marketing Manager	74 F
8	Specialty Biscuits, Ltd.	Peter Wilson	Sales Representative	29 I
9	PB Knäckebröd AB	Lars Peterson	Sales Agent	Kalc
10	Refrescos Americanas LTDA	Carlos Diaz	Marketing Manager	Av.
11	Heli Süßwaren GmbH & Co. KG	Petra Winkler	Sales Manager	Tier
12	Plusspar Lebensmittelgroßmärkte AG	Martin Bein	International Marketing Mgr.	Bog
13	Nord-Ost-Fisch Handelsgesellschaft mbH	Sven Petersen	Coordinator Foreign Markets	Fral
14	Formaggi Fortini s.r.l.	Elio Rossi	Sales Representative	Vial
15	Norske Meierier	Beate Vileid	Marketing Manager	Hatl
16	Bigfoot Breweries	Cheryl Saylor	Regional Account Rep.	340
17	Svensk Sjöföda AB	Michael Björn	Sales Representative	Brov
18	Aux joyeux ecclésiastiques	Guylène Nodier	Sales Manager	203
19	New England Seafood Cannery	Robb Merchant	Wholesale Account Agent	Ord
20	Leka Trading	Chandra Leka	Owner	471
21	Lyngbysild	Niels Petersen	Sales Manager	Lyn
22	Zaanse Snoepfabriek	Dirk Luchte	Accounting Manager	Verl

Current record selector

Record: 7 of 29

Current record number

New record selection

Total number of records

Often, multiple records contain the same data in certain fields (as is the case with city and state names in a table). When you are about to enter data in a cell and the previous record contains the same data, press Ctrl+' to copy the previous record's field value into the current field's cell.

19

As you enter data, take advantage of the Office AutoCorrect feature. Just as Word and Excel support AutoCorrect entries, so does Access. All the Office products share the same AutoCorrect abbreviations you have defined.

When you enter AutoCorrect abbreviations and shortcuts, Access substitutes the shortcut for the AutoCorrect correction. Access does not automatically enable automatic spell checking as you enter data because much of your table data contains data such as formal names and product codes that would appear to the spell checker as misspellings. You can check your table's spelling by selecting Tools, Spelling.

To change a mistake, such as a transposed number, click the mistake to display the insertion point inside the Datasheet view's field and correct the entry. You can also press the arrow keys to move to any field, and press F2 to edit the field's text.

Formatting Your Data

Access is forgiving when you enter special data such as dates, times, monetary amounts, and memo field values. You can basically enter data in these fields in whatever way seems best to you! You can enter a date in a date field, for example, using any of the following formats:

```
05/12/2003
5/12/2003
May 12, 2003
May 12 2003
```

Access uses a predefined date format to display dates and times in the Datasheet view, so after you type a date, it can be immediately reformatted to match this view. By default, Access uses the date format mm/dd/yyyy.

As with dates, you can enter time in several common ways. Add a.m. or p.m. or use 24-hour clock time. Access, by default, formats your time values to the hh:mm:ss format.

Quickly Entering Date and Time Values

You can press Ctrl+; to enter the current date in a field, and press Ctrl+: to enter the current time. Access gets these values from your computer's clock and calendar setting.

Ctrl+; causes the date to display using the format dd/mm/yy (unless your Windows International settings specify a different date format) although Access stores the date using the current four-digit year.

Access currency fields accept a wide variety of formats. You can type a dollar sign (or whatever currency symbol matches your Windows International Country setting), decimals, and you can even place commas in currency values. After you enter a currency amount, Access displays the amount with the default format. The default currency format is based on your International settings. For North America, the default will be a dollar sign. If you fail to type the dollar sign, Access supplies one automatically.

Your Windows Control Panel contains an icon labeled Regional Settings (Windows 2000 calls this icon Regional Options). The language specified in your PC's Regional Settings determines how Access displays data. Therefore, you can maintain one database for multiple users around the world. The PC running the Access database determines, therefore, how the data appears on the screen and in reports.

If you need to format a currency amount in a different format from your Windows International Settings, you can do so by specifying the format in the Design view's property settings.

If you enter a value that does not meet the Field Properties requirements, such as placing two decimal points inside a single dollar amount, Access displays a dialog box (shown in Figure 19.2), indicating that you should correct the value before entering the next field.

FIGURE **19.2**

Access lets you know if you enter an incorrect format.

Access does not let you leave a record that contains a bad format. As a matter of fact, Access will not even let you move to another row in the database if a field does not meet the Field Properties requirements. Therefore, when you close your tables, you can be assured that Access saves all the data with the proper data type. Although the data values might not be correct, you will know that the data does fit within the specified formats you have declared for the table.

Editing Data

All the editing skills you mastered with the other Office products work with Access. You can rearrange the order of fields and records by dragging the record or field selectors with your mouse. You can select more than one field or record at a time by dragging your mouse through the record or field selectors or by holding Shift down while you click record or field selectors. Press Ctrl+A to select all the records in the table.

To delete one or more records or fields, select the records or fields you want to delete and right-click the record selector to display a shortcut menu. Select Delete Column or Delete Record.

Access provides several shortcut menus that help you perform needed tasks. For example, when you right-click the selected records or fields, the shortcut menu that appears provides familiar Cut, Copy, and Paste commands as well as Insert and Delete commands for records and fields. When you right-click a record selector, a different shortcut menu appears that enables you to work with the rows.

Right-clicking a column selector produces a shortcut menu with the Hide Columns command that temporarily hides fields (they physically stay in the table). These fields stay out of the way while you work with other data, and choose Format, Unhide Columns to reveal the data when you are ready to work with the entire table again. Other right-click

19

options can be helpful too, such as the sorting commands. You can *sort* records in *ascending order* or *descending order* with the shortcut menu's options when you right-click over data in the table.

> If you often need to adjust the width or height of records and fields, consider changing your table's font size and style (by selecting Format, Font).

Navigating Large Tables

Use the Navigation buttons at the bottom of the Datasheet view (see Figure 19.3) to move through and jump over large blocks of records that don't interest you at the time. The Navigation buttons works similar to a VCR, enabling you to move forward and backward through your data.

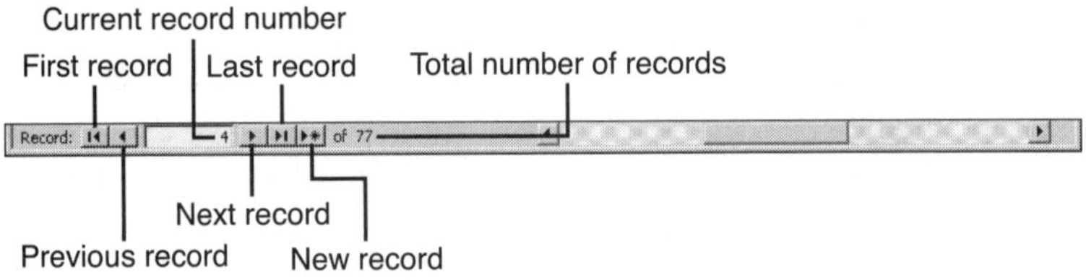

Current record number

First record | Last record   Total number of records

FIGURE 19.3

The Navigation buttons   Record: 14 ◄ ⌐ 4 ► ►I ►* of 77
help you navigate
through database   Previous record   Next record   New record
tables.

Here are a few pointers:

- Click Next Record to move the record selector to the next record.
- Click Previous Record to move the record selector to the previous record.
- Click First Record to move to the table's first record.
- Click Last Record to move to the table's last record.
- Click the Specific Record box, type a new record number, and then press Enter to jump directly to that record.

Simple Printing

Access includes powerful reporting tools, but they take some time to master. You learn about reporting in Hour 21, "Reporting with Access 2002." If you just want to print a listing of your data, however, you can do so easily from the Datasheet view. Access automatically prints the Datasheet view with field titles.

Perhaps you need to check a table listing for errors, or you want a printed listing (called a *hard copy*) so that you can proofread the data values that you entered. Before printing, display a preview (similar to the one shown in Figure 19.4) by selecting File, Print Preview. Move the magnifying glass mouse pointer over any portion of the preview and click to see a close-up.

FIGURE 19.4

Get a preview of printed datasheet tables.

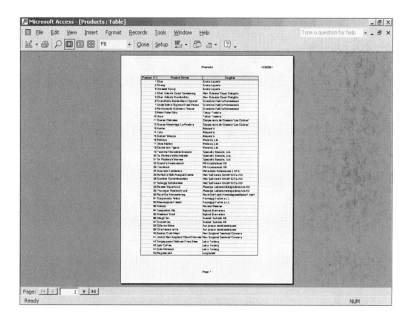

To print a Datasheet table, select File, Print (or click the Print button on the toolbar).

Using Forms to Enter and Edit Data

When you computerize your records, you want to make it as easy as possible for people to enter, edit, and view data in your database. Often, Access reduces paperwork. A credit agency might use Access to keep track of loan applications that borrowers fill out, for example. As borrowers bring in their completed applications, a clerk types the data from the application into an Access table. Although a Datasheet view would work fine for the data entry, a *form* works even better! The form can, while onscreen, mimic the look and feel of paper forms that many people are accustomed to using. You do not have to keep files of paper forms now that you use Access.

Using the Form Wizard to Generate Forms

You probably want to use the Form Wizard to create your first form. The Form Wizard generates simple forms that work well in most cases.

Follow these steps to start the Form Wizard:

   1. Display the Database window with your database open.

19

2. Click the Forms object to display the tasks you can perform with forms.

3. Click the Database window's New button to display the New Form dialog box (shown in Figure 19.5).

FIGURE 19.5

Creating a new form.

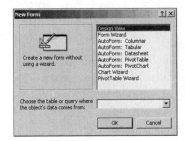

4. Click to select the Form Wizard option.

5. Select the table or query in the lower part of the dialog box to use as a basis for the form. If your database contains multiple tables and queries, each table and query appears in the drop-down list. You must select a table or query before continuing.

6. Click OK to display the opening Form Wizard screen (shown in Figure 19.6). This screen lists the available fields that you can include for your selected table.

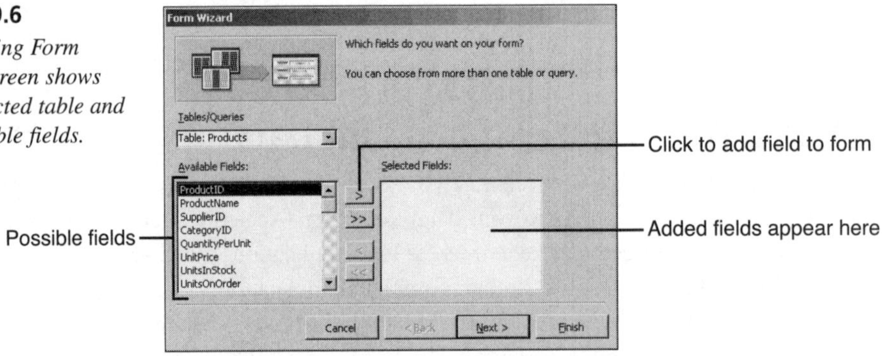

FIGURE 19.6

The opening Form Wizard screen shows your selected table and its available fields.

Possible fields —

— Click to add field to form

— Added fields appear here

You might or might not want to include every field on every form you create. Suppose, for example, that you want to create a form for your company's personnel that contains employee names and extension numbers, but not employee pay rates. The next step in creating your form is to indicate to Access which fields to include.

To add table fields to the form, select a field and click the button labeled >. Access adds that field to the selected field list. To include all the fields, click the button labeled >>. The Form Wizard sends all the table's fields to the selected field list.

If you send a field to the form accidentally, select that field and click the button labeled <
to remove the field from the form. Clicking << removes all the fields, so you can start
over if you want to rearrange the fields or copy new ones from scratch.

Click the Next button to display the Form Wizard Layout screen (shown in Figure 19.7).
Click the different options to see a preview of how that option changes the form's layout.

FIGURE **19.7**

*Select a layout for
your form.*

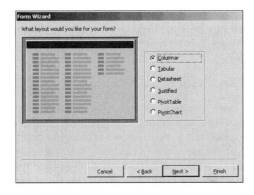

 The Tabular and Datasheet form layouts are similar to the Datasheet view.
The Columnar and Justified layouts look similar to typical paper forms. As
you click each option, Access displays that option's resulting form layout.

When you click the Next button, the Form Wizard displays a screen from which you can
select a form style (as shown in Figure 19.8). Click through the style selections to see a
preview of those available. Many styles have unique personalities that can add eye-
catching appeal to an otherwise dull form.

19

FIGURE **19.8**

*The Form Wizard sup-
ports several form
styles.*

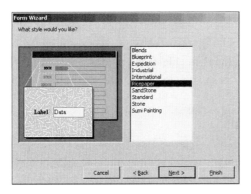

When you click the Next button, you see the Form Wizard's closing screen, which asks for a form title (the default title is the name of your selected table). Click Finish to generate the form.

After you learn more advanced Access commands (see Hour 21), such as how to use the form-creation and editing tools, you can open the generated form's Design view and change specific parts of the form. The Form Wizard generates your form, and you can then modify the form to look exactly the way you want it. For now, the Form Wizard's generated forms work well.

In some cases, generated forms contain problems but you can correct those problems with a little editing from the form's Design view. Figure 19.9 shows a generated form that needs slight editing. The Form Wizard automatically uses field names for the form prompts and data descriptions. If your field names are long, the Form Wizard might not display the entire field name for the prompt. Also, some data might not align properly because the data value's width might be longer than the form's field. In addition, if your table does not contain many fields, the form does not take up the full screen and might look too small. You can maximize the form onscreen or resize the form to a smaller window.

Figure 19.9 displays its form in the Form *view*. The Form view displays records in the form-like format. Access also contains a form's Design view (not unlike the table's Design view), in which you can edit the form and change its appearance.

When using forms, you must understand how all the data types appear. If your table contains Yes/No data-type fields, those fields appear with an *x* to indicate the Yes value. If you name a rental property's tenant field Pet Deposit?, for example, and assigned the Yes/No data type to the field, those owners who pay a pet deposit have an *x* for this field value.

Memo fields can hold a lot of data, so if you use a memo field, keep typing when the insertion point reaches the right side of the field. Access scrolls the field to enable you to continue. Form views display memo fields with scrollbars, so you can look at all the data in the fields.

Navigating Forms

Forms typically show only single records. Unlike the Datasheet view, the form is a much better tool for working with single records. In the Datasheet view, you can often see many records, but not all the fields in those records, because the fields rarely fit on the Datasheet view screen. The form shows only a single record, but often manages to include all fields from the records because of the form layout.

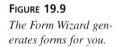
FIGURE **19.9**

The Form Wizard generates forms for you.

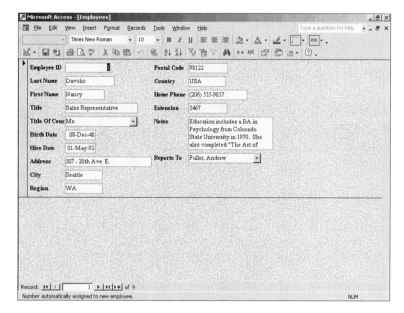

Access offers several ways to move through records in the Form view. Press up arrow, down arrow, Tab, and Shift+Tab to move from one field to another. Press PageUp and PageDown to move to the previous and next table record, respectively. The record number appears at the bottom of the form window's record selection control. As in the Datasheet view, you can click the record selection control to move from record to record.

> To jump to a record quickly, press F5, type a record number, and press Enter.

19

Editing Form Data

As you move through the form records, feel free to change data in the record. The record selector arrow changes to an editing pencil to show that you are editing the record. If you use Tab or Shift+Tab to move from field to field, press F2 when the highlight appears over the field you want to edit. When you change data from within the Form view, Access changes the data in the underlying tables.

> To add records from the Form view, click the New Record button to display a new one that you can fill out.

Printing Forms

If you select File, Print from the Form view, Access prints the forms. Unlike the onscreen Form view, Access prints as many forms on the page as fit (select the File, Print Preview to see what will print, such as the preview shown in Figure 19.10).

FIGURE 19.10

Access prints multiple records per form.

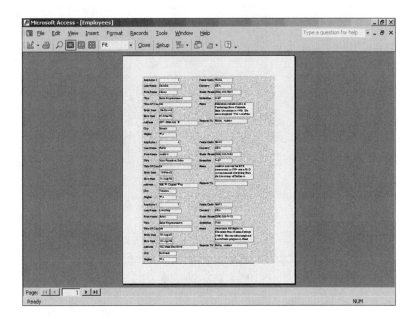

Summary

This hour extended your Access knowledge by showing you how to use the Datasheet view to enter and print data. You also learned how to create and use forms. Access replaces the paper forms you are used to and provides a form-like approach to data entry and editing.

The Form Wizard quickly generates nice forms for you from your table data. The Form Wizard is a great place to start designing your forms because it analyzes your table and generates a form based on your table's fields.

The next hour, "Retrieving Your Data," teaches you how to filter data and use queries so that you can work with subsets of table data.

Q&A

Q **When I open a table's Datasheet view, why does the data appear in a different order from the order in which I entered it?**

A Access sorts data, in ascending order, according to the table's selected key field. Your Datasheet views always appear in the order sorted by the key field unless you change the sort order by right-clicking the field that you want to sort by and then choosing Sort Ascending or Sort Descending. Access uses the key field to locate records quickly when you search for data.

Q Why should I use the Form Wizard but not the Table Wizard when I begin learning Access?

A You must understand tables, records, and fields before you use the Table Wizard to generate tables because you almost always have to modify the Table Wizard's generated table to suit your exact needs. Therefore, it helps, when starting out, to create tables from scratch and learn how tables work. After you learn how to use the table's Datasheet and Design views, you are better equipped to edit tables generated with the Table Wizard.

The Form Wizard looks at tables that you generated and creates simple data-entry forms with the format and layout that you request. Forms require less editing when you generate them from the Form Wizard than tables do. You will be pleased with the Form Wizard from the moment you create your first form.

Q Can I edit the AutoNumber field?

A If you let Access create and enter your table's key field, you should also let Access maintain the AutoNumber that it enters for you. When you create reports, you can hide the AutoNumber field so that the field does not appear with the data that others see. The AutoNumber field is Access's bookkeeping field when you fail to designate a key. Access keeps the table sorted in the key order, and you should not bother with this field. If you want, rearrange the table to move the AutoNumber field to the far-right side of the Datasheet view. Then you rarely see the field when you work with the data.

19

HOUR **20**

Retrieving Your Data

This hour teaches you about Access 2002 filters and queries. Although your database contains a lot of data, you rarely want to see all that data simultaneously. Generally, you want to see only data subsets. Filters and queries produce those subsets for you.

When you view data subsets, you prevent unwanted data from getting in the way of the information with which you need to work. The power of queries is that you can select records and fields from multiple tables and view that selected data subset from within a single Datasheet or Form view.

The highlights of this hour include the following:

- What a filter is
- Why you sometimes use Filter by Selection and sometimes use Filter by Form
- When a filter limits you
- Why queries are more robust than filters
- How to use the query wizards
- How to use the Query Design view to create and edit queries
- Where to specify advanced selection criteria

Using Data Filters

A *filter* is a subset of data from a table. Suppose that you want to see only certain records from a table, such as all customers who are past due. Instead of hiding the records that you don't want to see, create a filter. The filter removes unwanted records from view. The records don't go away, and you don't have to unhide the records later (as you do when you actually hide records by right-clicking over a column or row in the Datasheet view and selecting Hide Columns or Hide Row). A filter works similar to a short-term record hider, putting certain records out of the way while you work with the filtered data.

Access supports three filtering approaches:

- *Filter By Selection*—Filters data based on selected table data
- *Filter By Form*—Enables you to choose the data fields that you want Access to use for filtering
- *Advanced Filter/Sort*—Controls advanced filtering options from the Access menu bar

The easiest and most common filter options are Filter By Selection and Filter By Form, which the following two sections describe.

Access includes an Advanced Filter/Sort option on the Records, Filter menu, but you will almost always prefer creating a query to using the advanced filter. In addition, Access supports a Filter Excluding Selection that filters the opposite of Filter by Selection. A query is easier to save and work with in the future than a filter.

Filter By Selection

Filter By Selection works by example. Suppose that you want to display only those table records that contain a specific field value; for example, you need to work only with customer records from Brazil. If your customer table contains a Country field with scattered Brazil entries, you can filter out all those records that do *not* contain Brazil in their Country fields.

You can practice working with filters by opening the sample Northwind Traders database that comes with Access. (You'll locate this FPNWIND.MDB file in your Office Samples folder.) Perform the following steps to design a filter that filters out records that don't contain Brazil:

1. Display the Datasheet view for the Customers table.

2. Locate one record with Brazil in the Country field. You might have to click the horizontal scrollbar to see the Country field from the Datasheet view.

3. Double-click the single field value that contains Brazil to select that value. If you select only the first part of the field instead of selecting the entire field, such as the letter *B*, you would filter all records that do not start with *B*.

4. Click the toolbar's Filter By Selection button. Access filters out all records that don't match your selected *criteria*. Figure 20.1 shows a filtered Datasheet view that displays only records containing a Brazil entry in their Country field. Before the filter, this Datasheet view held more than 90 records. By locating the example field and clicking once, you just changed the display to those records that only contain Brazil for the Country field value.

5. To return to the full Datasheet view, click the toolbar's Remove Filter button.

As you can see, a filter removes unwanted records; Access filters those unwanted records from view.

To filter out records that contain your selected value (instead of all records that do not contain a value), select Records, Filter, Filter Excluding Selection. The Filter Excluding Selection option works similar to a reverse filter. Click the Remove Filter to revert the Datasheet view to its full table once again.

FIGURE 20.1

Filter By Selection filters out all unwanted records.

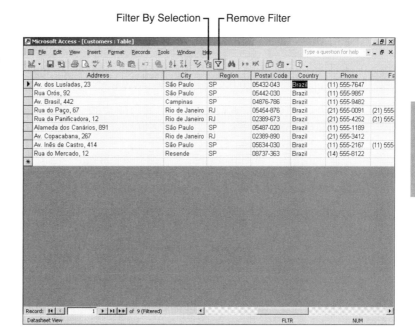

20

You do not first have to locate a customer record from Brazil to create the previous list's filter. If you right-click any field value in the table and then type a value in the shortcut menu's Filter For text box, Access applies the Filter By Selection command to your entered filter value. Therefore, you can type Brazil in the Filter For text box, press Enter, and more quickly create the same filter that the previous steps created.

Filter By Form

Filter By Form enables you to filter by multiple values rather than by only one value. You can apply a Filter By Form from both the Datasheet and Form views.

Perform these steps to use Filter By Form:

1. Click the Filter By Form button. Access displays a single blank record. If you have recently created a filter, that previous filter's selection value appears in the single row that displays. You can erase the value and enter a different one.

2. Scroll to the field you want to filter by or click on the empty field.

3. Click the field's drop-down arrow to display the list. Access displays a scrolling drop-down list of every value (without duplicates) that appears in that field within the current table.

4. Select the value by which you want to filter.

5. Optionally, click another empty field value and select from that field's drop-down list of available values. You can select as many filtering field values as you need. Unlike the Filter By Selection, which enables you to filter only by one field value, Filter By Form enables you to filter by several fields.

6. Click the Apply Filter button to display the filtered records.

7. Click the Remove Filter button (before you begin filtering, this button is called the Apply Filter button) when you are ready to return to the full-record view.

If you filter by a date field, Access surrounds the filtered value with pound signs (#). You often see pound signs around dates, such as #7/4/2003#; this enables Access to distinguish the date from a formula.

Access can perform an Or filter, meaning that Access filters to find all records that include one or more of your selected filter field values. If you want to find all customers who live in New York or who live in Maine, for example, select New York, click the Or tab at the bottom of the Filter By Form window, and select Maine. You can continue adding Or conditions to select from one of several fields.

Although Access uses an Or condition to select from one of several field values, it uses an *And condition* to select across fields. This means that if you select Brazil for the Country field filter and Rio for the City field filter, Access filters to find all records with both Brazil as a country and Rio for the city. If a record contains the country Brazil but São Paulo for the city, such a filter would not retain that record.

Using Queries

A *query* is really nothing more than a question you ask Access about your data. Access does not understand questions the way you generally ask them, so you must ask your question with its special query format. A query differs somewhat from a filter. A query is the request that produces a subset of data. A filter, on the other hand, just temporarily hides certain data from your Access views so that you can see only a subset of data from a table.

A query is an object, just as tables and forms are objects. Therefore, you see the Queries object page on the Database window, and you create, edit, and execute queries from this page. As with other objects, queries have names that you give them. Many queries are nothing more than named filters; however, filters go away when you are finished with them, whereas you can recall a query later by its name. If you want to reapply a filter, however, you must reproduce it.

Although you cannot name filters, you can turn a Filter By Form request into a named query. When you enter the Filter By Form request, click the Save As Query toolbar button. Access prompts you for a query name and stores the filter as a query. Often, creating a named query from a Filter By Form is faster than generating a new query from scratch if you only want to create a simple query that filters records.

20

Queries are often much more advanced than filters. A query enables you to specify selected records from a table or from another query. You can create a query that selects records and fields from multiple tables. The data subset that a query generates often becomes a table-like Datasheet view from which you can report. You can build a query that extracts certain records and fields from three tables, for example, and then generate a report from those extracted records and fields.

Not only can you create a query that extracts fields and records, but also you can specify the exact order of the resulting data subset, sort the subset, and use powerful extraction criteria to select data based on very specific requirements.

Once you generate a query, you can save that query just as you save tables and reports. The saved query will contain all the instructions necessary to once again generate the data so that you do not have to build that query again.

The created data subset is called a *dynaset*.

Creating a Query with the Query Wizard

Although you can build a query from scratch, the Query wizard can do the dirty work for you in most cases.

Access includes these four query wizards:

- *Simple Query Wizard*—Extracts fields from one or more tables and from other queries.
- *Crosstab Query Wizard*—Creates a worksheet-like query that summarizes field values and cross-tabulates matching values.
- *Find Duplicates Query Wizard*—Creates a data subset from two or more tables or queries that contain matching values in one or more fields that you select.
- *Find Unmatched Query Wizard*—Creates a data subset from two or more tables or queries that contain no duplicate records.

You use the Simple Query Wizard often because of its general-purpose design. When you create a new query by selecting Queries from the Database window's object list and then clicking New on the toolbar, Access displays the New Query dialog box (shown in Figure 20.2).

FIGURE 20.2

Begin creating your query in the New Query dialog box.

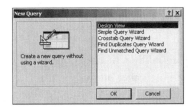

When you create a new query, a list of the four query-based wizards appears and you can select from that list. In addition, a fifth entry appears labeled Design View. The Design View entry is misleading because this is not a wizard, but a query-building screen from which you must build the query from scratch without the help from any wizard.

Follow these steps to build your first query using the Simple Query Wizard:

1. After opening your database, click Queries in the Database window.

2. Click the Database window's New button to open the New Query window.

3. Select the Simple Query Wizard from the New Query dialog box and click OK. Access starts the wizard and displays the Simple Query Wizard screen (see Figure 20.3).

FIGURE 20.3

Use the Simple Query Wizard screen to gen-erate your first query.

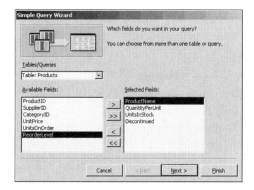

4. Select a table or an existing query that holds the data you want the query to extract. (You can build queries from tables or from other queries.) Access displays fields from the selected table (or query) in the Available Fields list.

5. Select one or more fields and click the button labeled >. Access includes these fields in the resulting query data subset. If you want the query to extract all cus-tomer names and balances from a customer table, for example, select those two fields and click > to send them to the Selected Fields list. The Selected Fields list is the query's resulting structure, and holds a description of the data subset that the query eventually produces.

6. Optionally, select another table or query from the Tables/Queries drop-down list and add more fields to the Selected Fields list. If Access prompts you to create a relation-ship between the tables, click Yes to create the relationship. Access relates the tables automatically if you have created the relationship link elsewhere. You are now build-ing a query that extracts data subsets from multiple sources. If you send the wrong field to the Selected Fields list, select the incorrect field and click < to remove it. To remove all your selected fields and begin again, click the button labeled <<.

7. Click Next to select either a detail or summary query. A detail query includes every field of every record; a summary query does not show duplicate selected records and includes summary statistics if you select them by clicking the Summary Options button.

20

8. Click Next and select a title for the query. Access bases the default name for the new query on the first selected table or existing query.

9. Click Finish to complete the query. Access builds the query and displays the selected records from the query in the Datasheet view. When you close the Datasheet view, you see the new query listed on the Queries page of the Database window. Again, you can often create a filter that produces the same extracted record subset as a query, but you can later re-extract queries by name instead of rebuilding them from scratch as you must do with filters.

Take a moment or two to reflect on what you just did. For the first time, you have the power to extract records from multiple tables to create a dynaset, or subset, of your database records.

You can also create a new form (using one of the form wizards) to display the results of a query. When you created a new form in the Hour 19, "Entering and Displaying Access 2002 Data," you knew only how to create forms from single tables. If multiple tables contain data you want to display in a form, however, create a query to extract from the two tables and base the form on that query.

To synchronize a multiple-table query, all tables must have a common field (such as a customer number), or you must use advanced Access commands to relate the two tables in some way. Without a relationship, such as a common field, the query cannot combine the fields from the two tables.

Access does not save your query results, just the query structure. Therefore, if you want to see a data subset twice, you must open the Database window's Queries page, select the query, and click Open to generate the query extraction once again. Although the extraction requires a little time to generate (usually the speed is negligible unless the tables contain many records), the query is always fresh. If you change one value in any table and open the query again, your most recent table edit appears in the query.

Another advantage of generating the query every time you need to use the data subset is that Access does not have to store the data twice (once in the source tables and again in the query).

If you edit data from the resulting query's Datasheet view (or from the query's Form view), Access updates the data in the original tables. Suppose that you want to edit the pay rate for every employee who works in your company's Northeast division; just create a query to extract only the Northeast division employees, make the edits, and close the query. Find and edit the Northeast employees' pay rates without the other employee records getting in the way.

Using the Query Design View

When you create or edit a query from scratch, you can use the Query Design view (such as the one shown in Figure 20.4).

FIGURE 20.4

The Query Design view enables you to create powerful queries.

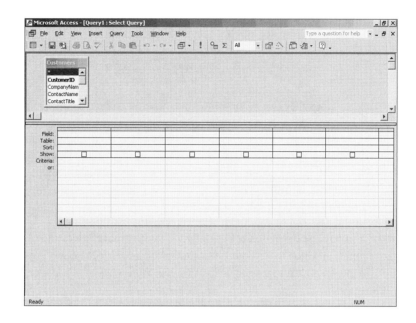

Although the Query Design view looks somewhat strange at first, the view's design is logical. The top of the Query Design view contains the source tables and queries, and the bottom of the Query Design view displays the criteria (the query-selection commands).

You use the Query Design view when you must:

- Create an advanced query that the query wizards cannot create.
- Edit an existing query.

After you learn to create a query with the Query Design view, you will also understand how to use the Query Design view to edit existing queries.

Creating a Query from Scratch

To use the Query Design view to create a query, follow these steps:

1. Select Queries in the Database window.
2. Click the New button to open the New Query dialog box.
3. Select Design View and click OK to open the Query Design view. Access displays the Show Table dialog box that contains all your table and query details (similar to the one shown in Figure 20.5).

20

FIGURE 20.5

Select from your database's tables and queries for the new query.

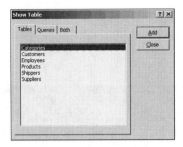

4. Click the table or tables that you want to include in the query and then click Add. As you add tables to the query, Access displays a new table in the Query Design view showing in the background. If you want to base your new query on another query, click the Queries tab to display a list of them from which you can choose, and then add the selected query. If you want to add both tables and queries, click the Both tab to display all your database tables and queries, and then select the ones you need.

5. Click Close to close the Show Table dialog box.

You have yet to build the entire query, but you have selected tables, existing queries, or both, on which to base your new query. Next, enter the query's criteria so that Access knows which records and fields to select from your tables and existing queries.

It's easy to accidentally add the same table twice to a query. If you do, just click the "extra" table in the upper pane of the query and press Delete.

Figure 20.6 shows the start of a new query. This query extracts from two tables, one named Customers and one named Employees. The line connecting the tables' common field, City, appears when you drag your mouse between the common field, as you do when you want to create a relationship. You might recall from the preceding section that Access must base queries on related tables and queries, and the common field relates the two tables.

Think of the top half of the query's design window as starting the request, "Given these tables and queries..." and the lower half of the window as finishing that request, "...extract all data that meets these conditions." The Query Design view contains your instructions when you want Access to extract data from one or more tables or queries and display the result in a table subset.

Relating two fields

FIGURE 20.6

This query can now extract from two related tables.

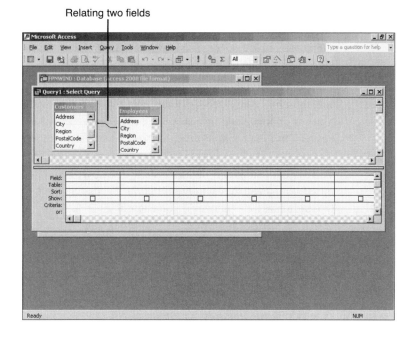

Each column in the Query Design view's lower half contains the resulting query's fields. Therefore, if you want the resulting data subset to contain four fields, you fill in four of the Query Design view's lower columns. These columns contain the instructions that indicate to the query how to extract the data from the table, tables, query, queries, or combinations of tables and queries that you have specified for the query.

Working with Complex Queries

To complete the query, follow these steps:

1. Click the first column's row labeled Table and select the table that contains the resulting query's first field. If you want the query's data subset to start with a field from the Tenants table, for example, you would select Tenants from the drop-down list.

2. Click the first column's row labeled Field and select the field that you want to place first in the resulting data subset. You might select Tenant ID from the list, for example.

3. If you want to sort the resulting query's subset based on the first field, select either Ascending or Descending from the row labeled Sort. You don't have to sort on the first field that you add to the query; you can sort on any field that you add. The query sorts all the resulting data based on the value of the field by which you sort. If you sort on two or more fields, Access sorts the data in the leftmost Sort column first.

20

4. Leave the Show option checked if you want the field to appear in the resulting query's data subset. Generally, you want the field to appear. If you want to sort the subset on a field but not send that sort field to the resulting extracted subset, uncheck the Show option for that field.

5. Click the first column's row labeled Criteria and enter a criterion. If you type a value, such as **JJ1**, Access extracts only those records with a field containing JJ1. You can continue adding criteria values beneath the first one. You can type the values **JJ1**, **BR1**, **BR2**, and **BE1** for five rows of criteria (still in the first column). This is like asking Access to extract only those tenants whose Tenant ID is JJ1, BR1, BR2, or BE1, for example. If the field is a text-data type, Access encloses the criteria in quotation marks (shown in Figure 20.7). Access encloses dates inside pound signs (**#1/6/1898#**, for example) if you enter dates in the criteria.

FIGURE 20.7

This query must match several criteria values for Customer ID.

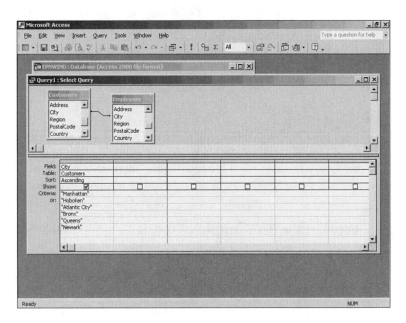

6. It gets fun here. Instead of selecting the field from the second column's drop-down list labeled Field, drag the field name from a table in the upper half of the Query Design view (such as the Order Date field in the Orders table). Access automatically fills in the table and field name in the second column of the query! (You might also double-click a field name from the table in the upper portion of the Query Design view to use that field name in the query.)

7. Enter the selection criteria for the new field. The criteria indicate exactly how you want to pull records from the table. If you want to extract all the records (all that fall within the criteria of the first field that you have entered), leave the second field's

criteria blank. You can further limit the extraction by entering an additional criterion for the second field. Suppose that you not only want customers with the IDs listed in the first criteria, but also want to limit the selection to any of those five who have an order date of January 6, 2003. You enter **#1/6/2003#** for the criteria.

8. Continue adding fields that you want to appear in the resulting query. When you execute your query, these fields appear in the resulting table.

As you work with the query, you might want to add more tables. Add the tables in the Query Design view by selecting Query, Show Table. Add as many tables (or queries) as you prefer to the query from within the Query Design view, but remember that the tables and queries must relate somehow. Remove a table or query from the Query Design view by right-clicking the table name and selecting Remove Table.

> You can use all the cut, copy, and paste methods that you learned earlier in the book for the query-extraction fields. You can move a field from one location to another by selecting, cutting, and pasting it, for example. You can also resize column widths by dragging the field column edges, and you can change any value by clicking that value in the Query Design view.

If you really want to get fancy, use the relational operators in Table 20.1 to add to your extraction power.

TABLE 20.1   Access's Relational Operators Improve Extraction Power

Operator	Description
>	Greater than
<	Less than
>=	Greater than or equal to
<=	Less than or equal to
<>	Not equal to
=	Equal to (not needed for simple matches)

Suppose that you want to include customer-order details in a query, but you only want to include orders with more than 19 units. Enter **>19** for the Quantity field's criterion to limit the selection to those records that match the other criteria and that have order quantities of more than 19 units. The relational operators work with numbers, text values that fall within a range of words, and dates.

The Between keyword is useful when you want to extract values that fall between two other values. If you type **Between #1/1/2005# And #1/31/2005#** for a date criterion, for example, Access extracts only records whose date falls between 1/1/2005 and 1/31/2005 (including the days 1/1/2005 and 1/31/2005).

Access uses an implied Or when you specify multiple criteria. Instead of typing five separate Customer IDs such as **101**, **102**, **103**, **104**, and **105**, for example, you could enter **101 Or 102 Or 103 Or 104 Or 105**. (Of course, entering **Between 101 And 105** would be even easier.)

Be sure to save your query when you finish with it. Click the Query Design view's Close Window button and name the query so that you are able to refer to it later. When you select the query and click Open from the Queries page of the Database window, Access runs the query, extracts the data, and displays the result in your Datasheet view.

Although Access queries are useful and not extremely complex, the screens might seem daunting at first for Access newcomers. The Access online help screens provide many examples and explanations that you might want to peruse to familiarize yourself better with database queries.

Summary

This hour showed you how to narrow your data and form subsets. Often, a table contains many more fields and records than you want to work with at any one time. Access's filter and query powers enable you to create subsets of data to make your work more manageable.

Filters provide quick subsets, but queries provide much more power and flexibility. After you run a filter or query to create a subset of your data, you can make changes to the subset and modify data in the underlying tables. Although the Query Design view takes some getting used to, it enables you to specify powerful query extraction criteria so that Access searches for and finds the data with which you need to work.

Now that you can produce subsets of data, you need a way to report that data. The next hour, "Reporting with Access 2002," explores some of the reporting capabilities. The Report Wizard makes quick work of report generation from your tables and queries.

Q&A

Q Should I use a filter or a query?

A When you quickly want to see a subset of a table, use a filter. You sometimes use the subset in another way (as input to a report, for example), so creating a query that you can name and execute makes more sense.

Q **If I save a filter as a named query, what does the query's Query Design view look like?**

A Filters are much less powerful than queries, but they are easier to designate. As you create more queries and get used to your data needs, you find that many of your queries are little more than filters. Instead of messing with the Query Design view to design the query, generate a simpler Filter By Form filter and save it as a query. If you then want to modify the filter-based query or add more complex criteria, open the query's Query Design view and you can see that Access selected the proper source table and field names for you. You can then add to the criteria lines and request additional fields if you want.

Q **Does the row on which I place criteria make a difference?**

A Yes, although you are getting into some confusing logic. The way you specify criteria between two fields often indicates how you want the combined criteria to work. If you place one field's criterion on the same row as another field's, an implied *and* relation takes place, and Access extracts only those records that contain a match for both criteria values. If you place one field's criterion on a different row from another field's, an implied *or* relation takes place between them.

Q **How can I see my data in two ways, say, with the field names arranged alphabetically and with the fields arranged in the order of my table's design?**

A Create a query that extracts all the fields from your table. The query's output, or data subset, will contain all data that the original table contains (the subset will be the same size as the table). Set up the query's output for ordering the fields alphabetically. Queries aren't just for creating smaller subsets of tables; you can create a query to report table data in an order that differs from a table's original design order.

20

HOUR **21**

Reporting with Access 2002

This hour shows you how to create custom Access 2002 reports. Access includes several reporting tools, both automatic and manual, that produce complex reports. You can create a simple report by clicking a toolbar button. If you spend a little time developing the report with a report wizard, you can create extremely professional-looking reports.

You do not have to master the Report Design view, an extensive and complex report-creating tool, to create most of your reports. Some people have never used the Report Design view to design an Access report from scratch because of the report wizards' power. The report wizards give you complete control over a report's design.

The highlights of this hour include the following:

- How to create report queries
- How AutoReport creates simple reports
- Which report wizards Access supports

- How to use the main Report Wizard to generate virtually any report you need by making a few selections
- When to request summary statistics
- Why you should preview reports

Introducing Access Reports

You often want printed listings of your data, and the Access reporting tools enable you to produce professional reports with ease. This hour explains how to use the report wizards and discusses the different reporting styles and options available. You learned how to produce printed listings in Hour 19, "Entering and Displaying Access 2002 Data." In this hour, you learn how to add flair to your reports.

Unlike forms, a report often displays multiple records in a view that resembles the Datasheet view. The difference between the Datasheet view and a printed report is that the report provides summary statistics, fancy headings, footers, page numbers, and styles that accent your data. In addition, you can pick and choose exactly what data the report is to include as well as group that data to subtotal and total certain pieces of data in the database.

A *report* is not only a listing of multiple data values. Anytime you need to send Access data to paper, you must create a report. Therefore, a report might be a series of checks or mailing labels that you print.

Before you print any report, use the Print Preview to see the report on your screen. Often, you notice changes that you need to make, so previewing a report can save you time and paper. Your computer's print *spooler* (the area of memory that holds your report while printing) is too fast to stop quickly, so you usually end up printing the first few pages of a report even if you attempt to stop the printing.

When you are about to print a report, click the Reports object in the left pane of the Database window, select a report, and click the Preview button on the Database window's toolbar. Access can generate nice reports (see Figure 21.1).

Rarely do you report all the data from a single table. Except for detailed reports, such as inventory listings and master customer listings, you almost always report part of a table or values from multiple tables.

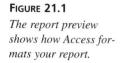

Figure 21.1

The report preview shows how Access formats your report.

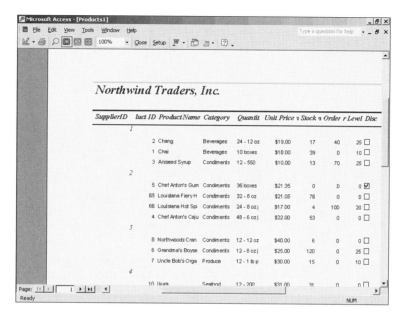

Almost all reports that you generate, therefore, get their data from queries that you have created. If you need to report from part of a table's data or from multiple tables, create a query on which to base the report. Your queries can order the data the way you want to see it, and Access can then print your query's results.

Generating Simple Reports Using AutoReports

Access includes an *AutoReport* feature, which quickly generates reports from your Datasheet views. As Figure 21.2 shows, the AutoReport feature is just a listing of field names and their corresponding field values.

Unlike the printed listings you get when you select File, Print from the Datasheet view, AutoReport formats your data in a readable manner without squeezing too much information on a single page. If you need to run a quick report from a table, follow these steps to enable AutoReport to generate the report:

1. Display your data in a Datasheet view. If you want to report from a subset of data or from a collection of multiple tables, display the query's Datasheet view or apply a filter to the data.

2. Click the down arrow next to the New Object button on the toolbar.

3. Select AutoReport from the button's drop-down list. Access generates a report from the current Datasheet view and shows a preview of the report (shown in Figure 21.2).

21

FIGURE 21.2

AutoReport generates simple reports.

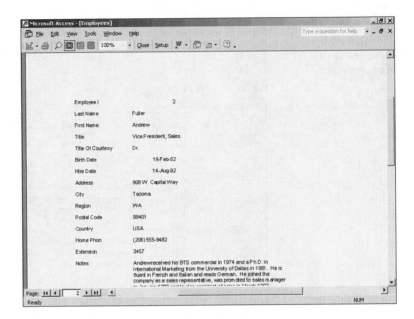

4. If the preview shows what you want, click the Database toolbar's Print icon to print the report.

5. Click the Design button to close the AutoReport preview and to display the Report Design view (shown in Figure 21.3). The Report Design view can be difficult to understand when you first see it. (The Form Design view looks similar.) For now, don't worry about the specific screen elements. AutoReport created the report's design and saved you from having to use the Report Design view tools that you see in Figure 21.3.

6. Close the Report Design view and enter a report name if you want to save the AutoReport's design. If you think you will ever edit an AutoReport design later or generate the same report often, save the report. Generally, you use AutoReport only to generate quick reports. You will use the report wizards (described next) to generate more standard reports.

AutoReport generates reports using Access's report-designing tools. After you learn how to modify a Report Design view, you can use AutoReport to generate the foundation of a report, and then change the report to make it look the way you want.

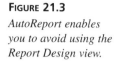

FIGURE 21.3

AutoReport enables you to avoid using the Report Design view.

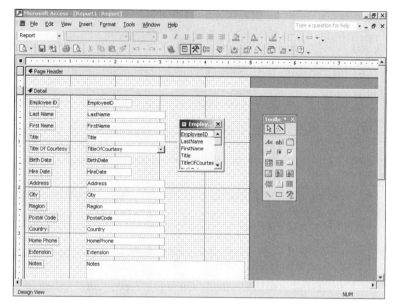

If you like using AutoReport for quick reports, check out the AutoForm feature. AutoForm creates fast and simple forms from your Datasheet views.

Generating Reports Using the Report Wizards

Access includes several report wizards that design reports according to the specifications you give. Select one of the report wizards by opening the Database window, clicking the Reports object (which displays the reports currently defined in the database), and clicking the New button to create a new report. The New Report screen (see Figure 21.4) appears.

The New Report dialog box enables you to access the following reporting components:

- *Design View*—A blank Report Design view on which you can add a new report's headers, footers, detail, and *summary* requests. When you want to generate a report from scratch, use the Design View in the New Report dialog box.

- *Report Wizard*—Walks you through the report-generation process by enabling you to select the source tables and queries as well as the fields that you want in the final report. You will probably run Report Wizard more often than the other options because it generates less specific reports than other reporting wizards. The next section, "Using the Report Wizard," explains how you can use Report Wizard to create reports.

21

FIGURE 21.4

Request a report from the New Report dialog box.

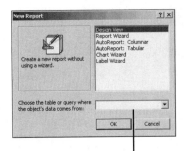

Click here to select a table or query

- *AutoReport: Columnar*—Generates a report that contains all the fields from the underlying table or query. The columnar report resembles the AutoReport, except that the columnar report makes better use of your report's page space and designs a more routine report. A columnar report can include titles and special fonts, and can emphasize field data.

- *AutoReport: Tabular*—Generates a report that displays on a single line the record of each source table or query by adjusting the font size to fit your report page. The tabular report looks much better than a simple Datasheet view, and is often more useful than the generic AutoReport you learned about in the previous section. Figure 21.5 shows a sample of the wizard's tabular report. As you can see from the figure, Access is not always able to fit the complete field name at the top of a column of data. You can adjust the report's design to allow more room for the field name if you prefer.

FIGURE 21.5

Tabular reports produce well-organized listings of your data.

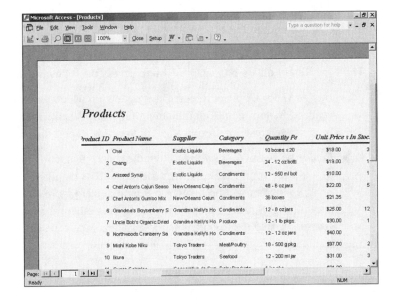

- *Chart Wizard*—Produces graphs from your data. Access graphs resemble Excel graphs, and you can control the format and style as well as the table from which Access graphs.

- *Label Wizard*—A generic mailing-list report that produces mailing labels for all common labels. The mailing label industry has a standard numbering system (the *Avery numbering system*, after the company that is perhaps best known for computerized mailing labels). Most office-supply stores sell mailing labels with an official Avery number, so you can format a report for your labels.

Using the Report Wizard

The second New Report screen option, Report Wizard, is probably the most common selection you make when you generate customized reports. The Report Wizard walks you through a series of steps to create a custom report from your tables and queries, and it includes many common reporting styles and special features that you need.

> You must create a named query before generating a report based on that query. You cannot create a report based on a query that you have not yet written.

To start the Report Wizard, follow these steps:

1. Display the Database window.
2. Click the Reports object to display any database reports you've defined and to generate new ones.
3. Click the New button to display the New Report screen.
4. Select Report Wizard.
5. Open the New Report's drop-down list box to select from a list of tables and queries that reside in your database.
6. Click the OK button to display the Report Wizard's field selection screen (shown in Figure 21.6). The field selection screen displays a list of fields from your selected table or query that you can select for use as the report's data.

21

FIGURE 21.6
*Select the fields you
want for your report.*

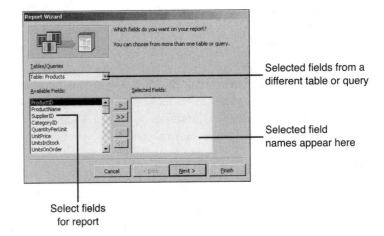

Selected fields from a
different table or query

Selected field
names appear here

Select fields
for report

7. Select the fields that you want in the final report by clicking the field in the
Available Fields list and then clicking > to send the field to the Selected Fields list.
You can also double-click a field name to send it to the Selected Fields list. As you
can see when you open the Tables/Queries drop-down list box, you can select
fields from several tables and queries in addition to the primary source you
selected in step 5.

8. After you select the fields for the report, click Next.

Grouping Report Summaries

Now that you have selected the report fields, you must indicate how the report is to be
summarized. Rarely will you want to print a data listing without requesting a *report summary* that includes totals and subtotals. Depending on the type of numeric fields you
have selected for the report, the Report Wizard prompts you for subtotal and total summary information or grouping information. If your report contains numeric data, the
Report Wizard lets you choose the grouping options (shown in Figure 21.7). Use this dialog box to indicate how you want Access to group your report subtotals.

FIGURE 21.7
*Indicate how Access is
to produce the subto-
tals and totals.*

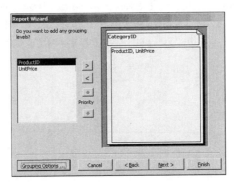

> Access totals and subtotals reports based on a group's numeric fields, not text fields. The numeric fields enable the Report Wizard to produce subtotals and total summaries, whereas no such summaries are possible with text fields.

If Access does not display the Summary dialog box, the Report Wizard prompts you for grouping information, and you can select the field on which you want your data grouped. When you request grouping, you are telling Access how to sort your report. If you grouped by a City field, for example, the report would sort the report in City order. The subtotals are then summed for each city in the report data.

You might have to run the Report Wizard a couple of times to group the report the way you prefer. Be sure to select only those numeric fields that produce proper subtotals. If you report a division number field and that field is numeric, for example, you wouldn't want Access to subtotal and total the division number. If you print a report with customer past-due balances, however, you do want to print a subtotal for each customer and an overall grand total of past-due balances.

The grouping field should be non-numeric groups, such as customer IDs, for which you are printing a detailed list. Although the same customer might appear on several report lines, you want Access to subtotal only when the customer ID changes to the next customer in the report. The grouping doesn't total or subtotal the customer IDs, but the totals and subtotals that appear all break (stop) when the customer ID changes. The grouping capability keeps multiple customer IDs from appearing down the column when you print multiple records for the same customer.

As you click each field that you selected, the grouping dialog box displays a preview of your report, showing how the grouping will fall out. Generally, the grouping options and preview give you enough information to decide on a grouping scheme.

If you want to group on multiple fields, the group order you select determines the priority that Access uses to group the data. The highest priority grouping level (if you select multiple groups) appears on the left of the report, the second grouping level appears to the right of the first one, and so on. Generally, multifield grouping gets confusing. If you want to add such grouping levels, click every group level from the series of fields that Access displays. The Report Wizard prioritizes the multifield groups in the order that you select the fields.

21

You can group by a maximum of four field-grouping levels. If you need to group by more than four fields, you have to edit the report design or create a report from scratch. Rarely do you need more than four groups.

If the Report Wizard has presented you with the grouping view screen rather than the subtotal and total summary screens described here, you need only click the field by which you want to group the report. If you are producing a customer balance report, for example, the Report Wizard might enable you to group by either the Customer ID field or the Customer Order Number field.

After you have set up the grouping levels that you need, click Next to select a sort and summary order for the report.

The Report's Sort and Summary Order

When you see the sorting and summary screen (see Figure 21.8), you are almost done creating your report. Select from one to four fields that you want Access to use for sorting your data. If you are reporting from a query that already contains sorted data, and if you generate the report so that the data groups in the order of those sorted fields, don't select any fields by which to sort. If you want to sort by one or more fields that do not enter the reporting system already sorted, however, select up to four fields and click the button labeled Ascending to sort in ascending order.

The Ascending button changes to Descending when you click it, so you can then select a descending sort.

Selected sort   Click for
fields   descending

FIGURE 21.8

Select from one to four fields by which to sort.

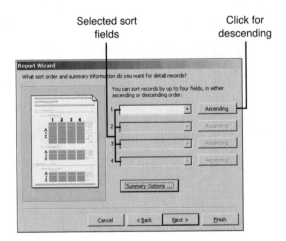

If you requested totals and subtotals in earlier Report Wizard steps, you will see a Summary Options button. These options display the Report Wizard's Summary Options screen. Each of your report's numeric fields appears in the box, so you can select any or all these summaries for that field:

- *Sum*—Requests a total for the field
- *Avg*—Requests an average for the field
- *Min*—Requests that Access highlight the minimum value in the field
- *Max*—Requests that Access highlight the maximum value in the field

> You cannot display summaries if your report has no numeric fields or if you are grouping by the numeric fields.

Choosing a Report Layout and Style

Click OK to close the Summary Options screen, and then click Next to choose a report layout. Click through the various layouts to select one that fits your needs. As you click layouts, Access displays thumbnail sketches of those layouts. If you click the Block style, for example, you see that Access displays boxes around your report fields.

After you select the layout, click Next to select from the Report Wizard's style screen (shown in Figure 21.9). From this dialog box, you can add the finishing touches to your report.

FIGURE 21.9

The Report Wizard's style screen determines the overall appearance of your report.

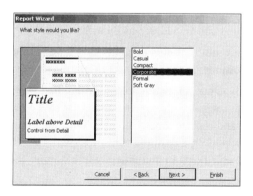

Click Next, enter a report title if you don't want to use the original source table or query name, and click Finish to generate the completed report. Sometimes Access takes several minutes to generate the report, especially if the source tables and queries contain many records and your report contains several grouping levels. When finished, Access prints a preview of your report so that you can look at your handiwork.

21

Summary

Access is certainly a powerful program. Despite its ease of use, it does take some getting used to before you fully master all its features. You will probably use the Access wizards more than any other wizard in any other Office product.

At this point, you are ready to begin generating sample databases and practicing with Access. As you create more databases, you learn how to partition your data properly into tables and generate data-entry forms and reports.

Hour 22, "Sharing Information Between Programs," begins the part of the book that explains how the Office programs work together to help you with your data-processing requirements. In addition, you learn more about using Office with the Internet.

Q&A

Q How does the toolbar's AutoReport differ from the AutoReport entries I see on the Report Wizard's opening screen?

A The AutoReport entries on the Report Wizard's opening screen create more finished reports than the AutoReport toolbar button. Use the AutoReport toolbar button to quickly generate a report from your Datasheet and Form views. Use the Report Wizard AutoReport entries to produce more complete reports without taking the time to set up summary and sorting features. Not all reports require summaries, and the two AutoReport wizards suffice for many reports that you will generate.

Q What is the largest page size that I can produce in an Access report?

A Access report pages can be as large as 22 inches wide by 22 inches long.

Q Do I subtotal on numeric fields or fields that I want to group by, such as Customer ID numbers?

A When you specify grouping instructions, the field that you group by is usually a nonnumeric field, such as a Customer ID field. Access collects all the customer ID records together and reports each customer's information in one group. When Access finishes reporting a customer's records (when the ID changes), Access subtotals the numeric fields in that group before starting the next group.

PART VII

Combining the Office XP Products and the Internet

Hour

Hour **22**

Sharing Information Between Programs

This hour explores how Office XP products work together. Office programs integrate so well that it is hard to know where to start describing the possibilities. Generally, if you need to combine two or more Office files, you are able to load or embed one product's file within another even though the Office programs that created the two files are completely different.

From inserting links in Word documents to combining an Access table and an Excel worksheet into a PowerPoint presentation, Office supplies the interaction you need. You can also add your own graphics to your Office documents by drawing with the Office drawing tools.

The highlights of this hour include the following:

- Why drag-and-drop operations work so well between Office programs
- How to control a drag-and-drop operation to produce a copy, a move, or a link
- How to edit, update, and break links between Office documents

- What requirements a Word document must meet to serve as a PowerPoint presentation
- Which steps you must take to import Access data into Word
- How to write letters to Outlook contacts quickly
- How to select WordArt styles when you want to add fancy text titles and banners to your Office documents

Sharing Data Between Applications

Office's cornerstone is data sharing among its programs. Office offers several ways to share information among products. Almost all the Office products support the inclusion of other Office files. For example, Word includes the Insert Microsoft Excel Worksheet toolbar button that inserts any Excel worksheet in a Word document.

Besides inserting entire files, you might want to insert part of a document in another Office application. The following sections explain the most common methods to embed part of one application's file inside another.

Drag and Drop

Suppose that you want to use part of an Excel worksheet inside a Word document. You might want to do this if you are preparing a report for management on last quarter's sales figures. If you have both Excel (with the relevant data loaded) and Word running at the same time, these steps quickly insert the worksheet into the Word document:

1. Resize your Excel and Word program windows so that you can see both the *source file* (the Excel worksheet) and the *destination file* (the Word document).
2. In the Excel worksheet, select the cells that you want to copy and transfer to Word.
3. You can use the keyboard or mouse to make the transfer. Select Edit, Copy to copy the selected cells to the Office Clipboard, click on the Word document's location where you want the cells to go, and select Edit, Paste to place the worksheet into Word. You can also hold the Ctrl key and drag one edge of the highlighted worksheet cells directly to the location in your Word document where you want to place the table and release the mouse to finalize the transfer. Figure 22.1 shows the result of such a copy.

If you use the mouse and do not first press Ctrl before dragging the cells, Excel will move the table from the Excel worksheet to the Word document instead of copying the table.

FIGURE 22.1
This table in Word came from Excel.

From here in Excel...

...to here in Word

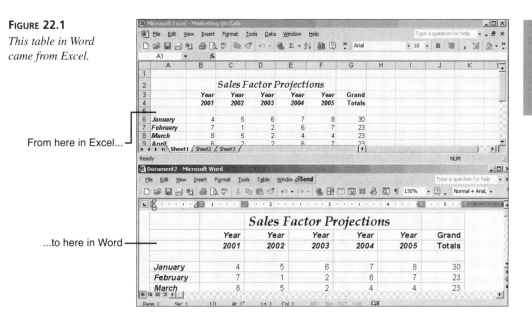

Depending on the size and style of your Word document, you might want to format the copied table differently from Excel's format. Right-click the table and select Format Object to display the Format Object dialog box. You can apply colors, lines, shading, and other formatting attributes to the copied object from the Format Object dialog box.

Creating Links

Suppose that you create a monthly sales report using the same Word document and the same Excel worksheet every time. Although the data within the Excel worksheet changes to reflect each new month's figures, the structure and formulas remain the same. You don't have to drag the updated Excel table to your Word document before printing the Word document each month. Instead of copying or moving the cells, you can create a *link* to the cells. A link points to another file.

As long as you have inserted a link to the Excel worksheet in your monthly report document's template, you need only change the Excel worksheet each month, start Word, create a report document from the template, and print the document. You won't have to copy or move the actual Excel cells into the report because the link points to the cells and displays their contents. The report always points to the worksheet cells via the link that you inserted when you created the Word document.

To create such a link, perform these steps:

1. Arrange and resize your two program windows so that you can see both the source document (the Excel worksheet) and the destination document (the Word document).

2. Select the cells in the Excel worksheet that you want to link and transfer to Word.

3. With the right mouse button, drag the edge of the highlighted cells to the location in your Word document where you want to place the table. You might have to practice doing this for a while if you are not accustomed to using the right mouse button for dragging.

4. Release the right mouse button. Word opens a shortcut menu with these options: Move Here, Copy Here, Link Excel Object Here, Create Shortcut Here, Create Hyperlink Here, and Cancel.

5. Select Link Excel Object Here to indicate to Word that you want to create an object link (as opposed to a move or a copy of the cells). Although the cells appear as though Office copied them into the Word document, the cells represent only the link that you created between the Excel source file and Word's destination document. Whenever you change the data in Excel's source file, the linked information in Word is automatically updated.

> The destination file (in this case, the Word document) always reflects the most recent changes to the source file (in this case, the Excel worksheet). Therefore, if you must keep archives of old reports with the previous monthly values, you want to copy the cells instead of creating a link.

> After inserting one or more links, select Edit, Links to produce the dialog box shown in Figure 22.2. The Links dialog box contains every link in your document and enables you to change, break, or lock any link. When you break a link, the data becomes embedded in the document and no longer updates when you update the source. When you lock a link, you temporarily prevent the link from being updated when its source is updated.

To watch the real-time nature of the links, change a value in the source Excel worksheet. The Word document immediately reflects your change. If the Word document does not reflect the change, select Edit, Links and make sure that the Automatic Update option is set. If Manual Update is set, Word will not update the link to reflect any changes in the Excel worksheet until you select Edit, Links and click the Update Now button.

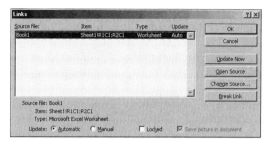

FIGURE 22.2

Use the Links dialog box to manage your document links.

Creating Shortcuts

Instead of inserting a copy or a link, you can insert a *shortcut* in the destination document.

You probably use shortcuts less often than links and embedded copies when producing reports because you usually want the reports to show actual data and not icons. If you often work with data from one program while in another program, however, the shortcuts are nice. The data does not get in your way until you are ready to work with it because you see only icons that represent the shortcut data. In addition, the icon loads much faster than the underlying data would load and speed becomes an issue if you work on older computers.

> When you create a shortcut from one Office program to another, Office displays a shortcut icon. If you double-click the data, Office opens the appropriate program and enables you to edit the original data using the source program that created the data. If you insert a shortcut into a non-Office program, however, Office inserts a shortcut icon that represents the data. If you double-click the icon from within the other program, the appropriate Office program begins, and you can edit the data.

Several scenarios exist where a link might work well. Suppose that you are working in Excel, modifying weekly salary figures for a large worksheet that you maintain. Each week you must study the salary amounts and enter a 10-line explanation of the salaries. Instead of typing the definition each week or (worse) using Excel as a limited word processor and editing the text each week, you could embed a shortcut to a Word document that contains a template for the text. When you double-click the shortcut, Excel starts Word, which automatically loads the template. You can create the final text in the template, copy the Word text into your salary worksheet (replacing the shortcut), and save the worksheet under a name that designates the current week's work.

To insert a shortcut, perform these steps:

1. Arrange and resize your program windows so that you can see both the source document (the Word template document) and the destination file (the Excel worksheet).

2. Select the Word template text that you want to use for the shortcut. (Press Ctrl+A if you want to select the entire Word template document.)

3. With the right mouse button, drag the edge of the highlighted template text to the location in your Excel worksheet where you want to place the shortcut.

4. Release the right mouse button.

5. Select Create Shortcut Here from the pop-up menu. Office creates the shortcut. As with a link, the shortcut data does not actually appear in the destination document. Unlike a link, you can drag the shortcut to your Windows desktop, to Explorer, or to another program to create additional copies of the shortcut.

Before inserting an Access table into another Office program, run a query to filter data that doesn't interest you. Hour 20, "Retrieving Your Data," explains how to develop data queries. Later in this hour, the section titled "Using Word and Access" describes how to insert Access data into a Word document.

Inserting Hyperlinks

Thanks to the Internet, more and more users are accustomed to using hyperlinks. A hyperlink is text (or an object) that describes the link to another document or to a Web page on the Internet. When you point to the hyperlink, the mouse pointer changes to the shape of a hand. When you click the hyperlink, that linked document appears.

Perhaps you want to insert a hyperlink to a corporate Web site that an employee can click to locate information on a product's specifications. You can insert hyperlinks to other Office products, but in reality, hyperlinks are typically used for Web pages.

The nature of hyperlinks means that you will use hyperlinks most often to point to Web pages. Office XP makes inserting hyperlinks extremely simple if you display the actual Web page address inside your Office XP files. For example, if you want to embed a hyperlink inside an Excel worksheet, you only need to type the hyperlink itself and Excel automatically turns that address into a hyperlink. As soon as you type the Web address, Excel underlines the Web address and turns the address into a hyperlink to that site.

You can turn the automatic conversion of Web addresses into hyperlinks on and off. Select Tools, AutoCorrect and click the tab labeled AutoFormat As You Type. Uncheck the option labeled Internet and Network Paths with Hyperlinks when you want to type Web addresses without the Office product converting that address to a hyperlink.

22

Remember that you don't have to use Web addresses for hyperlinks in Office documents. You can enter path and filenames that reside on your own PC. When you or another user clicks the link, the Office product displays that link's file. Therefore, you can easily link documents together, even documents from different products within Office.

Perhaps you want something other than the Web address to appear. In other words, one of your PowerPoint presentation slides might include the text `Click here to view our informative Web page` and, when clicked, during the presentation, the slide changes to show the actual Web page. To change a hyperlink to customized text, follow these steps:

1. Type the Web address or path to the Office file that you want to display when the user clicks the hyperlink.

2. Select the hyperlink.

3. Press Ctrl+K to display the Insert Hyperlink dialog box shown in Figure 22.3. The toolbar also displays an Insert Hyperlink button that displays the Edit Hyperlink dialog box.

Enter hyperlink text here

FIGURE 22.3

Use the Insert Hyperlink dialog to change the text on the hyperlink.

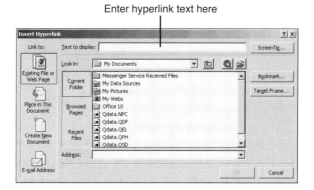

4. Type a new value in the text box labeled Text to Display.

5. Click OK. Your text appears in place of the hyperlink's address.

Turning a Word Document into a Presentation

Word and PowerPoint share a special link that enables you to turn a set of notes into a presentation. As you create your notes in Word, be sure to use the Heading 1 through Heading 5 styles. PowerPoint uses the Heading 1 style for each slide's title and uses the Heading 2 through Heading 5 styles for the slide's subsequently indented text.

If your Word document contains styles other than Heading 1 through Heading 5, PowerPoint ignores those paragraphs.

You can easily apply Heading 1 through Heading 5 styles to a Word document that you have already created by clicking a paragraph (or by moving the mouse pointer anywhere within the paragraph), and clicking the Style box's drop-down arrow, and selecting Heading styles from the drop-down list box. You can also select the style by opening the Style drop-down list box and scrolling to the heading style that you want to select.

After you create the Word document, open the document from within PowerPoint and save the presentation. From Word itself, you can convert your document to a presentation by selecting File, Send To, Microsoft PowerPoint.

Using Word and Access

A database can be extremely large with many tables. Often, you want to export a portion of an Access database to a Word document. The drag-and-drop method does not always offer exactly what you need to get the data you want into a Word document.

> If you want to use an Access table in a PowerPoint presentation, load the table into a Word document, and then convert the Word document to a PowerPoint presentation as described in the previous section.

To load Access data into a Word document, perform these steps:

1. Display the Database toolbar in Word (select View, Toolbars and then click Database).

2. Click the Insert Database toolbar button. Word displays the Database dialog box.

3. Click the Get Data button to begin locating the database to import. Before specifying the data to be imported into Word, you must locate the database.

4. Browse to the database file you want to import. When you locate the database, select the database and Word displays the Select Table dialog box shown in Figure 22.4.

FIGURE 22.4

Indicate exactly which table Word is to use.

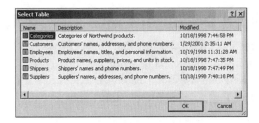

5. Select the table or query that you want to load into the Word document, and click OK to return to the Database dialog box.

6. Click the Query Options button if you want to limit the table's records or fields. (If you don't select the Query Options button, Word imports the entire table.) Word displays an Access query window, from which you can select records and fields using normal Access database-selection criteria. Select one or more fields that meet the criteria you specify. You can specify additional tables if you want Word to import data from multiple tables.

7. Click the Insert Data button to insert your selected data.

8. You now can format the data and use it in your Word document as if you typed the data yourself.

Outlook Letters

Users often keep Outlook loaded throughout the day, making appointments, calling contacts, and planning meetings. Outlook includes a handy feature that enables you to write a letter to any contact quickly and easily. A wizard makes the connection between Outlook and Word. The following steps explain how to access this often-overlooked feature from Outlook:

1. Click to select any Outlook contact.

2. Select Actions, New Letter to Contact to start Word's Letter Wizard shown in Figure 22.5.

FIGURE 22.5
The Letter Wizard takes care of the letter's formatting and address details.

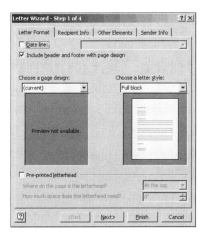

3. Select a page design and letter style from the dialog box.

4. Click the Recipient Info tab to display the letter's recipient information. The wizard will have already filled in the contact's name and address. Select or type the salutation that you desire on the Recipient Info tab.

5. Click the Other Elements tab to define other aspects of the letter such as the reference line and subject if those items are to appear.

6. Click the Sender Info tab to enter information about you, the sender. You can put
   your return address information as well as a company name and closing, such as
   "Best Wishes."

7. Click Finish and Word builds the letter using the elements you selected. Your only
   job now is to fill in the details such as the body of the letter and to complete the
   elements such as the attention and subject lines.

In a similar manner, you can send a letter you're writing in Word to an e-mail recipient.
With your Word document loaded, select File, Send To, Mail Recipient. Word opens an
e-mail message and copies your document to the message body. You then can click the
To button to select a recipient who is to receive the e-mailed document.

Sending Attachments

When you work on an Office file, such as a Word document or Excel worksheet, you can easily send the document to one of your Outlook recipients.
Simply select File, Send To, Mail Recipient (As Attachment). Office automatically opens a new e-mail message with your document attached to the message. You then can click the To button or type a recipient's e-mail address,
enter a subject, and send the e-mail with your file attached. The user on the
other end can then open your e-mail message from within her mail program
and save or view your attachment.

Enhancing Your Office Documents

Office enables you to insert images and other objects into your documents. Graphics
spruce up newsletters and other documents that require eye-catching images.

In Hour 6, "Advanced Word 2002," you learned how to use the Media Gallery to insert
images, sounds, and videos into presentations. In addition to producing the Media Gallery
for clip files, the Insert, Picture option produces a menu that includes the following options:

- *From File*—Enables you to insert an image from any graphics file. Use this option
  when you don't want to confine your images to the ones supplied in the Media
  Gallery.

- *From Scanner or Camera*—Enables you to scan an image into the Office document
  or receive a digital camera's image. You must have a TWAIN-compliant scanner or
  digital camera attached to pull such images into Office. (Most scanners follow the
  PC scanner standard called TWAIN; your scanner's documentation should indicate
  whether your scanner is TWAIN-compliant.)

- *Organization Chart*—Starts an Office add-in application that creates organizational charts.

- *New Drawing*—Enables you to use the Drawing toolbar to create your own artwork.

- *AutoShapes*—Inserts one of Office's *AutoShapes*, pre-designed shapes such as arrows and stars that you can resize and place where you want.

- *WordArt*—Displays the WordArt Gallery of styles (shown in Figure 22.6). WordArt enables you to convert text into shapes. Despite its name, WordArt is available from all Office products, not just Word.

- *Chart*—Displays asmall Excel-like worksheet (called a datasheet) in which you can enter data. The datasheet offers a sample set of cells in which you can enter your own values or import data from Excel. When you close the datasheet, the resulting bar chart appears in your document.

FIGURE 22.6

You can select a WordArt style from the WordArt Gallery.

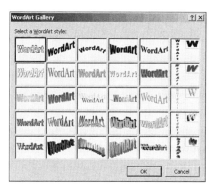

The next three sections describe the most common graphics insertions you can make into your Office files from the Insert, Picture menu.

Inserting Images from Files

To add an image (or sound or video) clip-art file to a document, select Insert, Picture, From File to display the Insert Picture dialog box. Locate the image on your disk (or on your network, or the Internet by selecting the source from the Look in list box) and click Insert to insert the image.

If you often insert the same image, sound, or video clip, consider adding the clip to the Office Media Gallery. The Media Gallery makes common clips easy for you to find, thus eliminating the need for you to search your disk drive every time you want to insert a clip file. Hour 6 explains how to use the Media Gallery's search feature to locate clips on your computer and place them in the Media Gallery.

Inserting WordArt

WordArt displays text in several shapes, colors, and styles to add pizzazz to your documents. You can add an eye-catching title at the top of an Excel worksheet, for example, to grab the reader's attention.

To add a WordArt image, perform these steps:

1. Select Insert, Picture, WordArt to display the WordArt Gallery dialog box.
2. Select the WordArt style that you want to use by double-clicking the style. Office displays the Edit WordArt Text dialog box (shown in Figure 22.7).

FIGURE 22.7

Provide text for
WordArt to format.

3. Enter the text that you want to format as WordArt and select the proper font and point size. The WordArt style that you select follows your font and size request as closely as possible.
4. Click OK to insert the WordArt text. Office displays resizing handles around the WordArt image, which you can use to resize or move the image. In addition, the WordArt toolbar that appears provides several editing techniques that you can apply to the image, such as rotation and color.

Figure 22.8 shows a sample WordArt image inserted at the top of a small imported Excel worksheet.

FIGURE 22.8

*A sample shows
WordArt's appeal.*

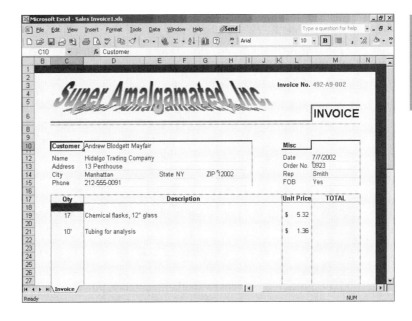

Summary

This hour described how to integrate Office products by sharing data files among the programs. One of the most elegant ways to copy or move data from one Office program to another is to use drag and drop. By holding your right mouse button, you can control how the drag-and-drop operation sends the data from one document to another.

Word and PowerPoint share data files easily as long as you use the proper heading styles. Presenters often use Word documents as a basis for a PowerPoint presentation, and you will appreciate the automation Office provides. After you convert your Word document to a PowerPoint presentation, you can adjust the presentation's format and add slides if you want.

When importing Access data into Word, you must be selective. Databases are often huge, and you usually want to import only a small part of the database into your Word document. Make sure to indicate to Word what data from what table you want to import so that you get only the data you need.

This hour also explained how to use the graphics-related tools to insert art and draw pictures inside your Office documents. As you might expect, the Office tools are easy to use and appear (along with their toolbars) when you request them, but stay out of the way when you don't need to work with them.

The next hour, "Office and the Internet," introduces the Internet and shows you how to access Web pages using the Internet Explorer Web browser included with Office.

Q&A

Q **What format does my data take when I drag and drop something from one Office product to another?**

A Office provides excellent intuitive conversions when you combine data from more than one Office product. When you drag a worksheet from Excel to Word, for example, the worksheet becomes a Word table. You then can use all the standard table-editing tools in Word to modify the appearance of the worksheet. Excel converts Word text to text-cell entries. Excel converts Access table data to worksheet cells, respecting the data types when possible (so the numbers stay numbers and the dates stay dates).

Q **Why would you ever want to copy data and not create a link to another document?**

A When you copy data, it is copied into the destination document, so the data resides in both the destination document and the source document. If you were to take the destination document to another computer, the document could not access its original link (if you had used a link). In addition, you might not want the destination document's data being hooked "live" to the source data. If you are creating archive files of older data, for example, you want always to copy the data and not form a link or shortcut to the original source data. Keep in mind that if you do copy or paste the data instead of forming a link, and if the data changes in its original location, the copied data will not reflect that change.

Q **Why wouldn't you import a complete database into Word?**

A A complete database contains tables, queries, reports, forms, macros, and modules, and all those items make little sense in a Word document. If you need to report data using the entire Access database, use Access to generate reports. Word is useful for printing database subsets. If you want to include part of an Access database table in a Word report, you can easily send the table's data into Word using the tools described in this lesson.

Hour **23**

Office XP and the Internet

If you are new to Internet technology, this hour introduces you to a whole new world. If you already use the Internet, you might want to peruse this hour's lesson anyway to pick up the Office specifics that relate to Internet access. The Internet is much more a part of computer users' lives than ever before. Microsoft recognizes this and includes Internet access capabilities in Office. The individual Office products all provide some level of Internet connectivity. Microsoft is committed to integrating Internet access more completely into future Office and Windows releases, and you see that commitment already in Office XP.

The highlights of this hour include the following:

- Why the Internet and the Web are so important
- How to start and use Internet Explorer
- How to surf the Internet to find and view multimedia information
- How to use search engines to locate the exact Internet information you need

- How to access the Internet from within an Office product
- How to view Office documents from within Internet Explorer
- How to include Web links in your Office documents

A Brief Internet Primer

The *Internet* began as a government- and university-linked system of computers that has since turned into a business and personal system that contains a seemingly infinite amount of information. The Internet is a worldwide system of interconnected computers. Whereas your desktop computer is a standalone machine, and a network of computers is linked together by wires, the Internet is a worldwide online network of computers connected to standalone computers through modems.

The Internet offers the most unique research and information-access tools ever invented. You can get up-to-date news, stock quotes, and sports scores. You can locate product information, purchase everything from cars to airline tickets, play games, listen to music, view videos, and chat with other Internet users around the world via your keyboard or microphone.

That vast amount and format of Internet data requires a standard so that all can share in the Internet's content. The Internet currently brings together a set of standard Web page formats (using HTML code), e-mail messages, and other protocols such as chat systems and graphics supported by all the major Web browsers and related programs. Users all over the world send electronic mail to each other, view each other's Internet material, send files back and forth, conduct business over the Internet, research from the Internet, keep up with the latest news, sports, entertainment, and business headlines, and chat with each other through the keyboard, voice, and video.

Introducing the Web

The *Web*, or *World Wide Web (WWW)*, is a collection of Internet pages of information. Web pages can contain text, graphics, sound, and video. The pages are linked to other pages to make for easy traversal back and forth between Web sites via hyperlinks. Figure 23.1 shows a sample Web page. As you can see, the Web page's graphics and text organize information into a magazine-like readable and appealing format.

FIGURE 23.1

Web pages provide Internet information in a standard format.

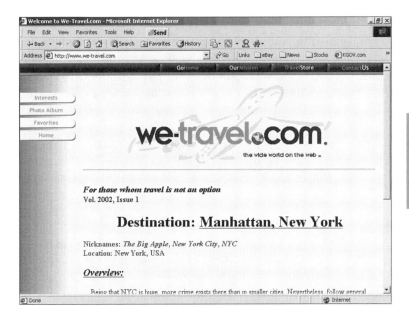

Generally, a Web site might contain more information than fits easily on a single Web page. Therefore, many Web pages contain links to several additional extended pages, as well as other linked Web pages that might be related to the original topic. The first page you view is called the *home page*, and from the home page you can view other pages of information. You can think of the home page as a table of contents for the entire Web site.

The Internet has standardized Web page locations with a series of addresses called *URLs*, or *uniform resource locators*, that are formatted like this: http://www.microsoft.com. You can view any Web page if you know its URL. If you do not know the URL, the Internet provides several search engines that find Web pages when you search for topics. You learn how to search the Internet later this hour in the "Searching for the Information You Need" section.

Using Internet Explorer

Internet Explorer is a *Web browser* (also called a *browser*) that brings Web data to your desktop. Microsoft's free Web browsing program, *Internet Explorer*, works closely with the Office products and integrates with them nicely as you'll see in this hour's lesson.

If your company offers networked Internet access, you need a network interface card in your PC so you can connect to the company's Internet connection. If you use the

Internet from home, or from an office that does not provide networked Internet access, you need to get Internet access through an *ISP*, an *Internet service provider*. One of the easiest ways to get access is through the Microsoft Network or America Online services, which have access programs that are available with all Windows 98, Windows Me, and Windows 2000 installations. If you want Internet access through another ISP, such as a local Internet provider, your provider will tell you how to use Internet Explorer or another Web browser to access the ISP's Internet system. You will also need modem access (56K is the minimum recommended speed these days) or another Internet connection that might be available in your area such as a cable modem or DSL (*Digital Subscriber Line*). Check your phone book for options that you can get locally.

Although Internet service is relatively inexpensive, it is not free. Most modem-based ISPs charge a flat rate, such as $21.95 a month, for unlimited Internet usage. Higher speed Internet access, such as DSL, will typically run more per month than the dial-up ISPs.

Web browsers such as Internet Explorer are easy to start. You literally can access the Internet with one or two clicks by running Internet Explorer. After you sign up with an ISP and get the Internet phone number to access the Web, you are ready to navigate the Internet.

To start Internet Explorer, double-click the Windows desktop icon labeled Internet Explorer. If you get an Internet Connection Wizard dialog box, you must contact your service provider to learn how to hook up Internet Explorer to the Internet. Internet Explorer prompts you for the username and password that you selected when you signed up for your Internet service.

Assuming that you have Internet access and have been set up with a provider, Internet Explorer dials your provider and displays the page set up to be your initial browser's *home page*. If you have high-speed, constant access, through a company connection or through cable modem service, you might not have to log on to the Internet to use it. Depending on the amount of information and graphics on the page, the display might take a few moments or might display right away.

The Home button on the Internet Explorer toolbar displays your home page. You can return to the home page by clicking the Home button.

You can change your home page address by entering a new home page address within the Tools, Internet Options dialog box's General page (see Figure 23.2). When you enter a new home page address, Internet Explorer returns to that page whenever you click the Home toolbar button or start Internet Explorer in a subsequent session.

Figure 23.2

You can change your browser's home page.

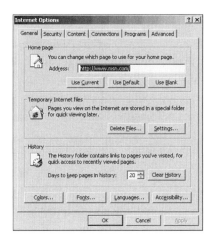

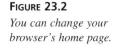

Managing the Internet Explorer Screen

You can navigate Internet pages easily with Internet Explorer. If you are new to the Internet, study Figure 23.3 to learn the parts of the Internet Explorer screen. Internet Explorer displays your home page and lists the home page's address in the address area.

Figure 23.3

Learn the Internet Explorer screen so that you can maximize the power of the Internet Explorer browser.

Web page address

Starts your e-mail program

Previous Web page

Keeps track of favorite sites

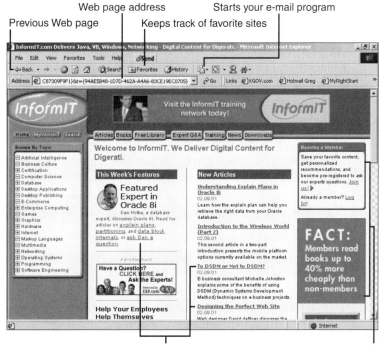

Hyperlinks to other sites

Web page viewing area

Use the following guidelines to familiarize yourself with the Internet Explorer screen:

- Some Web site addresses are lengthy. Drag the Address bar left or right (giving more or less room to the link buttons) to adjust the address display width.

- Click the down arrow at the right of the address entry to open a list of recently traversed site addresses. If this is the first time you or anyone has used your computer's Internet Explorer, you might not see sites other than the current home page sites.

- Use the scrollbar to see more of your home page. Most Web pages take more room than fit on one screen.

- Use the View menu to hide the toolbar and status bar so that you have more display room for the Web page. The Address list box can be hidden as well. You can still enter site addresses that you want to traverse from the File, Open menu.

- Display the toolbar and status bar again by clicking the appropriate View menu options.

You will probably spend a lot of time on the Internet, so the better you understand Internet Explorer the more effective you will be online.

Surfing the Internet

Remember that the Internet's Web is a collection of interconnected Web pages. As you *surf* the Internet using Internet Explorer, you run across Web pages that contain *links* to other sites. These links (also called *hot spots* or *hypertext links*) can be underlined, appear in different colors from the surrounding text, or can even be activated by clicking on an image. After you click a link on a Web page, if you return to that Web page, the link appears in a different color to let you know that you have already gone there. You can locate these links by moving your mouse pointer over the underlined description. If the mouse pointer changes to a hand icon, you can click the hyperlink to display that page in your browser. After a brief pause, your Web browser displays the page.

Suppose that you view the home page of your financial broker to update an Excel investment worksheet that contains your stock portfolio. The page might include links to other related pages, such as stock quotation pages, company financial informational pages, and order-entry pages in which you can enter your own stock purchase requests.

One of the most useful features of Internet Explorer and every other Web browser is the browser's capability to return to sites you have visited both in the current session and in former sessions. The toolbar's Back button takes you back to a site you just visited, and you can keep clicking the Back button to return to pages you have visited in the current session. The Forward toolbar button returns you to pages from which you have backed up. Because this back-and-forth feature is so popular with Web browsers, Microsoft chose to add the Back and Forward buttons to all of the Windows operating system windows.

At any point, you can click the Address drop-down list arrow to see a list of URLs you have typed previously. You find addresses from the current as well as previous Internet Explorer Web sessions.

If you know the address of a Web site that you want to view, you can type the site's address directly in the Address text box and click Go or press Enter. Internet Explorer takes you to that site and displays its Web page. In addition, you can select File, Open to display an Open dialog box in which you can enter an address. When you click OK, Internet Explorer displays the page associated with that address.

If you find a location you really like, save that location in Internet Explorer's Favorites list. If you run across a site that discusses your favorite television show and you want to return to that site again quickly, for example, click the Favorites, Add menu option to add the site to your Favorites list. When you store your favorite sites in the Favorites folders, you can quickly access them during future Internet sessions.

As you familiarize yourself with the Internet, you will want to visit Web pages that interest you. After you visit a site, you can easily return to it again. Use the following steps to become comfortable surfing Web pages:

1. If you have not started Internet Explorer, start it and log on to the Internet.
2. Click the Address list box to select the URL of your home page (or whatever URL is currently shown in the Address list box).
3. Type the following Web page address: **www.informit.com**. You see InformIT's home page appear, as shown in Figure 23.4. (Depending on the changes that have been made to the site recently, the site might not match Figure 23.4 exactly.)

FIGURE 23.4

Practice surfing the Web to InformIT's home page.

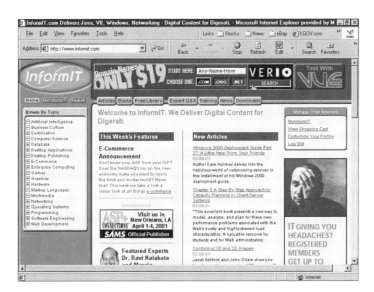

> Often, you see Web addresses prefaced with the text http://. This prefix indicates both for you and your browser that the address to the right of the second slash is a Web page's URL. This prefix is optional for today's Web browsers. If you type the prefix, be sure to type forward slashes and not the MS-DOS or Windows backslashes you might be used to typing for PC folder locations.

4. Click any link on the page. After a brief pause, you see the linked Web page.

5. Click the toolbar's Back button. Almost instantly, the first page appears.

6. Practice building a favorite site list by clicking the Favorites, Add to Favorites menu option. Internet Explorer displays the Add Favorite dialog box.

7. Enter a description for the page in the Name text box. Make the description something by which you can remember the page (such as InformIT Digital Content).

8. Click OK.

9. Click the Favorites toolbar button. You see the new entry. When you click the hyperlink for the favorite entry, Internet Explorer looks up that entry's stored URL address and goes to that Web page.

> If you add too many favorites, your favorites list might become unmanageable. As you add to your favorites list, you can create new folders from the Add Favorite dialog box using the Create In button. By setting up a series of folders named by subjects, you can group your favorite Web sites by subject so that they are easier to manage and find.

Some Web pages take a long time to display. Often, Web pages contain a lot of text and graphics, and that data takes time to arrive on your computer. Therefore, you might click to a favorite Web site but have to wait a minute or longer to see the entire site.

To speed things up, Internet Explorer attempts to show as much of the page as possible, especially the text on the page, before downloading the graphic images. Internet Explorer puts placeholders where the graphic images are to appear. If you view the page for a few moments, the placeholders' images begin to appear until the final page, with all graphics, displays in its entirety.

Searching for the Information You Need

How can you expect to find any information on a vast network of networks such as the Internet? Web pages offer linked sites in an appealing format that enable you to comfortably view information and see related pages, but you must know the location of one of the site's pages before the links can help.

Fortunately, Internet Explorer offers a searching mechanism that helps you locate information on the Web. By clicking the Search toolbar button, you can access a search page, such as the one shown in Figure 23.5. As you can see, the search page consumes the left pane of your Internet screen. You can still see the Web page you were viewing while you perform a search. After you click on a link in the Search pane, the resulting search page that you find will appear in the right pane when you make the search. You can easily return the browser to a single-pane Web view by clicking the X in the upper-right hand corner of the Search pane (or simply clicking the Search button a second time).

FIGURE 23.5

Locate data on the Web.

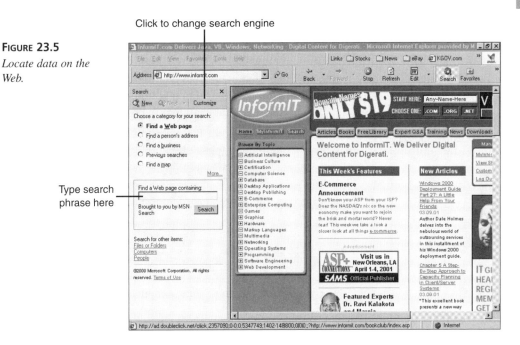

The Internet Explorer search pane offers the benefit of multiple search engines. The accuracy of the search depends on the words and phrases you enter, as well as the capability of the search engine. Some search engines you can choose from search only Web pages, for example, whereas others search *newsgroups*. To search with a different search engine, click the search pane's Customize toolbar button. The right pane displays a list of search engines that you can use for subsequent searching.

After the search engine locates its information, Internet Explorer displays from zero to several address links in the left pane that you can click to find specific Web-based information about your topic. (Figure 23.6 shows the result of one search.) By scrolling down the page (and by clicking the additional pages of links if your search turns up a lot of sites), you can read the descriptions of the pages. The descriptions often contain the first few lines of the located Web page text.

Result of clicking a topic

FIGURE 23.6

The results of a search might produce several pages of Web sites.

Search phrase

List of found topics

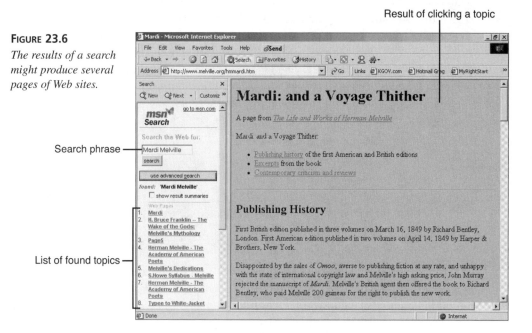

Each search engine locates information differently and each also has its own rules for the words and phrases you enter. Keep in mind that the more specific your search phrase is, the more accurately the search engine can find information that helps you.

Generally, you can use these guidelines with most search engines:

- Enclose a multiple word phrase in quotation marks if you want the search engine to search for those words in the order in which they are listed. If you enter "West Virginia", for example, the search engine searches for that specific name. If you enter West Virginia (without the quotation marks), however, most search engines locate every site that contains the word *West* and every site that contains the word *Virginia*, most of which would have nothing to do with the state you originally wanted to locate.

- Place a plus sign (+) before each word for which you want to search. Entering +Tulsa +oil would find only those sites that contain both the word *Tulsa* and the word *oil*.

Remember that these search criteria rules are only guidelines that usually work well with the most popular search engines. Some of the search engines follow slightly different rules, and you have to look up that search engine page's help references for specific information if the previous rules do not seem to work the way you expect.

How Office Products Combine with the Web

23

Office offers a complete set of tools that integrate the Office products and the Internet. From any Office product, you can access files and Web pages on the Internet. The following sections describe how you can access the Web from Office.

Viewing Web Pages from Within Office Products

You don't have to start Internet Explorer to view a Web page from within an Office product. All you need to do is display the Web toolbar and type the address you want to see. While creating an Excel worksheet, for example, you might need to locate financial information from your company's Web site. Follow these steps to surf the Web from Excel:

1. Select View, Toolbars, Web to add a new Web-browsing toolbar to Excel.

2. Click the Address text box of the Web toolbar.

3. Enter the Web address that you want to see. (Alternatively, you can click the Favorites list on the Web toolbar to view and select the Web page that you want to view.) If you access the Internet from a modem, Excel dials your ISP to get Internet access.

4. Excel's menus and toolbars change to match that of Internet Explorer and displays the Web site that you want to view. You can switch between the Web and Excel by pressing Alt+Tab. In addition, you can copy and paste information from Web pages to your Excel worksheet.

Viewing Documents in Internet Explorer

In addition to starting Internet Explorer from an Office product, you can view Office documents directly from within Internet Explorer. Whenever you are browsing the Internet, select File, Open and type the full path and filename you want to view (or click Browse to locate the path and file) from within Internet Explorer.

Internet Explorer opens and displays the file within the browser window. Not only does Internet Explorer display the file, but all Internet Explorer menus change to enable full editing capabilities for that Office document. If you open a Word document, for example, Internet Explorer menus change to Word menus; you can then insert a table or format the text as if you were using Word. If you click the Internet Explorer Tools toolbar button while viewing the Office document, the Word toolbars appear beneath the Internet Explorer toolbar so that you have full Word toolbar capabilities from within Internet Explorer.

Figure 23.7 shows an Excel worksheet viewed from Internet Explorer. All of Internet Explorer's toolbars appear, but the menus change to reflect the actions possible in Excel. Also note that the worksheet's row numbers and column names appear around the worksheet so that you can manipulate the worksheet from Internet Explorer.

FIGURE 23.7

You can view an Excel worksheet from within Internet Explorer.

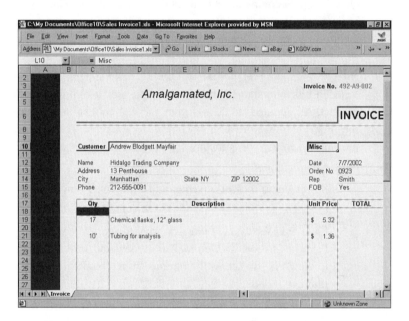

If you click the Back button, Internet Explorer displays the preceding Web page or whatever else you were viewing from Internet Explorer, and the menus change so that you can surf the Web normally.

Excel As a Browser?

You might wonder why Excel displays browser menu options and toolbar buttons when a Web page appears, but Excel reverts back to a worksheet program when you view worksheets in Excel. What is Excel, a Web browser, a worksheet program, or both?

Excel actually does not access the Web; for that, you need a Web browser such as Internet Explorer. Nevertheless, the Web toolbar that you find in all the Office products does enable you to navigate between Office files and the Web without changing programs. Through a process known as *DLLs* and

ActiveX controls, the Office programs are able to borrow some characteristics of a Web browser as long as the browser resides on your computer.

Perhaps someday, the only program you will need is a Web browser. The browser menus and toolbars can change depending on the document with which you want to work. Internet Explorer integrates with Windows itself so that the browser becomes part of your Windows environment. The Internet is so important to computing today that companies such as Microsoft are incorporating Web technology into all products as well as operating systems.

23

Creating Links in Office

As you learned how to use Office products throughout the previous hours, you learned that you can type a Web address in an Office document to create a link to that address. When you type a Web address in a PowerPoint presentation, for example, that address becomes a link to an active Web site address. If you click that address, the Office product starts Internet Explorer, logs you on to the Internet if needed, and displays the Web page located at that address.

Keeping Current

The Office programs help you utilize the Internet to its fullest. Conversely, the Internet helps you keep your Office applications running smoothly as well. For example, from any Office program, you can select Help, Office on the Web to view the latest information about the topic on which you're requesting help.

In addition, you can use the Web to download the latest updates, bug fixes, and patches to your Office programs. When you browse `http://officeupdate.microsoft.com/`, you will see the Web page similar to the one in Figure 23.8. (Figure 23.8 lists information about Office 2000, the Office version that predates Office XP, because no Office XP Web pages were publicly available at the time of this writing.) You will be able to read the latest news about Office products, see how others use Office, and download sample files, templates, and updates to your software.

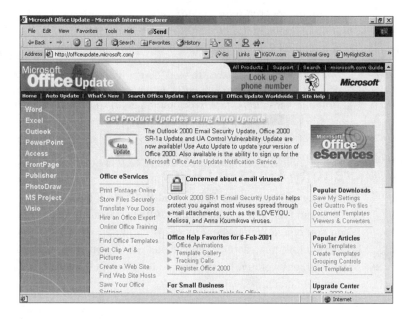

FIGURE 23.8

Microsoft maintains a huge Office-based Web site.

If you click on the Web page's AutoUpdate link, you'll be able to install an automatic update feature that instructs Office to check the Internet regularly and if updates are posted that will bring your installation up to date, the update process starts automatically so that you can keep current.

Use Internet Explorer More Effectively

Now that you have gotten a taste for what Internet Explorer can do (in this and the previous lesson), you are ready to take the browser to the next step so that you can utilize Internet Explorer, along with Office, at their fullest potential.

Keeping Links

If you want your most important Web sites located even closer than the Favorites list, add the site to your Links bar. At the top of Internet Explorer, as well as on your Windows taskbar if you choose to display the Links toolbar, resides a series of links to Web sites. As Figure 23.9 shows, your links appear on your screen ready for your click to jump to that site. Your links can appear on the toolbar to the right of or below the Internet Explorer menu depending on where you drag them. If your links are not currently displayed, right-click a blank area of your toolbar (you can also do this with your Windows Taskbar) and select Links.

Links   Click here to see more links

FIGURE 23.10
*Your links are ready
for one-click access.*

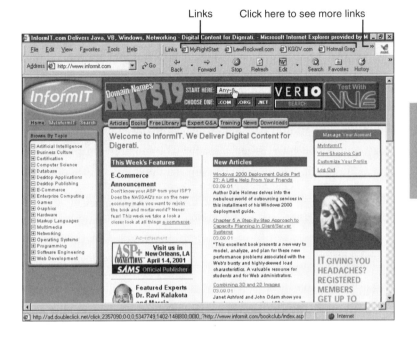

To remove or change a link, right-click over the link and select the appropriate menu item from the pop-up menu. To add a link, drag its Web site icon from the Internet Explorer Address text box to the Links bar. You can rearrange links by dragging them to a different location. To see the links that don't fit on the Links bar, click the arrow at the far-right of the Links bar.

Internet Explorer helps improve the way that you view Web pages with graphics. Some Web pages take several seconds, and possibly longer, to display. Although the text appears right away, the graphics take some time to load. Internet Explorer puts a status bar at the bottom of the browser so that you know how much (by percentage) of the current page is loaded and how much is left. If you don't want to wait on a long load, click Stop or simply select another page to view.

More Internet Explorer Tips and Tricks

Internet Explorer supports these two shortcut keys that will save you time:

- *F4*—Opens the Web address's drop-down list box so that you can quickly jump to a site you have visited recently.

- *Alt+D*—Places the text pointer in the Web address list box so you can type a Web address to display.

If a Web address meets this common format: `http://www.SiteAddress.com`, all you need to type is **SiteAddress** and Internet Explorer searches for the correct site using the fully formatted Web site address.

One final tip can provide multiple Web pages from one browser. Suppose that you are viewing a Web page with links to another page. You want to read both pages, perhaps to compare notes in resized windows. You can open a second Internet Explorer browser window by right-clicking over the hyperlink and selecting Open in New Window from the pop-up menu that appears. (You can also hold your Shift key while clicking the link with your left mouse button to open the page in a new window if you find that easier.) A second Web browser window opens with that linked Web site there, but your original browser window will still be open displaying the Web site you started from. By judiciously opening new Web sites in additional windows, you can view several Web pages at the same time without having to browse between them each time you go back to one.

Summary

This hour introduced you to the Internet, the Web, Internet Explorer, and showed you how Office and the Internet work together. The Internet is a vast collection of networked computers all around the world. You can access the Internet as long as you have access through an Internet service provider. Although Internet information appears in many forms, the most useful Internet information often appears on Web pages that contain text, graphics, sound, and video.

Internet Explorer includes searching tools as well as a history system that keeps track of recent Web pages. Not only can you view Web pages with Internet Explorer, but you can also view other kinds of files on your computer. As the Internet becomes more organized and Internet access gets faster and cheaper, the Web browser will become part of your daily computing routine. One day, you will find that you do most of your work from Web browsing software such as Internet Explorer.

The next hour continues the Internet discussion by explaining how to create Web pages from within the Office products.

Q&A

Q I have clicked the Internet Explorer icon, but I don't see Web pages. What do I have to do to get on the Internet?

A Do you have Internet access from Microsoft Network or from another Internet service provider? Generally, unless you work for a company that offers Internet access to its employees, you have to sign up for Internet access, get the access phone number, pay a monthly fee (most Internet service providers offer unlimited access for a flat monthly rate), and set up a browser, such as Internet Explorer, to access that provider.

Q Does all Internet information appear on Web pages?

A The Internet's information appears in many forms, sometimes in a form known as an FTP site or a newsgroup. The Web page standard, however, has become one of the most popular ways to organize and view Internet information. As more people used the Web-page standard, more modern technology enabled that standard to evolve into a uniform container of multimedia-based information. Therefore, with a Web browser, you can view all kinds of information over the Web.

23

Hour 24

Creating Web Pages with Office XP

You don't just have to be a user of Web pages. You can create them yourself with the tools available in Office. By utilizing the Office wizards and design tools, you can quickly create Web pages that equal those from the pros. With Office you can hone text, graphics, and data tables and present that data to the world on the Web.

Most Office users implement Word as their primary Web page development tool and import other Office product data into their Word Web pages. All the Office products are Internet-aware; they all enable you to convert their data to Web pages.

The highlights of this hour include the following:

- What you need to publish pages on the Internet
- How to save Word documents as Web pages
- When to use the various Office wizards to generate your initial Web pages
- How to export Excel and Access data to your Word-based Web pages

- Why you should limit the amount of Access information that goes into your Web page
- How to save individual Access objects in a Data Access Page
- How to modify the way a PowerPoint presentation looks and behaves on the Internet

Preparing to Publish Web Pages

Before you can publish pages on the Web, you must have access to a *Web server*. Perhaps your company uses a Web server for its site; if so, you can store your Web pages on that computer. If you have access to an online service, such as Microsoft Network, your online service might offer an area for one or more Web pages that you can copy to the online site's Web server free or for a small charge. Several free Web hosting sites exist, such as http://www.geocities.com/ that allow you to post Web pages that others can view. Most of these free services require that you and your users view ample advertisements to pay for the free services the host offers.

If you want to publish a personal Web page for fun, you will enjoy telling the world your stories and sharing your family photos with others. If you want to start a business on the Internet, however, or offer timely information that you want others to visit often, you need to be aware that Web page *maintenance* is costly and time-consuming. You don't just create a Web page, load the page on the Web, and expect to keep people's interest if you don't keep the material up-to-date. In addition, performing *e-commerce* (selling goods and services over an Internet connection) often requires the help of an outside agency such as a bank or credit card service, so you might want to get help when you first go online with your organization. In addition, the free Web hosts typically offer only to serve personal Web pages and not business Web pages, so you will always have to factor in extra costs for hosting.

Many homes and small businesses are now getting fast Internet connections. Many of these connections, such as the DSL connections (*Data Subscriber Lines*) enable you to set up a fixed *IP address*. An IP address, or *Internet Protocol address*, always anchors your position on the World Wide Web so that you can set up your own Web server and host your Web pages directly from your own computer if you're inclined to do such a thing. Keep in mind that you will need to address storage, speed, and security issues (the dreaded s's of Web hosting) before you can safely and successfully host your own site.

Perhaps you are beginning to realize that data communications, by its very nature, is technical. When you begin to develop Web pages and manage Web sites, you will see that you must master some network terminology and phrases just to understand what is taking place.

Office and the Web

One of the reasons you should consider using Office to create Web pages is that you already have the Office tools. Office offers several wizards and templates that you can use to create your Web pages. Nevertheless, Office is not necessarily the best tool you can use to create Web pages. Office offers good tools with which you can create and maintain a Web page. If your Web page generates a lot of interest, however, you might want to use a more specific tool for Web page creation such as Microsoft FrontPage and Internet Explorer. FrontPage is to Web pages what Access is to databases; FrontPage offers specific Web page tools that create advanced Web pages with very little effort on your part.

24

FrontPage is part of the Office suite of programs but this text does not cover FrontPage. Web design and development is more involved than creating files in the other Office products. If you are interested in using FrontPage to create professional Web sites, consider getting *Sams Teach Yourself Microsoft FrontPage 2002 in 24 Hours* by Rogers Cadenhead (ISBN: 0-672-32104-1) and learning the FrontPage application in depth.

All the Web-related aspects of Office support both the Internet and *intranets*. Therefore, if your company maintains an intranet (which is an in-company Web site viewed only from computers on your company's network), you can save Web pages to that intranet as easily (and sometimes more easily) as on the Internet.

Each of the following sections describes how you can use Word, Excel, PowerPoint, and Access to generate Web-page information. If you connect to your Web server with your PC, you can offer live content on the Internet. In other words, as soon as you update your database, viewers of your Web site who access that database see the updated values.

Most of your early Web page creations will probably take place in Word until you master a more full-featured Web-page creation program such as FrontPage. Even if you embed an Access database on a Web page, you will probably do most of that Web page design in Word. Therefore, most of this hour focuses on Word's Web-editing tools. The final sections describe how to integrate the other Office products into your Word Web pages.

Word and Web Pages

Word offers two ways to create Web pages: You can save Word documents in a Web page format, or you can create a Web page using one of the Word wizards. The following two sections explain each method.

Saving Word Documents As Web Pages

One of the easiest ways to create a Web page from a Word document is to save the document in an *HTML format*. Suppose you create a company report that you want to publish on your Web server. All you have to do is select File, Save As Web page, and then click OK. Word then saves the file in an HTML Web page-compatible format that you then can transfer to the Web server.

You can view your document from the Internet Explorer Web browser by selecting File, Web Page Preview. By viewing the document from the Web browser, you see how your Web page will appear to other Internet users. The format will differ slightly from the document in its native Word format (especially italicized fonts).

Figure 24.1 shows a Word editing session that includes a rather complex Web page being edited. Figure 24.2 shows how that same Web page looks when viewed from Internet Explorer when you select from Word's File, Web Page Preview menu option. The lines and other editing marks inside the Word document help distinguish the Web page's alignment and table cells that work together to form the final page.

FIGURE 24.1

When editing a Web page with Word, the page's alignment grids and other element marks show.

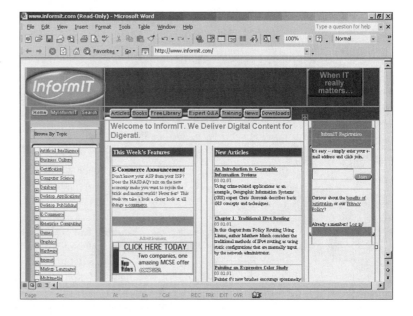

FIGURE 24.2

By viewing your document as a Web page, you learn how the document will look as a Web page.

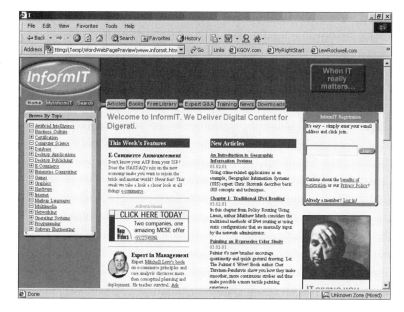

When formatting your Web page, keep your end user in mind and write for the largest audience possible. You can select a fancy font for your Web page text. If you stick with the standard fonts that come with Windows (such as Courier, Times New Roman, and Arial), however, you ensure that all viewers of your Web page will have those same fonts and the page will look the way you intend for it to look on their browsers.

Remember that Web pages are often colorful. Color fonts can spruce up a Web page dramatically as long as you don't overdo the colors. Use the toolbar's Font Color button to select a new font color quickly.

For Web Masters Only

If you have written HTML code before, you can embed HTML commands in your Web page from within Word. Format your HTML code with the HTML Markup style, and Word embeds it as HTML code. The code does not appear on the Web page, but the browser that displays the Web page formats the page according to your HTML-based instructions.

Figure 24.3 shows HTML code for a Web page being edited in Word. The HTML code can be tedious if you are unfamiliar with it, but Word does offer itself as a text editor (as opposed to a word processor that would incorrectly wrap words inside the HTML code) when you work with HTML code.

FIGURE 24.3

You can view the HTML code for your Web page.

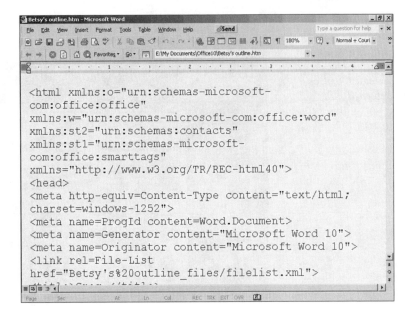

Using the Web Page Wizard

When you create a new document by selecting File, New and select General Templates from the New Document Task Pane, Word offers a dialog box with a series of templates and wizards. If you click the Web Pages tab, you find Web options such as the following:

- *Column with Contents*—A Web page designed for informational purposes with topics at the left and hyperlinked details from those topics in the right pane.

- *Frequently Asked Questions*—A Web page designed to ask a series of questions at the top of the page and include hyperlinked answers to those questions for the remaining portion of the page.

- *Left-Aligned Column*—As you can see from Figure 24.4's sample from the resulting template option, the left-aligned column includes a figure in the page's left pane and information flowing down the right pane. As with all the samples from the Web Page Wizard and templates, you can easily replace the figure and placeholder text in this sample.

- *Personal Web Page*—A Web page that is simple and laid out well for personal, nonbusiness informational home pages that a family might use to provide news to other family members who live elsewhere.

- *Right-Aligned Column*—A Web page that is the mirror-image of the left-aligned column page with the figure in the page's right pane and information flowing down the left pane.

FIGURE 24.4

Word produces a clean sample you can work from.

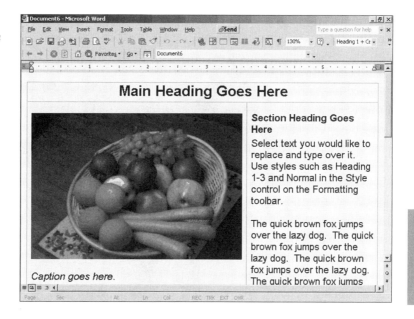

- *Simple Layout*—A Web page with its information down the middle column of the page.
- *Table of Contents*—A Web page with a table of contents section flowing down its middle.
- *Web Page Wizard*—The step-by-step wizard that creates a Web page according to your specifications.

The easiest way to create a Web page according to your specifications is to start the Web Page Wizard. (Figure 24.5 shows the opening screen.)

Microsoft's Web site at www.microsoft.com includes several additional Web-specific Word templates that you can download.

As you follow the wizard, you see the underlying Word Web page take shape. The wizard prompts you for the style of the Web page. As you can see from the personal Web page outline built for Figure 24.6 by the Web Page Wizard, the pages can be interesting.

After the wizard does its job, you can edit the Web page and change the general text to the specific text you want on the page. As you edit, check out the Web tools toolbar that you can add from the View, Toolbars option as well as the Insert menu; when working with a Web page in Word, the Insert menu and Web tools toolbar include several items you can insert in your Web page, including pictures, videos, text boxes, background sounds, scrolling text, and hyperlinks.

FIGURE 24.5

Word builds a Web page as you respond to the wizard.

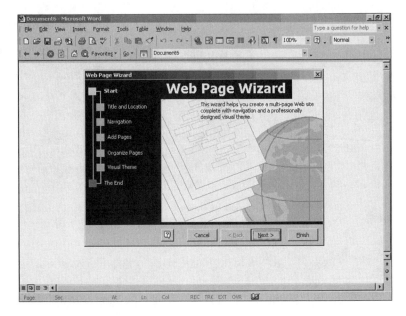

FIGURE 24.6

The Web Page Wizard generates many varieties of Web page styles.

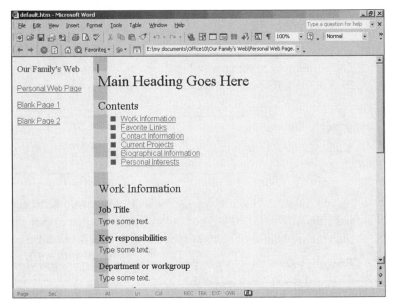

If you want to add callout graphics to your Web page, Word offers the drawing tools you learned about in Hour 22, "Sharing Information Between Programs."

Now that you have seen how to use Word to create Web pages, you already know a lot about how the other Office products create Web pages. Many of the Web page features in the other Office products work the same way as in Word. You can save an Excel worksheet as a Web page, for example. When saving Office documents as Web pages, most of the formatting and editing features you get with the products' native formats remain. In other words, an Excel worksheet that you save as a Web page contains all the same elements that the worksheet contains when you save that worksheet as an Excel file with the normal worksheet extension, .XLS. Revision markings do not appear in Web pages, but all other Office document elements do appear in the Web page.

The remaining sections build on your knowledge of using Word and the Web by showing you how Excel, PowerPoint, and Access also support the Web.

Excel and Web Pages

Excel supports most of the same Web features that Word does, including the capability to save worksheets in the HTML format. After you create the worksheet, select File, Save As Web page to save the worksheet in a format readable to any browser.

In addition to the Web-based HTML format, Excel also supports the Web toolbar that you can display by selecting View, Toolbars, Web. From that toolbar, you can select other Office documents to display and edit from within Excel as well as enter an Internet Web site address to view. All Office products support the Web toolbar, and you can display any document from Internet Explorer (the browser engine used by all Office products when you work with Web-based objects and pages). Because of these two facts, all Office products enable you to view any of the other Office products' documents or any Web page just by typing that document or Web page address in the address text box of the Web toolbar.

If your company stores worksheets on the Internet or on an intranet, the File, Open option in Excel can open those worksheets. When you select File, Open and then enter the URL and filename, such as `http://www.mycompany.org/accts.xls`, Excel opens that worksheet. (Excel offers you the Internet Log On dialog box if you are not already logged on to the Internet.)

If you type a hyperlink Web address or a hyperlink to another Office document in an Excel cell, Excel takes you to that document and displays the Web toolbar automatically (if the toolbar is not already displayed). When you click the Web toolbar's Back button, Excel takes you to the preceding Web page.

Rarely does a Web page contain just an Excel worksheet. Web pages contain other text and graphics; that's why you probably want to create the general Web page in Word using the Web Page Wizard and then import (using the Windows Clipboard or Insert menu) your Excel data into the Web page. If you insert a link to your Excel data instead of inserting a copy of the worksheet, your published Web page always contains "live" worksheet data that changes as you update the worksheet.

If you use an online service to publish your Web page and not a local Web server networked to your PC, you have to update the Web page manually each time you want to update the worksheet data.

Access and Web Pages

Access supports hyperlinks in its database forms, reports, and fields in datasheets. Access supports Word, PowerPoint, Excel, as well as Internet or intranet hyperlinks. In addition to other documents, the hyperlink can point to other Access tables, forms, and reports.

One reason you might want to store hyperlinks in a database field is to store Web pages for vendors, competitors, and customers in tables. When you view forms that display the hyperlink to those tables, you can click the hyperlink to see the Web site.

Obviously, a hyperlink is not active when it appears in a printed report or onscreen in Preview mode. If you import the report into a Word document, Excel worksheet, or an HTML page, however, the hyperlink is active.

The Hyperlink data type is one of the Access data types that you can designate as you create your table (shown in Figure 24.7).

As you know, Access databases contain several objects, tables, forms, reports, and queries. A simple File, Save As Web page option cannot, without more information, determine exactly how you want to export the objects to the HTML document. You could use such an option for the other Office documents because they had fewer objects than an Access database. Therefore, to save a table or other object to its own Web page, select File, Save As and select Data Access Page for the type of file to save. Access stores the object as a Web page using the HTML format.

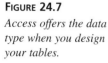

FIGURE 24.7
Access offers the data type when you design your tables.

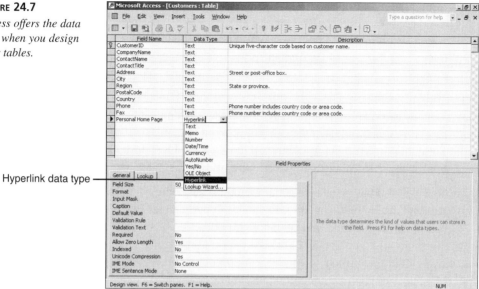

Hyperlink data type

24

PowerPoint and Web Pages

When you save a PowerPoint presentation as a Web page, PowerPoint does not immediately save the file. Instead, it presents you with the Save As dialog box that contains a Publish button that, when you click the button, produces the dialog box shown in Figure 24.8. The dialog box determines how your presentation appears over the Internet when a remote site displays the presentation's Web page.

FIGURE 24.8
The Publish As Web Page dialog box determines how your presentation will appear on the Internet.

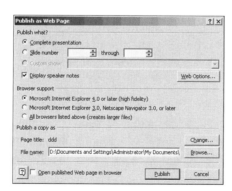

PowerPoint actually lends itself well for Internet presentations. When generating a presentation for display on the Internet, keep your graphics to a minimum so that the slides load quickly inside the user's browser. The user can control the presentation by clicking the mouse or pressing PageDown.

Summary

This hour showed you how to use Office products to create Web pages. Word certainly offers the advantage in your initial Web page design, unless, of course, you want to put a PowerPoint presentation on the Web; in which case, the PowerPoint templates offer the best place to start your Web page design.

You can use Word as your primary Web page development tool and import other Office products as needed to add their elements to the Web page that you save from Word. PowerPoint offers a unique Web page design wizard that designs Web-based presentations with the same look and feel as other Web pages.

Now that you have concluded your preliminary introduction to combining Office products and the Internet, you are ready to hone your Internet Explorer skills in the next lesson so that you use the Internet more efficiently.

Q&A

Q Can I use my Windows 98 or Windows Me PC as a Web server?

A Surprisingly, you can with Windows 98 but not with Windows Me. Even if you could use a server with Windows Me, you probably don't want to tie up your PC by using it as a Web server. Windows 2000-based computers are better equipped to be Web servers. If you want to try, however, Windows 98 contains a special program you can install called Personal Web Server. This program provides the tools needed for your PC to operate as a Web server. If you use a slow PC and if you use a dial-up Internet connection, your PC offers slow Web page viewing. Therefore, no matter how effective your Web page content is and no matter how well you used the Office tools to develop an attention-getting Web page display, your Windows 98-based Web server is probably too slow to keep your viewers' interest. At the time of this writing, Windows XP has not been released but preliminary information makes it appear that XP will fully support the serving of Web pages.

Q Can I include Excel graphs on my Web pages?

A Certainly. You can copy the graph to your Windows Clipboard, and then paste it directly into your Word- or PowerPoint-based Web page. An Excel graph is no different from any other kind of data that you can copy and paste into a Web page from any of the Office products.

Windows supports *OLE (Object Linking and Embedding)* technology that enables you to insert virtually any object inside any other kind of document. If you want to insert an Excel graph or a video file with sound into a Web page, you can do so by using the Insert menu from the Office product's menu bar.

Glossary

absolute address—A cell reference in a formula that remains fixed when you move the cell to another worksheet location.

Access—The Office program that manages and reports database files.

action button—A button you place on a presentation's slide that, when clicked during the presentation, performs a preset action.

action settings—Settings that determine what happens when the user clicks an action button.

active cell—The cell where the next action will take place in a worksheet.

adjustment handle—A diamond-shaped handle that enables you to change the shape of AutoShape images by dragging only a portion of the image further in or out.

and conditions—Conditions that specify a method of searching in which all specified fields are used to select data.

animation tag—Numbers that attach themselves to portions of a slide to label specific animation effects on the slide.

argument—A value operated on by a function.

ascending sort—Sorting data from low to high values.

AutoComplete—An Office feature that completes common entries you begin to type, such as dates and weekday names.

AutoContent Wizard—A series of dialog boxes that help you generate PowerPoint presentations.

AutoCorrect—An Office feature that corrects spelling and makes pre-defined corrections to text.

AutoFormat—An Office feature that changes the appearance of data in your Office documents.

AutoNumber—A sequential number applied to all records in a database as a primary key field.

AutoReport—An Access tool for quickly generating reports from your Datasheet views.

AutoShapes—Pre-designed shapes such as arrows and stars that you can resize and place in documents.

AutoText—A tool that enables you to quickly insert completely formatted text.

axis— One of the reference lines in a coordinate system, chart, or graph.

banner—A highlighted heading that appears at the top of an Outlook calendar day indicating special occasions.

boilerplate text—A publishing term used for text that appears frequently.

caret—See insertion point.

cell—A specific location inside a worksheet that holds data values.

cell reference—The row and column intersection of a worksheet cell, such as F12.

Chart Wizard—A wizard that generates charts from Excel worksheet data.

comment—A note that attaches itself to a cell for subsequent reminders to worksheet users.

conditional formatting—The appearance of a cell that is based on the cell's contents.

copy—The sending of a copy of selected data to the Office Clipboard.

criteria—Instructions for locating data in a table.

cut—The removal of selected data from a file to the Office Clipboard.

Data Access Pages—Internet-ready data table pages that you can view with Internet Explorer from Web pages.

database—An organized collection of data.

database management system—A system that creates, organizes, manages, and reports from data stored in databases.

Database window—The primary Access window from which you manage your database's objects such as tables, forms, and reports.

data fill—The process of completing a sequence of data in a range of cells.

data series—A single group of data that you might select from a worksheet column or row to graph.

data table—A table that explains data values on a chart or graph.

datasheet view—An Access view of a table that looks similar to a worksheet with the table's rows and columns resembling a worksheet's rows and columns.

default value—A value that automatically appears in a field, but that you can override by entering a new value.

demote button—The left arrow on the Outline toolbar that moves an outlined entry down one level.

descending sort—Sorting data from high to low values.

Design View—The Access view from which you create and edit database objects such as tables and forms.

destination file—The file you are copying to when transferring data from one Office program to another.

digital subscriber line—See *DSL*.

document—Typically, a Word data file, but can apply to the other Office product data files.

DSL—A high-speed Internet connection that travels by regular telephone wire into homes and businesses. Also called *digital subscriber lines*.

dynaset—A subset of data, usually generated by a database query.

e-commerce—The selling of goods and services over the Internet.

endnotes—Footnotes that appear at the end of your document.

event—An Outlook activity not specifically tied to a time frame, such as a holiday or birthday.

Excel—The Office program that enables you to manage numerical information in a worksheet format.

exponentiation—The raising of one number to another power.

field—An area in a template or on a form where you enter data. Also, columns in a database table.

fill area—A chart or graph's background.

fill handle—A small black box located in the bottom-right corner of a cell that extends the cell's data when you drag the fill handle.

filter—A subset of data from a table.

flat file database—A simple database that requires much redundant data.

font—A set of characters that determine a typeface's look and style.

footer—The area at the bottom of every page reserved to display information such as page numbers, dates, or a company's name.

footnote—Text that appears in the bottom margin on a page.

forms—Onscreen representations of paper forms that you and others use to enter data into tables.

Form view—The view that displays records in the form-like format.

format—To change the appearance of your document's layout and contents.

Format Painter—A feature that applies an existing data's format to other data in an Office document.

formula—An expression that computes numeric results.

Free Rotate tool—A graphics tool that enables you to rotate text to any angle.

function—A built-in routine that operates on data.

grayscale—The output of a color image when printed on a black-and-white printer.

gutter—The inside margin of your text.

hanging indent—A format that extends the first line of a paragraph to the left margin and indents subsequent lines.

hardcopy—A printed listing of data.

header—Text that appears at the top of pages in your document.

hidden cell—A cell that has been formatted to remain hidden from normal worksheet views.

home page—The first page you see when you visit an Internet site.

Hotmail—An free online e-mail service offered by Microsoft.

HTML—Stands for Hypertext Markup Language, the programming language used for Web pages.

hyperlink—A location in a document or Web page that you can click to display other information stored in documents and files. Also called a *link*, *hypertext link*, and *hot spot*.

import—The transferring of data into an Office program.

Inbox—A collection of e-mail messages, organized in topic folders that you set up or contained in the default Inbox folder.

indention—The space between the page margin and where the text aligns.

index field—A field inside a database table you've indicated that you want to use for fast sorting and searching.

insertion point—A straight cursor that indicates where the next character typed will appear on the screen. Also called the text cursor or the caret.

insert mode—The mode in which newly-typed characters push existing text to the right.

Intelliprint—A feature that suppresses the printing of extra, blank worksheet pages that often appear because of the way worksheets often appear on the printed page.

Internet—A system of interconnected computers from all around the world.

intranet—An internal networked set of computers, usually inside a company or school, that interact with each other using Internet protocols.

IP address—A numeric value that specifies your Internet connection.

ISP—Also known as an *Internet service provider*, the company that provides you with your Internet connection.

Journal—An Outlook feature that keeps track of all your interactions such as contacts, phone calls, tasks, and other activities.

justify—To align text to the left, center, or right margin.

key field—See *primary key field*.

kiosk—A name applied to a self-running presentation.

label—A text value such as a name and address.

Label Wizard—A wizard that helps you generate labels from your database data.

leader—A character that provides a path for the eye to follow across the page within a tab stop.

legend—The area of a chart that identifies the color or pattern associated with each data series.

line spacing—The amount of blank space between lines.

link—A pointer to another file that connects the two files so that the user can see the contents of the linked file from the file where the link resides.

locked cell—A cell that cannot be changed.

macro—A set of written tasks that execute when a specific keystroke is pressed.

Master Style—A collection of headings, colors, and fonts that give a presentation its personality.

Media Gallery—A collection of clip art, sound, graphic, and video files you can place in Office documents.

Messenger—Microsoft's online chat service in which you can use to communicate with other Messenger users.

Microsoft Office Shortcut Bar—A Windows toolbar from which you can click buttons to start Office programs.

module—A program written in Visual Basic for Applications that controls an Office product.

motion path—The path that the animation follows if the animation moves around, onto, or off of your slide.

mouse pointer—An arrow that moves around the screen as you move your mouse. Also called the mouse cursor.

network—Two or more computers connected in order to share files, printers, and other resources.

newsgroups—Internet-based discussion and file-sharing boards.

nonbreaking hyphen—A hyphen that keeps certain words together so they do not break at the end of a line but will fully wrap so they always appear together.

Notes Page view—The view that enables you to create and edit notes for the presentation's speaker.

Office Assistant—An animated character that provides help for the Office programs.

Office Clipboard—An area of memory that holds up to 24 items you send there.

OLE object—An object that conforms to the *object linking and embedding* technology that enables you to insert non-Access data in an Access database table.

operator—A symbol such as a mathematical symbol that manipulates data, for example a minus sign.

operator hierarchy—A pre-defined set of rules that determines the order of math operations.

or conditions—Conditions that specify a method of searching in which only one of a list of specified fields are used to select data.

orphan—The name for the first line of a paragraph that prints on the last line at the bottom of a page.

Outbox—The holding folder for messages that are queued to be mailed.

Outlook—The Office program that keeps track of your e-mail messages, contacts, schedule, to-do lists, notes, and journal entries.

Outlook Bar—The bar of the left side of the Outlook window that organizes available folders and shortcuts.

Outlook Today—A view that shows an overview of messages, to-do tasks, and appointments for the current time period.

overtype mode—The mode in which newly-typed characters replace existing text on the screen.

Passport—An online account you can register with that enables you to log in to different Web sites automatically but safely and securely.

paste—The insertion of data from the Office Clipboard to a file.

Personal Information Manager—A program such as Outlook that keeps track of information such as a schedule, messages, contacts, and to-do lists.

PIM—See *Personal Information Manager*.

point—A measurement that approximates 1/72nd of an inch.

PowerPoint—The Office program that enables you to create and manage presentations.

presentation—A collection of slides comprised of individual screens.

Preview Pane—A window that shows the first part of a selected e-mail message.

primary key field—A field that contains no duplicate entries. Also called the *key field*.

Print Preview—An onscreen representation of how your printed Office file will look.

promote button—The right arrow on the Outline toolbar that moves an outlined entry up one level.

promotion arrows—A control on an outline that you click to indent data within an outline.

property—Information related to a specific file or object on the screen such as a file's name or a paragraph's background color.

queries—Stored instructions that select data from one or more tables for reporting, analysis, and data-management purposes.

range—A selected group of worksheet cells.

range name—A name that you assign to a range of cells.

records—Individual rows, or entries, in database files.

relational database—A database that uses data from multiple tables instead of requiring you to duplicate data in two or more places.

relative address—A cell reference that changes when you move the cell to another worksheet location.

Report Wizard—A wizard that helps you generate reports from your database tables.

Rules Wizard—An Outlook wizard that analyzes your e-mail, automatically places e-mail messages in appropriate folders, and responds to e-mail based on the e-mail message's properties.

scientific notation—A shortcut for writing extremely large and small numbers.

ScreenTips—Pop-up descriptions of toolbar buttons and other screen elements.

selection—Highlighted onscreen data, such as text in Word, that receives the next action such as a formatting or deletion command.

shortcut—An icon located in a file that represents data from another file.

shortcut menus—Menus that appear when you right-click over an object on the screen.

sizing handles—Small black boxes around graphs and other selected screen items with which you can drag to expand or shrink the objects on the screen.

slide—A screen you design that is part of a presentation.

slide layout—The PowerPoint view that shows an individual slide's setup for editing, such as the type and location of the placeholders.

slide show—Another name for a PowerPoint presentation that you present from a computer onto an overhead screen.

Slide Sorter view—The view that displays your entire presentation so that you can easily add, delete, and move slides.

smart tag—Special Office data that fits within a category, such as a person's name, time, or place.

sort—The arranging of data in sequential order.

source file—The file you are copying from when transferring data from one Office program to another.

spooler—The area of memory that holds reports while printing.

spreadsheet—See *worksheet*.

style—A collection of character and paragraph formats you can apply to your document.

suite—A collection of programs that work together such as the Office programs.

symbols—Special characters that don't appear on the standard keyboard.

synonym—A word that means the same as another word.

tab stop—A point within your margin where the insertion point moves to when you press the Tab key.

table—A grid of columns and rows used to organize data.

task—Any job in Outlook that you need to track, perform, and monitor to completion.

Task Pane—A window that can appear to the right of Office program screens that provides context-sensitive help for actions you can take.

template—A formatted outline of a file that serves as a blueprint to model the appearance of other files you create from the template.

text box—A box that holds text that you can format.

text cursor—A straight cursor that indicates where the next character typed will appear on the screen. Also called the caret or the insertion point.

themes—A set of predefined and unified elements that often appear in documents.

thesaurus—A dictionary that lists synonyms of words.

transition—The changing effect when one presentation slide changes to the next slide.

undo—An Office feature that reverses your recent actions.

uniform resource locator—The address of a Web page, also known as an URL.

URL—See uniform resource locator.

view—A way of looking at an Office program's document.

Voice Command—The Office feature that supports voice-activated commands and dictation.

watermark—A lightly-colored, faded graphic image that appears behind text.

Web browser—A program that enables you to view pages on the Internet.

Web server—A computer that sends Web pages to users who request the pages from over the Internet using a Web browser.

World Wide Web (WWW)—A collection of Internet sites. Also called the *Web*.

widow—The name given to the last line of a paragraph that prints alone at the top of the next page.

wizard—A step-by-step guide that helps you, through a series of question and answer dialog boxes, create documents and other files.

Word—The Office program that performs word processing.

WordArt—Drawing objects with special text effects that you can insert to create fancy headlines and titles.

workbook—A file that holds multiple worksheets.

worksheet—A file divided into rows and columns that forms cells and organizes data such as financial information. Also called a spreadsheet.

INDEX

X-Y-Z

.xls file extension (Excel),
  111, 123
XY (scatter) chart type
  (Excel), 172

Yes (True) fields (Access
  databases), 273

zones, hyphenation (Word),
  85
Zoom (Word)
    command, View menu, 72
    dialog box, 72